THE NON-NATIVE TEACHER

Updated edition with new material

Published by
SWAN COMMUNICATION
Teithside House
Bridgend
Callander
Scotland UK

SWAN

© Swan Communication Ltd
ISBN 978-1-901760-11-8

Edited by: Jen Shearer
Designed by: Susan Martin, The Write People for Design Ltd, Stirling

Printed in Scotland by J Thomson Colour Printers

3.   2.   1.
2021   2020   2019   2018   2017

First edition published 1994 by Macmillan Publishers Limited.
Second edition published 1999 by Max Hueber Verlag.

The publisher would like to dedicate this book to the memory of Donn Byrne, who was a strong supporter of non-native teachers through his work in India, South America and Italy, and in his writing.

CONTENTS

CONTENTS

Foreword

Péter Medgyes' voice was the first and one of the most prominent speaking out for many teachers whose first language is one other than English, whose own voices had been silenced after almost a century of systematically being considered failed native speakers, deficient communicators and second-best teachers.

Ever since the publication of the first edition of *The Non-native Teacher*, many others have found and lent their own rich and deep voices to expose the plight of non-native English Speaking Teachers (NNESTs) in many parts of the world. In particular, Enric Llurda, Ali Fuad Selvi, Ahmar Mahboob, Eva Bernat, Marek Kiczkowiak among many others have inspired me and shaped my own thinking. However, we all owe an enormous debt of gratitude to the first spokesperson who prepared the way for the NNEST movement. It is, therefore, a great privilege for me to have been invited to write this foreword to the third edition of *The Non-native Teacher*.

Warning to the reader

You are about to embark on a rich and complex reading experience. Be prepared for a distinctive voice like no other you might have read before, a confident voice that expresses original ideas in a highly personal, idiosyncratic style. A voice deeply rooted in a specific geographical setting (the Hungarian educational context), which informs much of the thinking, examples and experiences that shape the book. This is a rare occurrence indeed in the English Language Teaching literature – a unique, clearly situated voice which dispenses with the numbing restrictions imposed by political correctness and the controlled, measured niceties that come with the language in which it is written, characterised by politeness and understatement. For understated and measured, this work is not. And it cannot be. Get ready to be surprised, amused, interrogated, provoked or even irritated - and perhaps all of these - in the space of the very same page or paragraph. But more importantly, dare to read this text as a productive and potentially transformative activity and to make sure you notice its impact on you.

As I read this new edition, I found myself nodding in agreement, drawing big exclamation marks on the margin and smiling with complicit joy at some of its more subversive and provocative parts. I also noticed that a few other sections caused me to shake my head in disagreement – but more about this later. Here are a few of my favourite disarming moments: in Chapter 2, as the author's major objections to the definitions of the term *native speaker* are being discussed, all of a sudden the unexpected, almost childlike simplicity of the statement *'To say that a native speaker has a native-like command [...] is the same as suggesting that a good bus driver has the ability to drive a bus well.'* made me chuckle with delight. In Chapter 3, 'A "teacher-centred" approach', the one sentence almost concealed within a paragraph discussing the multiple roles of the teacher and listing teacher roles from two different sources brought the key issue of the non-native teacher back into focus without even mentioning it: *'Oddly enough, the role in which she [the teacher] could act as herself is not mentioned on either list, or anywhere else.'*

It is often statements like this, hidden in broader discussions, that cut to the heart of the non-NEST matter with the sharpness of a double-edge sword and speak intimately to those teachers who, like me, have experienced the profoundly damaging experience of having to hide the fact that we had been raised speaking a language other than English, or felt we had to do so, for fear of losing face in front of our students, their parents or sponsors. Being able to act as ourselves - to walk into the classroom without having to shed the fullness of our identity and personal history at the door; to tap into the richness of our own experiences as English language learners explicitly for the benefit of our students; to recognise and be proud of our hard-won knowledge and expertise: in short, to feel and behave comfortable and confident in our own skin as legitimate teachers of English. This is the ultimate goal, and yet, the one that is often glossed over or denied in the literature, and indeed in many teacher education programmes. And this is why it is important that you do not get distracted by the singular voice and style that permeates the whole book, for a lot of what Péter Medgyes has to say about the NEST/NNEST issue in this new edition remains as relevant and insightful today as it was when the first edition of *The Non-native Teacher* was published over 20 years ago.

It is certainly possible that some readers might find the current edition of *The Non-native Teacher* rather alien – an overall subjective book, with elements of research about someone else's context and circumstances, far removed from theirs. However, for readers like me, this book offers nothing less than an opportunity for bibliotheraphy – a possibility of reading for healing. For teachers for whom, no matter how long or hard we have studied it, and despite the well-meaning contemporary discourses around its ownership, English remains as ever 'an-other language', it is natural to identify with the arguments, examples and anecdotes woven through these pages, because they provide a mirror in which our own experiences and professional life stories are reflected. This identification inevitably helps us feel a little bit less alone in an industry that is still inequitable and discriminatory against the so-called non-native-English-speaking teacher in many parts of the world. It also allows us to have deeper insights into our own situations.

Reading the current edition gave me unexpected moments of epiphany, as a given line or sentence spoke to my history or my own thoughts with the force of a lightning bolt and helped me understand myself a little better. Let me give you an example: during a plenary at a recent EFL teachers' conference, the speaker put forward the argument for English as Lingua Franca (ELF) in terms of English now being the medium of communication of choice in a globalised world. While nobody can dispute the fact that English is currently by far the most powerful language in the world, I found myself reacting vehemently against that statement.

A few days later, as I was reading Péter's analysis of the impact of the global spread of English in Chapter 1, the line about immigrants for whom 'English remains a surrogate language, a substitute vehicle for communication **forced upon them** by the speech community that surrounds them' (*emphasis mine*), I finally understood my irrational reaction at that conference. I felt much closer to the truth about my own complicated, ambiguous and contradictory relationship with the English language - a language I both love and to which I have devoted long years of study and hard work, and one that I deeply resent when is it the only possible medium I have to express myself if I want to be understood - particularly at times when I would much rather communicate the full force of my anger, joy, despair, love, fear or anxiety, in no uncertain terms, in the language of my childhood, my family and my first life experiences.

When people who were born and bred speaking English, and have fully enjoyed the benefits and entitlements that come with that -including having relatively disproportionate opportunities to be heard or read as authors and experts in the field, given that they only represent less than 20% of the EFL teachers in the world - when such colleagues disseminate the naive view that English is now a universal property, a world heritage site of communication belonging to humanity, or blithely justify the

---

[1] With a score of 0.889, English features as almost twice as powerful as Mandarin, the next most powerful language in the Power Language Index. https://medium.com/world-economic-forum/these-are-the-most-powerful-languages-in-the-world-2f7d042b9342#.likur9vmh

omnipresence and almighty power of English in terms of choice, Péter Medgyes' voice still expresses a necessary, dissonant, liberating view for many.

I have stated above that I also found myself disagreeing with some of Medgyes' ideas. In my case, it was particularly those which reflected what could be interpreted as an introjected, negative view of the linguistic proficiency of multilingual teachers who have learnt English as a second, additional or foreign language, and which is described in the book as a 'handicap' when compared to that of 'native speakers.' And this is precisely where the damage inflicted by the long-lasting, pervasive deficit view of the NNESTs, which dominated much of 20th century thought in the fields of Applied Linguistics and English Language Teaching, can be seen at work only with the benefit of 21st century hindsight, courtesy of the recent Multilingual Turn in Languages Education, which offers a more balanced shift in perspective, from a deficit to an asset view of the NNEST. Seen in this light, my disagreement swiftly melts, to give way to compassion at the poignant recognition of a lonely prophet preaching ahead of his time, a physician in need of healing himself.

This updated edition of *The Non-native Teacher* is an essential book, a must-read for everyone involved in the ELT industry and, in certain respects, a classic in that, while some of its contextual detail, and a few of the ideas put forward, may at times sound slightly out of step with contemporary thinking in some quarters, its key messages have stood the test of time. You might be forgiven for thinking that this might sound like an accolade of sorts, even a virtue. In this case, however, the fact that this text is still relevant today is symptomatic of the scale and magnitude of the non-NEST issue in our industry over the twenty years after the book was first published.

When English Language Teaching ultimately becomes an equitable profession, then this book will be read as a significant contribution to NNEST studies in the history of ELT and will no longer be regarded as other than a historical work. Until then, it needs to be actively read and discussed in every teacher training, trainer training and management programme.

Silvana Richardson, Cambridge, December 2016

Publisher's Note

Publishing history

The first edition of *The Non-native Teacher* was published by Macmillan in 1994, as part of its MEP Monographs methodology series. This edition went on to win the English Speaking Union (ESU) Duke of Edinburgh prize in 1995.

The second edition, with some additional material, was published by Max Hueber Verlag in 1999.

Both editions established themselves as key titles on the topics and were widely used in training courses throughout the world. However, following various publishing company changes, both eventually went out of print.

Over the last few years, it has become clear that the questions raised in the earlier editions are still relevant, and warrant further discussion in relation to the developing range of teaching contexts and political, economic and educational change. The reactions to Silvana Richardson's plenary at the 2016 IATEFL Conference – and to both her and Péter Medgyes' subsequent sessions – confirmed the feeling that a new edition would make a worthwhile contribution to the debate.

The present edition: black and blue

The first thought was to simply 'revise and update' the original text. But this quickly proved to be unrealistic. It would require much rewriting to incorporate the developments over the last 25 years and risked being confusing for those who knew the original. It also risked watering down the author's distinctive and individual voice.

The decision was made to leave the original content largely as it was (apart from some essential updating of detail), to form the main text (printed in black) , and to add substantial new material from the viewpoint of 'today' (printed in blue).

New material (in blue)

Each chapter is now framed by totally new material:

- Focus points to provide an easy way in.
- Margin notes – arising from the points in the original text and suggesting ways in which the reader/user can relate these to their own current and local situation.
- Further reading – a few current titles related to the content of the chapter.

The aim is to provide an interactive continuum between situations and views from several decades ago and today, and looking ahead to possible future developments both internationally and within different teaching contexts.

Potential readers/users

Our aim is for the material to provide useful points of discussion on teacher training and continuing professional development (CPD) courses, while also encouraging individual readers to relate it to their own teaching situations, and raising questions that might encourage academic readers to explore different teaching classroom situations further.

We hope you enjoy it.

Susan Holden, Swan Communication, March 2017

Style and Factual Content

Terminology

NEST and non-NEST

In the original editions, the author used the terms 'NEST' and 'non-NEST' to denote 'native-English-speaking teachers' and 'non-native-English-speaking teachers'. Elsewhere, abbreviations such as NS and NNS have been used, as well as various other forms, which are apparent from the papers and book titles in the Bibliography. Some people have objected to the negative connotation of 'non-', but, for the sake of continuity, this current edition continues to use the terms NEST and non-NEST.

'she' and 'he'

Throughout this text, the teacher is referred to as 'she', and the learner as 'he' for the sake of convenience.

Spelling

The original text used British English spelling, while many of the quotations cited are from American English sources. We have continued this practice of using both conventions, as appropriate.

In addition, as 'fossilization' was first used with its linguistic connotation in an American context, we have used that spelling throughout.

SURVEYS

This edition contains results from the following three surveys:

Survey 1   28 respondents from the US, plus a follow-up interview with 7 of them.
Survey 2   216 respondents from 10 countries.
Survey 3   81 Hungarian non-NESTs, followed by 10 interviews.

Acknowledgements

The author and publisher are very grateful to the following people, reflecting a range of teaching backgrounds and contexts, who gave their opinions on this project at an early stage and offered subsequent advice and suggestions.

Gail Ellis, Simon Greenall, Nayr Ibrahim, Alan Maley, Vinicius Nobre, Uwe Pohl, Catarina Ponte, Silvana Richardson, Margit Szesztay, Scott Thornbury

In particular, we would like to thank Shelagh Rixon for her invaluable 'running commentary' on the project as it developed. She provided useful – and often challenging – comments and ideas which have helped to shape it.

We hope that this final published form reflects this range of views, although we take full responsibility for its final form. We hope you will find it useful, challenging and thought-provoking.

The author would also like to thank his two co-authors Valéria Árva and Eszter Benke and adds:

'I have talked about the NEST/non-NEST issue at dozens of teachers' conferences in the past quarter century. My thoughts have generally been warmly welcomed and this has encouraged me to believe that a third edition of this book might not be such a bad idea after all. I wish to extend my heartfelt gratitude to both my NEST and non-NEST colleagues the world over.'

Permissions

We are grateful to the following for permission to reuse two previously published papers:

- Árva, V. & P. Medgyes (2000) 'Native and non-native teachers in the classroom' *System 28* (pp. 355-372), Elsevier. (see Chapter 11).
- Benke, E. & P. Medgyes (2005) 'Differences in teaching behaviour between native and non-native speaker teachers: as seen by the learner' in E.Llurda (Ed.) *Non-native Language Teachers: Perceptions, Challenges and Contributions* (pp. 195-215), Springer. (see Chapter 12)

Introduction

Rationale

This book aims to study the major differences in teaching attitudes between native-speaking teachers of English (*NESTs*) and non-native-speaking teachers of English (*non-NESTs*). My primary concern is to examine the characteristics of non-NESTs by comparing them against NESTs. Once the distinctive features have been identified, I shall suggest ideas about how non-NESTs may become better teachers on their own terms. Although the message is hopefully relevant to all kinds of ELT experts, I wish to reach practising teachers first and foremost.

Until recently, ELT literature has barely dealt with the native/non-native division and, quite often, has openly challenged it. There are several possible reasons for this negative attitude.

Those who dismiss the idea of distinction usually refer to the ambiguities with which it is so obviously loaded. First of all, they say, it is difficult to divide the world into two neat groups: English-speaking and non-English-speaking countries. What about places like India, Nigeria or South Africa, where English is the first or second language for a significant number of citizens?

Opponents of this distinction raise similar problems when the native speaker is contrasted with the non-native speaker of English. What about children in immigrant families who speak the language of their parents at home and the language of the community in the street and at school? Are they native or non-native speakers of English?

The issue is also rich in politico-educational implications. For example, if we accept the native/non-native distinction, we may unwittingly abet discriminatory practices against non-NESTs who seek job opportunities abroad.

Nevertheless, it seems to me that most teachers, as well as their students, fall outside these fuzzy areas. Most of us *do* come from English-speaking or non-English-speaking countries; most of us *are* native or non-native speakers of English. But even those teachers whose identity is equivocal seem to show dominant features of belonging. In my view, the native/non-native distinction *does* exist not only in reality but also, and more significantly, in the minds of millions of teachers. It should not be rejected, overlooked or blurred, simply because it runs in the face of certain theories or ideologies; it deserves the researcher's attention. It is for this reason that the present book draws the line between NESTs and non-NESTs, if only for sake of convenience, and endeavours to highlight points of divergence by grasping them as they feature in our everyday teaching behaviour.

As a matter of fact, the native/non-native distinction has usually been neglected for far more prosaic reasons than the ones mentioned above. Let me draw attention to a few of them.

Firstly, the study of NESTs and non-NESTs is at the interface of several disciplines: linguistics, sociolinguistics, psycholinguistics, pedagogy, educational politics and several other fields of research all seem to have a bearing. These ramifications of the topic have prevented the researcher from seeing the forest for the trees.

Secondly, non-NESTs are scattered around the globe; the differences between those working at opposite ends of the world may be staggering. Blinded by the multitude of divergences, researchers have often overlooked the features all non-NESTs have in common.

Thirdly, most professional literature gets written in English by researchers who speak English as their native language. Although non-natives also conduct research, their activities are largely restricted to their home environment and few find their way into the mainstream of international communication. This applies with particular force to researchers living in the so-called developing countries.

Finally, for quite some time ELT researchers were reluctant to write about the teacher at all, whether NEST or non-NEST. 'Learner-centredness', the buzzword of the 1970s and 1980s, implied that teachers should keep a low profile in the teaching/learning operation. As a consequence, research focusing on the teacher was pushed to the periphery. Nowadays efforts to bring the teacher back onto the stage are gaining momentum – I wish to join this movement.

The structure of this edition

The book is symmetrically arranged in six parts and twelve chapters. *Part I* is like a runway for take-off, placing the issue of the native/non-native speaker in a general framework extending beyond ELT. While Chapter 1 discusses problems arising from the hegemony the English language enjoys in international communication, Chapter 2 is an attempt to clarify certain ambiguities inherent in the dichotomy between the native and the non-native speaker.

In *Part II*, the focus shifts from the speaker in general to the teacher in particular. Chapter 3 seeks to justify why it is the teacher, and not the student, who is the focus of my attention. By drawing the line between NESTs and non-NESTs, in Chapter 4 I advance a few hypotheses and then introduce the three surveys whose purpose it is to validate those hypotheses.

Part III carries the central messages of the book. Chapter 5 and Chapter 6 respectively scrutinise the negative and positive aspects of being a non-NEST in great detail.

Chapter 7 in *Part IV* is meant to round off the debate by suggesting an answer to the question: 'Who's worth more: the native or the non-native?' In a reconciliatory tone, Chapter 8 suggests forms of collaboration between 'them' and 'us'.

Part V is essentially a collection of practical ideas about how non-NESTs can improve their English-language proficiency. Chapter 9 offers activities related to teachers' professional lives whereas Chapter 10 recommends activities they can do in their leisure time.

Part VI opens avenues for further research in the area. Whereas the empirical studies shown in earlier chapters are based on teachers' self-perception, Chapter 11 examines mismatches between stated and actual teaching behaviour through video-recordings and interviews. The final chapter, Chapter 12, investigates the learners' take on the issue.

In conclusion, I freely admit that this book is slanted towards non-NESTs for at least two good reasons. One is that, although we greatly outnumber NESTs, there is relatively little on the market to address our special problems. The second reason is that our difficulties are often more daunting than those confronting NESTs. Let's face it: my full sympathy is with the non-NEST – what other attitude would you expect from an author who himself is a non-NEST?

Péter Medgyes, Budapest, March 2017

CHAPTER 1

The juggernaut called English

Focus points

- The reasons why English has become the *lingua franca* of the world
- Positive and negative effect on the use of non-native English speakers' L1
- The changing varieties of English
- Attitudes towards the 'English as a Lingua Franca' (ELF) movement

1.1 English as the language of international communication

Whether we like it or not, English has become the primary language of international communication, the *lingua franca* of the world, and it is rolling ahead like a juggernaut. More people speak English today than have ever spoken any single language in the recorded history of the world. According to conservative estimates, it is spoken by 700 million people; more radical estimates put this figure between one and two billion. Even more strikingly, the number of those who speak English either as their mother tongue or as a second or foreign language has grown by 40 per cent since the 1950s (Crystal 1987). English is the official or semi-official language in more than 60 countries over the six continents, or as Fishman puts it, 'The sun never sets on the English language'(1982: 18). If the current trend continues, by the end of the 20th century people who speak English as a second or foreign language will outnumber those for whom it is the mother tongue (Kachru 1982). ◎¹

English has become the dominant language in many fields of activity, such as business and banking, industry and commerce, transportation, tourism, sports, international diplomacy, advertising, pop music and so on. But above all, English has become the common language of scientific discourse in a world where the relative 'development' of a nation can best be measured in terms of its access to science through English (Kaplan 1983).

EXAMPLE

Garfield reports that 88 per cent of all articles in the Science Citation Index are in English and 96 per cent of all citations refer to articles written in English (quoted in Grabe 1988). ◎²

In fact, the rise of English as a universal language is an accident of historical circumstances. As the British Empire faded, so the influence of the United States rose. Since World War II, military development, economic stability and the invention of computer networking have all been instrumental in securing a privileged status for the nations who speak English as their first language (Kaplan 1987). Although the spread of English is not due to any superiority of the language itself, it cannot be denied that the extensive use of English has contributed to a relative enrichment in every area of its use.

◎¹ Kachru was writing in the early 1980s, not today.

Did his prediction come true? Search for data on the internet.

Further reading:
Graddol (2006)

◎² Do you think the percentages have increased or decreased in favour of English since then? What makes you think so?

Governments on either side of the Atlantic have long recognised that the English language is their greatest 'God-given' asset. Unlike oil extracted from the North Sea or Alaska, the supply of the English language is inexhaustible. Phillipson was right in claiming that Britain, for example, is amply compensated for the loss of the British Empire. Metaphorically speaking,

> 'whereas once Britannia ruled the waves, now it is English which rules them. The British empire has given way to the empire of English' (1992a: 1).

The promotion of the English language is thus an excellent form of investment. No wonder that government agencies, as well as some official bodies and private organisations, invest huge amounts of money in exploring new markets for English.

EXAMPLE

Along with the collapse of Communism, in Eastern European countries, Russian, which had been the compulsory first foreign language in the school curriculum, was de facto replaced by English (and German in certain countries). In quick response, the 1991–92 ELT budget of the British Council in Hungary, for example, rose by 500 per cent compared to the 1989–90 budget, while the American government sent a contingent of 100 Peace Corps volunteers. At the same time, the World Bank decided to provide aid amounting to 12 million US dollars to support foreign-language teaching, primarily ELT, in Hungary (Medgyes 1993) ⊙³

The English language is merely a tool to help achieve economic and political goals – but it is an extremely effective one. As a consequence, some non-English-speaking countries are unenthusiastic about the onslaught of English and those who regard it as a sign of 'linguistic imperialism' often try to hold up the process of 'linguistic genocide', that is the degeneration of the native language. Indeed, a study of English including 102 countries established that poorer countries are more dependent on English as a language of instruction and communication (Fishman *et al.* 1977). ⊙⁴

At an individual level, too, non-native speakers of English find it hard to compete with native speakers on equal terms (Chapter 2.2). Referring to multi-lingual and multi-ethnic societies where English is often the primary medium of instruction, Phillipson says that

> 'For children whose mother tongue is not English, English is *not* the language of their cultural heritage, *not* the language of intense personal feelings and community, *not* the language most appropriate for learning to solve problems in cognitively demanding decontextualized situations, etc. English does *not* necessarily have teaching materials which are culturally appropriate, *nor* experts with the appropriate linguistic and cultural understanding for all learning contexts' (1992a: 286). ⊙⁵

His arguments may also apply, albeit to a lesser degree, to monolingual cultures who may feel threatened by the omnipresence of English.

On the other hand, the spread of English may also be regarded as a boon. Apart from those native and non-native speakers for whom English primarily serves some utilitarian purposes, there are a number of people who appreciate English for its role of promoting cross-cultural communication and global

⊙³ Since the mid-1990s, support from foreign agencies has gradually dried up in Hungary. As the United States Information Agency was closing its office in Budapest, I asked its last Director why they had decided to move out of Hungary. His curt answer was: 'You know, Péter, Hungary is no longer sexy'.

Has your country ever been the beneficiary of financial assistance from foreign donors?

Further reading:
Bolitho & Medgyes (2000)

⊙⁴ Is this statement about the lack of official enthusiasm for English still true? How do you account for the rise in its popularity for ever-younger learners in some countries?

⊙⁵ Download 'Dreams and Realities' (2011) from the internet. Select the chapter you find most relevant for your local educational environment.

Do your experiences support the author's claims?

understanding (Smith 1983). Today, English is no longer the carrier of essentially one culture, but that of the cultural heritage of all those individuals and communities who use English in their everyday lives, each of them giving it a distinct identity of their own. In terms of its significance, Kachru (1982) likens the spread of English to the modern use of computers.[1]

Be that as it may, the demand for English far exceeds the supply. Since English is a precondition for countries to gain access to, or remain in, the mainstream of global communication, many governments do all they can to satisfy this insatiable demand. From the individual's point of view, too, English is the language of social empowerment (Eggington 1992): as knowledge of English is a passport to a better job and, conversely, the inability to speak and write in English is a disadvantage (Krasnick 1986), millions of young people spend thousands of hours trying to come to grips with the English language. Some researchers warn, though, that the majority *waste* their time learning English, because they will not have the chance to use it in their future careers (Rogers 1982).

In some countries native-speaking teachers of English enforce the rule of the English language. In other countries, however, which cannot afford (or do not wish) to invite NESTs in significant numbers, non-NESTs, such as myself, are the 'prophets'. In view of the concerns referred to above, we should be aware of the ambivalent nature of our job and the responsibility that it entails. ⊙⁶

⊙⁶ Do NESTs in your country typically teach in state education, universities, or private language schools?

1.2 The Inner Circle, the Outer Circle, the Expanding Circle

The Anglo-Saxon tribes forced their language on the ancient inhabitants of the British Isles. In 1620, the *Mayflower* dropped anchor in America with 120 Pilgrim Fathers on board, who brought their puritan convictions together with the English language. About 150 years elapsed before deported convicts and their guards established the first British settlements in Australia and shortly afterwards New Zealand was annexed to the British Empire, only just in time to prevent the French taking over the islands.

Basically, these are the countries belonging to Kachru's (in Quirk & Widdowson 1985) *Inner Circle* (**Figure 1**) in which the majority of the population speak English as their mother tongue.

Figure 1: The three concentric circles

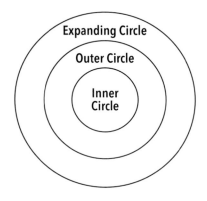

---

[1] Mind you, many people call into question the efficacy of computers.

First Britain and, in her wake, some other Inner Circle countries, took over half the world. As a concomitant of their rule, they imposed the English language on the indigenous people with whom they came into contact. Thus English spread in the colonies and became the second language for a privileged elite. Countries such as India, Pakistan, Singapore, Nigeria, Zambia and Kenya belong to what Kachru calls the *Outer Circle*. Different as they are, these countries have one feature in common: English is the institutionalised language in many spheres of life, an *intranational* means of communication.[2]

Although virtually all former colonies have now achieved independence, the influence of Inner Circle countries today is stronger than ever. As a consequence, English is the first foreign language in countries as far from each other as the Czech Republic is from China, or Brazil is from Tadjikistan; the *Expanding Circle* in effect includes the rest of the world.

In accordance with the three concentric circles, English speakers can be classified into three broad and indistinct groups: those for whom English is the *native language* (or mother tongue), those for whom it is a *second language*, or those for whom it is a *foreign language* (Chapter 2.1).

There are several other ways of grouping English- and non-English-speaking countries. Phillipson (1992a), for example, speaks of *core-English countries* as opposed to *periphery-English countries*. In this binary distribution, second and foreign language speakers of English have been grouped together; they are both peripheral

> 'in the sense that norms for the language are regarded as flowing from the core English-speaking fountainheads' (Phillipson 1992a:25) (Chapter 6.6).

People living in different parts of the world speak English in their own ways, displaying linguistic features which reveal their roots. Thus British speakers can immediately be distinguished from American speakers, who can in turn be distinguished from Indian speakers of English. Similarly, a German accent is easily identified, and so is a Persian or Japanese accent. Furthermore, within each Inner Circle country, English speakers represent different varieties. Those of us who have experienced difficulty in understanding, for example, Texan English in the US, or Geordie in Britain, are only too well aware of the richness of dialects. ⊙⁷

⊙⁷ Of course, it's not only accent which is varied, but vocabulary and grammar too. Can you suggest examples?

⊙⁸ Do you have difficulty in understanding any specific English accent? Can you recall an awkward situation similar to the one I related?

EXAMPLE

I remember spending a few days in Newcastle, England. As I was exploring the town, I lost my way. I asked a man the way. He said something I couldn't understand, so I asked him to repeat his directions. He repeated it – not a word did I catch. After one more try, the guy smiled at me, shrugged his shoulders and went on his way. Even today I'm not sure whether he was speaking English with a Geordie accent, or whether it was Norwegian or Icelandic. ⊙⁸

---

[2] Certain countries are even less amenable to arbitrary grouping; consider Jamaica or South Africa, where English is the native language of only one segment of the population.

In addition, speakers from the Inner Circle use a sociolect which indicates what section of society they belong to. Thus a university professor tends to speak differently from a carpenter, a teenager typically differs in his or her English usage from a seventy-year-old, and so on.

EXAMPLE

Legend has it that 'Gregory's Girl', a film about Scottish teenagers, was so crammed with Scottish school slang that it had to be subtitled for the American audience.

Indeed, there are so many 'Englishes' in the world that some researchers once predicted that English would fall into separate languages one day, due to mutual unintelligibility (Lewis 1971). They liked to remind us of Latin, which broke into separate Romance languages many centuries ago. Were this fate to await English, it would cease to be the language of international communication, they speculate.

Challenging this grim prophecy, moderates refer, for instance, to Pidgin English, which has not ousted English from its pride of place. Kachru (1982) contends that educated Indian English will surely survive even if a code-mixed variety such as 'Hinglish' should become unintelligible, and Quirk points out that English cannot fall into separate languages, because today

'we have easy, rapid and ubiquitous communication, electronic and otherwise [...] Moreover, we have a strong world-wide will to preserve intercomprehensibility' (Quirk and Widdowson 1985: 3). ☉⁹

1.3 Standard Englishes

The problem of varieties of English inevitably leads to the issue of *Standard English*. Should a particular variety of English be favoured as a model and taught to learners? British English, or American English, or some other major variety? If a British variety were chosen, which one could it be? A Scottish, a Northern English or a Southern English variety? Or *'The Queen's English'* with *Received Pronunciation (RP)*, of which a speech therapist once said:

'No unbiased listener would hesitate in preferring [RP] as the most pleasing and sonorous form' (Wyld 1934: 608). ☉¹⁰

However, such arrogant claims can still be heard in schools, despite the fact that RP is unlikely ever to have been spoken by a more than three or four per cent of the British population (McArthur 1992). ☉¹¹

With reference to norms in their own language use, native speakers tend to adopt either a purist or a liberal attitude. Purists claim that the 'decay' of the English language is, among other things, due to the lack of a codifying body, such as the Academy in France. Others counter that no academy is needed for English to become standardised: the educational system, mass media, publishing and other institutions can do that job (Thomas 1999).

☉⁹ Which force do you think is more powerful: the one that breaks up the English language or, rather, the one which holds it together? What are your reasons?

☉¹⁰ On YouTube, find someone who speaks with an 'authentic' RP accent. Do you find this any more 'pleasing' or 'sonorous' than other accents? Do you have a favourite accent?

☉¹¹ On YouTube, find a short sketch where the character speaks with a typical non-native accent. Can you guess where the speaker comes from?

In response to purists' claim that there was, as it were, a vintage year when the English language achieved a measure of excellence, Aitchison says that

> 'in fact, there never was such a year. The language of Chaucer or Shakespeare's time was no better and no worse than that of our own – just different' (Aitchison 1981: 26).

Although the battle between liberals and purists is camouflaged in linguistic or pseudo-linguistic arguments, it is often motivated by ideological and socio-political interests.

Ordinary native speakers tend to be much less divided over the issue of non-native use of English. As a rule, they do not expect foreigners to speak a standard variety and any accent is accepted, as long as it is understandable without undue effort. This tolerance is particularly perceptible in relation to non-natives who do not aspire to be integrated into the society as full members and are content with the role of the 'foreigner' (Corder 1973). In fact, there may be a point on the scale of proficiency beyond which a non-native speaker risks evoking a belligerent attitude in the native speaker: 'How dare you trespass on my private property?' (Janicki 1985) (Chapter 2.3).

Let me return now to the concept of the three concentric circles in the context of norms. Kachru (in Quirk & Widdowson 1985) calls those in the Inner Circle the *norm-providing* varieties (mainly British and American English). Potentially, there are as many varieties as there are Inner Circle countries, plus countless dialects and sociolects within each, but most of them are rejected as models.

In the Outer Circle, by contrast, there are the *norm-developing* varieties (such as Singapore English or Tanzanian English), which for a long time had little validity beyond the national borders and, quite often, even within them. Although such varieties were widely used in everyday communication, they were regarded as deficient models, hence they were not accepted as alternatives of Standard English (Davies 1989). Some speakers retorted that their nativised variety was not deficient, it was just deviant from the 'Mother English', in other words 'British English', norm, or *different* from it (Smith 1983).

EXAMPLE

An African student, after he was criticised by the native-speaking teacher for using a non-standard form, burst out like this: 'It's our language now and we can do what we like with it!' (Povey 1977: 28). ⊙¹²

⊙¹² Do you agree with the African student in the example? As a native speaker of English, is it all right if you 'speak with an accent'? What if you are a non-native speaker of English?

The status of norm-developing varieties is rapidly changing these days. On the one hand, ELT conducted in the Outer Circle is becoming 'de-Britishised': teaching materials once imbued with British culture are now often set in the native milieu. On the other hand, countries in the Outer Circle have begun to diffuse their own linguistic and cultural norms to the Expanding Circle – partly through the teaching of English as a major international enterprise.

Finally, the varieties in the Expanding Circle are labelled as *norm-dependent*, because non-native speakers' language goals are largely determined by norm-providers. Or to use Kachru's metaphor,

⊙¹³ How would your students react if you spoke with an Australian or South African accent? Or a norm-developing variety, such as Indian or Tanzanian English?

> 'the non-native Englishes are linguistic orphans in search of their parents' (1982: 50). ⊙¹³

As for the relationship between the three categories, Kachru (1982) warns that they should not be regarded as closed sets, but rather as a spectrum of Englishes. Under favourable conditions, norm-developing countries can become norm-providing ones, whereas norm-dependent countries can turn into norm-developing ones. In Phillipson's (1992b) view, too, the dividing line between English as a second language (ESL) and English as a foreign language (EFL) countries is in a constant state of fluctuation.

EXAMPLE

Sweden might be a good example of a country which is in the process of shifting from norm-dependency to norm-development. Due to the fact that the overwhelming majority of the population can speak good English, Swedish English may soon be recognised as a variety in its own right.

Although norm-providing countries seem to have lost the exclusive prerogative to control the standardisation process, the debate about the need for a standard variety remains lively. Some protagonists favour the choice of a Standard English for reasons of economy (Nickel 1987) while Quirk, the distinguished grammarian, argues that

'the existence of standards [...] is an endemic feature of our mortal condition [...] People feel alienated and disoriented if a standard seems to be missing' (Quirk & Widdowson 1985: 5-6).

In similar vein, Kennedy (1985) acknowledges the importance of a certain degree of homogeneity, although he notes that it may be beyond the bounds of the possible to adopt any single set of norms.

The concept of a standard model has come under repeated attack. Liberals challenge it on ideological grounds, saying that the acceptance of any exclusive model engenders discrimination against those coming from non-standard backgrounds. Instead of a single model, they propose that two, or even more, should be specified. In disagreement, Svartvik (in Leech & Svartvik 1975), a well-known Swedish linguist, warns against the idea of multiple norms for fear of the negative consequences they might have on the spread of global English.

Extremists totally reject the model concept: let everyone speak as they please! Quirk angrily lashes out against them:

'Disdain of elitism is a comfortable exercise for those who are themselves securely among the elite' (Quirk & Widdowson 1985: 6).

What matters more, however, is that if this relativistic view were consistently enforced, it would impair mutual intelligibility (Davies 1991), while the profession of ELT, in particular, would become impossible to practise.

Indeed, what is Standard English? Has anyone ever tried to describe it? Kachru cites Ward:

'No one can define [Standard English], because such a thing does not exist' (quoted in Kachru 1982:34).

⊙**14** These terms have now largely been replaced by the umbrella term 'English as a Lingua Franca'.

After reading the Sowden-Cogo debate, explain the principles of the ELF movement.

Further reading:
Sowden (2012) vs.Cogo (2012).

⊙**15** Watch Jay Walker's TED talk, 'The world's English mania' (2009). In his opinion, is the spread of English a tsunami or an opportunity?

What do you think?

Further reading:
Phillipson (1999a/1999b) vs.Crystal (2000).

Standard English is obviously an idealisation, an amalgam of beliefs and assumptions about rules and norms to which certain people attempt to adhere with varying degrees of success. And apparently there are several Standard Englishes available to both native and non-native speakers.

And a final point. Standard English is often used interchangeably with the term *International English* or *International Educated English*. ⊙**14** It is obvious that English is a tool of communication in innumerable human encounters between natives coming from different English-speaking countries, between natives and non-natives, as well as between non-natives. The settings for International English can range from multi-national conferences through business negotiations to tourism and so on. The question now is whether International English is (a) a special kind of Standard English with norms distinct from those of other standard Englishes, or (b) any kind of Standard English used in international settings. In agreement with Davies (1991), I claim that a separate 'international' variety of English does not exist, therefore we had better speak of *English as an International Language* rather than as *International English*.

From the point of view of non-NESTs, the choice of a specific English variety is probably determined by a host of factors. To the extent that this choice is within our scope, we should offer a variety which will help our students perform effectively in their future lives as speakers of English. ⊙**15**

Summary

In this chapter, I have set the scene for the central topic of my book: the native/non-native issue. I have shown that English has become the universal language of international communication. After referring to the ambivalent attitudes towards the hegemony ascribed to the English language, I have presented ways of classifying countries on the basis of their use of English. Speaking of norms, I have argued that today there are several Standard English varieties for teachers and learners to select as a model.

During my discussion, I have used the terms *native speaker* and *non-native speaker* rather freely as though they expressed obvious, universally accepted concepts. In Chapter 2, I shall argue that the native/non-native distinction is, in fact, one of the issues that needs to be most carefully debated.

Further reading

- **Bolitho, R. & P. Medgyes,** (2000) Talking shop: from aid to partnership. *ELT Journal 54* (pp. 379–386).

  This is a dialogue between a Brit and a Hungarian, both of them having been intensively involved in various language development initiatives in Central and Eastern Europe. They discuss their respective priorities and perspectives concerning aid projects.

- **Graddol, D.** (2006). *English Next*. The British Council (available from the British Council website).

  This is an update and extension of Graddol's earlier work, *The Future of English?* (1997). After giving an in-depth analysis of the role the English language plays in our rapidly changing world, the report provides plausible scenarios about the future of the 'World English Project'.

- **Phillipson, R.** (1999a) Voice in a global English: unheard chords in crystal loud and clear. *Applied Linguistics 20* (pp. 265–276).
- **Crystal, D.** (2000) On trying to be crystal-clear: a response to Phillipson. *Applied Linguistics 21* (pp. 415–421).
- **Phillipson, R.** (1999b) Closing word. *The European English Messenger VIII(1)* (p. 65).

  In his review article, Phillipson criticises Crystal for his claim that the English language has been a vehicle for progress at global and local levels. Crystal counters by accusing the reviewer of being led by his political creed rather than by rational thinking.

- **Sowden, C.** (2012) The overnight growth in English as a lingua franca. *ELT Journal 66* (pp. 89–96).
- **Cogo, A.** (2012) English as a lingua franca: concepts, use, and implications. *ELT Journal 66* (pp. 97–105).
- **Sowden, C.** (2012) A reply to Alessia Cogo. *ELT Journal 66* (pp. 106–107).

  In this inspiring debate, the authors argue about the relationship between Standard English and ELF, and the implications of ELF on the teaching of English.

CHAPTER 2

Is the native speaker really dead?

> ## Focus points
> - Defining the concept of the native speaker of English
> - Native and non-native speakers on a continuum
> - Different forms of motivation

In Chapter 1, I used the terms *native speaker* and *non-native speaker* without qualification[1], and indeed, in everyday usage there is no problem with them or with the distinction they suggest. In professional circles, however, one would do well to avoid them these days. ⊙[1]

⊙[1] Check the data on the internet for the number of native vs. non-native speakers of English in different parts of the world. Account for any similarities and differences.

EXAMPLE

*As part of my research for this book (see Chapter 4.2, **Survey 1**), I circulated a questionnaire among my colleagues at the American Language Institute of the University of Southern California. My purpose essentially was to explore whether they found any difference in teaching attitudes between native- and non-native-speaking teachers of English.*

Attached to a completed questionnaire she returned, a virtually bilingual respondent wrote a critique of my research hypothesis. What upset me was not the objections that she raised, for they were relevant and well founded, but the fury with which she used them to attack my innocent proposal. As it turned out in the follow-up interview, her anger was motivated by her repeated failure to get a job in Japan and other countries, merely on the grounds that she had not been born and brought up in an English-speaking country. She had not even been granted the opportunity of a job interview to prove her native-like proficiency.

Since this experience, my conviction that there is more to it than meets the eye has repeatedly been confirmed: the native/non-native distinction reaches far beyond applied linguistic research. It is a hornet's nest, fraught with ideological, socio-political and stinging existential implications, factors which may at times carry far more weight than the rigour of scientific investigation. In fact, academic jargon often serves as a disguise to conceal other considerations.

Nevertheless, in this chapter I hope to provide an overview of the native/non-native distinction under the spotlight of applied linguistic research alone, divesting it of other aspects which might blur my focus. Nor do I touch upon its validity in the context of ELT, an issue I address in **Part II**.

---

[1] Some researchers have begun to replace the term *native speaker* with the term *native user* to emphasise that language includes writing and print as well as speech.

2.1 Defining the native speaker

The native/non-native division is one of the most complex and elusive areas in applied linguistics. At different points in time, researchers have thrown doubt on the categories of native or non-native speaker. Even in the 1980s, Paikeday (1985) confidently entitled his book 'The native speaker is dead', while Rampton in the 1990s was more nuanced, with an article entitled 'Displacing the native speaker'. Ferguson (1982) formulated the radical approach as follows:

'In fact, the whole mystique of native speaker and mother tongue should probably be quietly dropped from the linguist's set of professional myths about language' (1982: vii).

To replace the native/non-native speaker, new terms have been coined, such as *more or less accomplished* (Edge 1988) or *proficient users of English* (Paikeday 1985), *expert speakers and affiliation* (Rampton 1990), *English-using speech fellowships* (Kachru 1985), and so on. What all these labels have in common is the heavy stress on what Kachru (1992) calls 'WE-ness' instead of the *us and them* dichotomy. The trouble is that these well-sounding terms are no less spurious than the weathered terms, native/non-native speakers (Medgyes 1992). ⊙²

Native and non-native speakers: a dichotomy or a continuum?

In an effort to pin down the native speaker, let me present a summary of the major points found in oft-quoted definitions (Stern 1983, Crystal 1985, Richards et al. 1985, Davies 1991). Thus the native speaker of, say, English is someone who:

1 was born in an English-speaking country; and/or

2 acquired English during childhood in an English-speaking family or environment;

3 speaks English as his/her first language;

4 has a native-like command of English;

5 has the capacity to produce fluent, spontaneous discourse in English;

6 uses the English language creatively;

7 has reliable intuitions to distinguish right and wrong forms in English. ⊙³

Sure enough, all of these are fuzzy and inconsistent criteria. Let me mention a few major objections:

1a After birth, many children move with their family to a non-English-speaking country; hence they do not acquire English, but rather the language of the new community.

1b Even those who acquired English as children may partly or completely lose this knowledge once they move to live in a non-English-speaking country.

1c Anyway, which countries count as 'English-speaking countries'? Can someone born in a norm-developing country be regarded as a native speaker of English (Chapter 1.3)?

2a What is the range of childhood? A three-year-old is a child, but what about a nine-, a twelve- or a sixteen-year-old? With regard to language acquisition, the 'critical period' is often mentioned in the literature, but its scientific validity is dubious (Stern 1983).

⊙² 'L2 users should be judged by what they are, L2 users, not what they can never be by definition, native speakers' (Cook 2005:50). What do you think Cook means by this?
Further reading: Cook (2005)

⊙³ According to this list of criteria, are you a native or a non-native speaker of English? Do you know of anyone who is an 'in-between case'?

⊙⁴ Kramsch (2014) argues that bilingualism is not the same as double monolingualism.

In your opinion, what is the difference between them?

Further reading:
Kramsch (2014)

2b There is no problem so long as both parents speak English to the child. But what if one of them happens to be a non-native speaker of English and speaks to the child in his/her L1? In that case, the child is likely to become a bilingual. But then which one is his/her native or first language? Can one be a native speaker of two languages? ⊙⁴

2c What about eight-year-old Juan? His father is Mexican, his mother is Norwegian, but the family have been living in Australia for five years. Thus Juan is acquiring two languages at home, plus English outside home. As a trilingual, which will he have as his dominant language: the home languages or the language of the community?

3 How can we define the *native language* in relation to the *mother tongue, first language, L1, home language* or *dominant language*? Let alone such phrases as the *second language* or *foreign language*? To what extent are these labels interchangeable? The confusion in this regard is apparent.

4a Similarly messy is the use of concepts such as *command of English, knowledge of English, competence in English*, or *proficiency in English*.² The term *native-like* proficiency clearly reveals the insecurity of researchers.

4b To say that a native speaker has a native-like command is sheer tautology; it is the same as suggesting that a good bus driver has the ability to drive a bus well.

4c As language teachers, we all know that there are many ways of measuring language proficiency. Nevertheless, there is no yardstick with which natives can be distinguished from non-natives. Where does nativeness begin on a test with, say, a hundred items?

5 By the same token, nor can the degree of native versus non-native fluency and spontaneity be identified. For example, in certain types of discourse, such as creative speaking or writing, native speakers stop and search for the right term or structure, possibly more often than non-natives. On the other hand, even elementary learners are able to use simple structures at a native level of automaticity.

6 Or how could differences in the creative use of English be specified? Furthermore, who would deny the creative genius of non-native writers of the English tongue, such as Conrad, Nabokov or Soyinka?

7 'When in trouble, consult a native speaker', runs the adage. Yes, but which native speaker: the linguistically naive or refined native speaker (Crystal in Paikeday 1985)? Unfortunately, it is common experience that the intuitions and judgements supplied by even the most educated native speakers are not always reliable. And they seldom agree amongst themselves... (Chapter 11.2)! ⊙⁵

⊙⁵ I have reservations about each of the seven criteria. Which one(s) do you take issue with? Why?

Needless to say, all these issues imply far more subtle and diverse ambiguities than I have been able to demonstrate. For lack of space, however, I would prefer not to dig deeper.

---

² Throughout this book, I refrain from using the term *competence*, because I would need to contrast it with *performance* and then bring in *linguistic competence* and *communicative competence* – a daunting task which would force me into digressions.

2.2 The interlanguage continuum

By supplying this list of quibbles, however, I do not wish to challenge the existence of the native speaker or, logically, that of the non-native speaker. Fugitive concepts as they are, they may still be legitimate and in everyday usage the native/non-native division does not normally pose problems. To all intents and purposes, my next-door colleague X is a native speaker of English, while I am not. Only a fool would call into question the obvious differences between us. True, at our present state of knowledge, the distinguishing features between us cannot be specified with any great degree of precision. But the same is true of a number of other phenomena in the world, and yet we regard these as separate entities.

EXAMPLE

To my knowledge, no one has been able to draw the line between such opposites as life and death or sanity and insanity, except in legal or practical terms.

I suggest, therefore, that we retain the terms 'native' and 'non-native' speaker, if only for sake of convenience. Let us accept Halliday's paradox (in Paikeday 1985): the native speaker is a useful term, precisely because it is not too closely defined. ☉⁶

There is general agreement that all *users* of English are simultaneously *learners* of English, granting that native speakers *have acquired* English in comparison with non-native speakers who *are still acquiring*. By virtue of speaking a more or less advanced degree of interlanguage (Selinker 1972), every speaker can, metaphorically, be placed on the interlanguage continuum at any stage of his/her learning process (**Figure 2**). ☉⁷

Figure 2: The interlanguage continuum – Version A

Zero proficiency point → Absolute proficiency point

Movement between the imaginary zero and absolute points is determined by various factors, among which the country of birth and the environment are supposed to play a decisive role. Thus, if born and brought up in an English-speaking community, a person would probably be a more accomplished user of English than if born and brought up in a non-English-speaking one. Hence native speakers are, *potentially*, more accomplished users of English than non-native speakers.

The question now is whether or not *all* native speakers are closer to the absolute proficiency point on the continuum than even the most advanced non-native speakers. In other words, can non-native speakers outweigh native speakers' advantage, by dint of other variables, such as a higher degree of motivation, better aptitude, longer experience, better education and so on? Are they handicapped in any absolute or relative way? Let us examine the two alternatives separately.

If non-NESTs are unable to ever catch up with NESTs, the interlanguage continuum looks like this (**Figure 3**):

☉⁶ While most researchers reject the native/ non-native dichotomy, it 'cannot be simply "magicked-away"' (Pacek 2005: 243).

What do you think Pacek means by this?

☉⁷ The term *interlanguage* privileges the native speaker by implying that 'the goal of a second language learner is to be just like a native speaker' (Mahboob 2010:4).

Do you agree?

Further reading: Mahboob (2010)

Figure 3: The interlanguage continuum – Version B

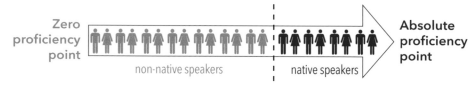

Figure 3 suggests that non-native speakers may constantly move along the continuum as long as they learn-to-use/use-to-learn English, but at a certain point their progress is halted by a glass wall. They can catch a glimpse of natives thronging on the other side of the wall, but they cannot walk through it or climb over it. The wall is bullet-proof, entirely isolating natives from non-natives. ◉⁸

One explanation for the assumed impermeability between natives and non-natives may lie in the different routes they have taken to acquire the target language.

> 'Native speakers move from a position of insecurity to one of security, while non-native speakers move in the reverse direction. Native speakers, however defined, start off seeking meaning: they learn the language offered them in order (in part) to gain the meaning they seek. As they progress, the gain in meaning gives them greater and greater security as they come, through the medium of L, to control their environment. Non-native speakers, on the contrary, already have that control in their L1. Their learning of an L2 means that they must abandon the security of their L1 to become less and less sure in the L2 of what was so familiar in the L1. Eventually, of course, if they make sufficient progress, they also gain security in the L2 as well as in their L1.' (Davies 1991: 35-36).

An even stronger argument for the total separation, it seems, is that non-natives, by their very nature, are norm-dependent as opposed to natives. Their use of English is but an imitation of some form of native use. Just as copyists never become genuine artists, runs the argument, non-native speakers can never be as creative and original as those whom they have learned to copy. They may have some degree of freedom in choosing the native-speaking membership to which they want to belong, but the model and the goal that membership represents should remain their basic preoccupation.

An obvious defect of this line of reasoning is that it runs in the face of everyday experience. We all know of non-natives who can speak English in a more sophisticated manner than the majority of natives, or whose writing abilities are more advanced than most natives'. Now, does native-like command in one or two areas of proficiency entitle the non-native to wear the 'native speaker' badge?

I have to ask at this point: what constitutes language proficiency? Well, there are the four skills, grammar, vocabulary, pronunciation, functions, and so on. But, to use the analogy of cooking, this is not yet a full recipe. The list of ingredients alone does not indicate the relative quantities to be used, nor does it give instructions about the steps to be taken. Without such information, we may arrive at two or more entirely different dishes or, worse still, bungle the whole meal.

Rejecting this alternative, let me offer a second route. This suggests that the non-native speakers' handicap is *relative*, with the implication that they have the potential to catch up with native speakers. By offering this compromise, I let non-native speakers into the much-coveted land of native-like proficiency (**Figure 4**):

◉⁸ Can non-native speakers break through or jump over the 'glass wall'? Have you met any non-native speakers of English whose language competence was on a par with that of natives – or even better?

Figure 4: The interlanguage continuum – Version C

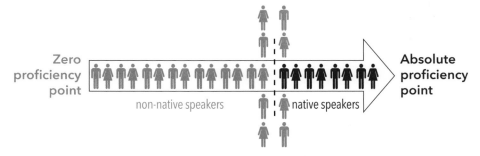

As the figure shows, a few non-natives have overtaken natives – or very few, as Davies (1991) admits. After all, it verges on the impossible for the non-native to outperform the native who spent much of the first five or six years of his/her life acquiring L1. ⊙⁹

2.3 Pseudo-native speakers

The acknowledgement that there are non-natives with a native-like command of English – whom I have come to call *pseudo-native speakers* for want of a better term[3] – does not necessarily imply that they are indistinguishable from natives. There is some evidence to confirm that even pseudo-native speakers display certain characteristics that reveal their non-nativeness – if scrutinised by expert native-speaker observers (Ellis 1985). In everyday situations, however, they pass as natives (Gardner 1985).

Let me list some of the linguistic features that are likely to give pseudo-native speakers away. ⊙¹⁰ In a native/pseudo-native comparison, pseudo-natives:

1   are most frequently and easily recognised by their divergent pronunciation or, to use Kachru's (1982) term, by the 'accent bar'.

EXAMPLE

A Hungarian friend of mine is a pseudo-native speaker of English. However, in England people often reckon that he comes from Australia, in Australia that he must have spent a long time in the US, and in the US that he is British. Some suspect, though, that he is French.

2   have a lower or higher level of idiomaticity than average. ⊙¹¹ Some pseudo-natives, consciously or unconsciously, prefer unmarked forms, refraining from the use of colloquialisms, catch-phrases, let alone slang, while others tend to be over-idiomatic, perhaps in an effort not to sound too drab.

EXAMPLE

The English usage of a Hungarian colleague of mine is full of slang expressions which are just a bit outdated. In appreciation of his bold attempts, a native speaker likened him to an Elvis Presley fan from the 50s.

---

[3] Deliberately, I avoid the term near-native speaker. In my view, a near-native speaker is someone whose proficiency is very good but does not reach native levels, whereas a pseudo-native speaker's proficiency may even surpass the native's in one or several aspects of proficiency. Incidentally, Gimson (in Paikeday 1985), somewhat jokingly, sets up the distinction between the natural native speaker and the honorary native speaker.

⊙⁹ On YouTube, watch the interview extract 'The Late Prof. Alan Davies discussing the concept of the native speaker' (2015).

Select a couple of points worth considering further.

⊙¹⁰ In my opinion, pseudo-native speakers differ from natives on these six counts. Can you add some more? Give examples from your own learning experience.

⊙¹¹ '[M]any so-called NSs can be far less intelligible in global settings than well-educated proficient speakers of a second language' (Moussu & Llurda 2008, p. 318).

If you agree, supply a couple of examples.

3 have gaps in the conceptual knowledge usually acquired by children during their linguistically most formative years (games, stories, nursery songs, the environment, basic school subjects and so on).

EXAMPLE

Do you know the names English-speaking children call each other (copy-cat, fibber, tell-tale, coward, swot, nosey parker)? ⊙[12] *Can you do basic arithmetic operations in English? Can you do them in your head, too? Are you familiar with the conventions of fairy tales (from 'Once upon a time' up to 'And they lived happily ever after')? Does the English for basic terms of biology such as* monocotyledon, thorax, stamen, abdomen *ring a bell? Could you define Thales' or Pythagoras' theorem or laws in English?*

⊙[12] Children's spoken language changes all the time. Do you recognise the terms 'wuss' or 'wally'? Have you come across any other recent examples?

4 use repetitions and routinised language less efficiently (Firth 1957). What pseudo-native speakers tend to miss in conversational situations is not the message content, since often there are no messages exchanged, but rather the ritual of the conversation (Davies 1991). In the English-language use of pseudo-native speakers, the balance between transactional and interactional language tilts towards the former (Corder in Brown & Yule 1983:1-3). ⊙[13]

EXAMPLE

Non-native speakers, including pseudo-natives, communicate in a business-like fashion, reducing small talk that everyday conversation is embedded in. Typically, they produce curt, to-the-point utterances which the native speaker may interpret as signs of rudeness or hostility.

⊙[13] Chinese by birth, Li calls herself a 'between-the-worlds resident'.

This status, she says, 'does give me the licence to march to a different drum, to some extent' (1999:50).

Explain this metaphor.

5 are less aware of the context at large. This may imply referential gaps in certain situations, or slips in register, which may lead to social gaffes. It goes without saying that insensitivity to context often results from deficient knowledge of English-speaking cultures.

EXAMPLE

On the first (and last) occasion I visited a McDonald's in the US, I ordered a hamburger. The girl behind the counter listed a number of what I inferred were fantasy names for various kinds of dressing. After a few abortive attempts to make out their meaning, I gave up and said: 'Give me that last one on the list'. Her non-verbal reaction clearly implied: 'This guy is nuts'.

6 are less coherent and consistent both in their own language use and in their judgement of other people's language use (Coppieters 1987). This has repercussions for ELT and especially for error correction practices (Chapter 6.4).

EXAMPLE

A pseudo-native colleague has complained that she still mixes up 'The same to you' and 'You too' in quick exchanges. So when a native wishes her a merry Christmas, she says 'You too', and when somebody says 'Take care', she often replies with 'The same to you'.

2.4 The 'average' non-native speaker

But let us enter the world of the rank-and-file non-native speaker – a far more densely populated land than that of the pseudo-native speaker. There are two important points to consider here.

One concerns motivation. Non-native speakers fall into two categories in terms of their aspirations. The first group consists of individuals for whom English is an instrument to achieve limited personal or professional goals, such as engaging in simple conversations with foreigners, carrying out routine tasks at work, understanding the gist of an English-language magazine or passing an examination. The second group includes people for whom English is a matter of the utmost importance, such as immigrants, or people for whom English is a major medium in their profession. Non-NESTs obviously belong to this latter category. It is in this sense that Gardner & Lambert (1972) distinguish between *instrumental and integrative motivation*. ⊙**14**

For non-natives with integrative motivation, a deficient command of English is a source of constant dismay. And this handicap is all-embracing: compared to native speakers, they do less well in every aspect of language performance, as a rule. This feeling of under-achievement is particularly troubling when their performance is compared to that of native speakers with similar variables in terms of age, sex, education, intelligence and, especially, profession. Let me mention in passing that we non-NESTs go through this painful experience day in, day out (Chapter 5).

Compared to their own L1 performance, the non-native speakers' handicap in English is even more glaring. Logically enough, they are far more effective in their mother tongue implying, among other things, that they are capable of reaching their communicative goals more directly and with less effort (Medgyes 1989).

The other thing I want to suggest is that even people with strong integrative motivation do not necessarily desire to qualify as native speakers. ⊙**15** The wish to attain native-like proficiency is not the same as an attempt to repudiate one's L1 identity. Even immigrants, for whom full integration may be vital, often keep a distance between themselves and the English-speaking community in which they have chosen to reside. English remains a surrogate language, a substitute vehicle for communication imposed upon them by the speech community that surrounds them.[4]

Fair enough, but then who can decide whether, for instance, Mr Gagnon, an excellent (pseudo-native?) speaker of English, is to be regarded as a native or a non-native? As the native/non-native dilemma is far from being resolved on a theoretical plane, let me suggest, somewhat complacently perhaps, that he be allowed to self-identify. After due reflection, let Mr Gagnon and every one of us decide whether we belong to the group of native, pseudo-native or non-native speakers of English, or perhaps somewhere else. In agreement with Davies, I believe that membership

> 'is largely a matter of self ascription, not of something being given' (1991:7–8). ⊙**16**

⊙**14** Are your students spurred to improve their language competence by instrumental or integrative motivation? Or a mixture of the two, perhaps? What about yourself?

⊙**15** Another pair is *intrinsic* vs. *extrinsic motivation*. What is the difference?

⊙**16** 'Ultimately, what appears to be the most distinguishing feature is simply whether one considers herself a native speaker of a given community and is recognized as such by other speakers' (Moussu & Llurda 2008: 337).

Do you satisfy both conditions?

---

[4] Oddly enough, the reluctance to give up one's native origins and personality may be a major obstacle to achieving a near-native command of English and may lead to fossilization (Chapter 9).

We should bear in mind, however, that such a choice carries responsibilities in terms of confidence and identity. Confidence in the sense that once we claim, say, pseudo-native status, we are not to suffer from the stress syndrome (Chapter 5.3). And identity in the sense that we need to be accepted as such by our fellow-teachers, possibly including native speakers. This implies allegiance to the norms of English, both in a linguistic and cultural respect.[5]

EXAMPLE

> *'I know several foreigners whose command of English I could not fault, but they themselves deny they are native speakers. When pressed on this point, they draw attention to such matters as [...] their lack of awareness of childhood associations, their limited passive knowledge of varieties, the fact that there are some topics which they are more 'comfortable' discussing in their first language. 'I couldn't make love in English,' said one man to me' (Crystal in Paikeday 1985).* ⊙[17]

⊙[17] Watch the TED talk 'Who am I? Think again' by Hetain Patel and Yuyu Rau. There are a few key words in it: *language, accent, imitate, pretend.* How are these related in their performance? Why the title?

Summary

In this chapter, I have examined whether the native/non-native division is indeed no more than a myth. A brief analysis of the definition of 'native speaker' showed that it is unquestionably an elusive term. I have offered three versions of the interlanguage continuum to demonstrate the controversial relationship between native and non-native speakers. I have claimed that even 'pseudo-native speakers' can be pinpointed under close scrutiny, not to speak of non-natives with a moderate command of English. I have concluded this chapter by suggesting that, for the time being, the native/non-native distinction should be established on the basis of self-ascription.

From now on, I shall divert my attention from the general aspects of the native/non-native distinction and study its particular manifestation in the world of ELT. But before I narrow down my focus, let me digress one more time. In Chapter 3, I shall briefly explain why this book, in sharp contrast to many other books published these days, is about the teacher and not the learner.

---

[5] Cultural allegiance does not, of course, equal allegiance to one particular English-speaking culture.

Further reading

- **Cook, V.** (2005) Basing teaching on the L2 user. In E. Llurda (Ed.) *Non-native Language Teachers: Perception, Challenges and Contributions to the Profession* Springer (pp. 47–61).

  The author explains in detail why he prefers the term L2 user to describe the non-native speaker. After presenting the four major characteristic features of L2 users, he passionately argues that they should not be treated as failed native speakers, because difference is not the same as deficit.

- **Kramsch, C.** (2014) Teaching foreign languages in an era of globalization: introduction. *The Modern Language Journal 98* (pp. 296–311).

  This paper explores the impact of globalisation on the ways foreign languages are taught and learned today. These changes, Kramsch argues, 'call for a more reflective, interpretive, historically grounded, and politically engaged pedagogy than was called for by the communicative language teaching of the eighties'.

- **Mahboob, A.** (2010) The NNEST lens. In Mahboob, A. (Ed.) *The NNEST Lens: Non-native English Speakers in TESOL* Cambridge Scholars Publishing (pp. 1–17).

  The opening chapter in this collection of papers defines the 'NNEST lens' as one which combines the concepts of multilingualism, multinationalism and multiculturalism. It then moves on to questioning the privileged status of the native speaker and providing an overview of the non-NEST movement.

CHAPTER 3

A 'teacher-centred' approach

Focus points

- Ongoing interaction between the teacher and the learners
- The complexity of the language teaching operation
- From organised forms of language learning to self-study
- Acquiring IT skills: independently or with support

3.1 Negotiations and responsibilities

'Most people do not realize how much even of their private life is taken up with amateurish teaching and haphazard learning' (Highet 1950: 5). ◎¹

◎¹ Can you give any examples of 'amateurish teaching' and 'haphazard learning' outside the language classroom?

Indeed, we incessantly teach and learn, both at home and at work. There is some kind of teaching and learning going on wherever there are parents and children, experts and beginners, superiors and inferiors. But the best place for a systematic and intensive form of teaching and learning is obviously the school.

In the classroom, there are two main characters: the teacher and the students. On occasion, there may well be a few extras present, such as a group of parents on an open day or a stray school inspector, but they are not entitled to interrupt the lesson.

In this model of the classroom, the teacher's job is to do the teaching and the student's job is to do the learning. In its crudest form, the teacher gives commands which the students try to carry out. A.R. Tom calls this concept, metaphorically, the *billiard ball hypothesis*:

'The pool player (the teacher) aims the cue ball (his behaviour) so that it will strike the target billiard ball (the student) at exactly the right angle to cause the billiard ball (the student) to go into a pocket (the achievement of what the student is supposed to learn'(Tom 1984: 55). ◎²

◎² How do you interpret the 'billiard ball hypothesis'?

EXAMPLE

A group of fifteen-year-olds have just read an article about the dangers of passive smoking. After a few exercises, the teacher tells the students to discuss this issue in pairs. In each pair, one student is instructed to be the smokers' advocate, the other one is the anti-smokers' advocate. After a couple of minutes, however, the pairs begin to flounder. Seeing this, the teacher makes wild gestures to prod the students on and even threatens the most jaded ones. In response, some students make desperate efforts to drag on, others switch into an L1 discussion of their evening schedule, still others give up in a sulk.

As this example is intended to show, no matter how hard the teacher hits the target billiard ball, it won't go into a pocket, because he has not reckoned with the fact that the target billiard ball is the cause of its own movement in a particular direction.

Ideally, classroom interaction is a *two-way process*, in which both parties endeavour to adapt to each other's goals and procedures. First, the teacher initiates an activity, but remains alert for the students' reactions. Thus, in a critical situation like the one in the example, a flexible teacher would take turns to join those pairs where work was about to peter out, and if this didn't help, she would set up a different task. In return, there is a good chance that the students would cooperate. As opposed to her inflexible colleague, the flexible teacher would succeed in sustaining motivation, by being ready to negotiate. The teaching-learning process should consist of *an endless series of negotiations* between the teacher and her students. ☉³

Of course it is possible to learn by slavishly carrying out the teacher's instructions and indeed by self-study.

EXAMPLE

> *On buying my first computer in 1986, I asked a friend, a computer buff, to teach me the basics. He started out by explaining the theoretical underpinnings, using incomprehensible jargon. After half an hour, I interrupted and asked him if he would now please teach me which keys to strike for what purpose. Undeterred, he continued as before: I gave up trying. We never had a second lesson. Instead, I set about the formidable task of learning from a manual.*

My friend may well have been the best computer expert on earth, but clearly he was a pathetic teacher, unable to establish a two-way flow of communication.

In an auspicious learning situation, the student is an active participant assuming partial responsibility for his own progress. At a basic level, responsibility involves making strenuous efforts to acquire the knowledge and skills imparted by the teacher – there is no learning taking place through osmosis.

At a more conscious level, the student not only carries out the instructions, but keeps the teacher informed about his progress by giving positive and negative feedback. The fact that he seeks opportunities to exercise control means that he is willing to *share responsibility* with his teacher. This kind of attitude is an essential condition for successful learning.

Shared responsibility does not imply that teacher and student roles become interchangeable. The idea of interchangeability is absurd since

> 'teachers are expected to know what learners are expected not to know' (Breen 1985: 147).

Breen calls their relationship an asymmetrical and non-egalitarian one, involving different rights and duties.

In fact there is a tacit agreement between the teacher and the students. This means that the students empower the teacher with the dominant role, expecting her to harness it to their benefit. The teacher, in turn, relinquishes some of her power, thus making the students responsible for their own

☉³ Think back to your own schooldays. What were your English teachers like – controlling or flexible? If you (also) had a NEST teacher, was she any different from the non-NESTs in this respect?

⊙⁴ The American writer H.Crews claims 'Teaching – real teaching, is – or ought to be – a messy business'.

Do you agree? Why (not)? How can teaching be made tidier?

Further reading: Underhill (2013)

learning. Their responsibility is, of course, restricted because, unlike the teacher, the students generally arrive at the lesson with no specific plans of their own: they are able therefore only to 'navigate' rather than 'negotiate' (Dickinson 1987), leaving the task of orchestrating, coordinating, adapting, altering, and substituting to the teacher (Gaies 1987). I believe that the skill of manouevring this tug-of-war is one of the distinguishing features of the good teacher. ⊙⁴

3.2 Teacher-centred and learner-centred approaches

Unfortunately, some teachers are not content with their leading role – they seek absolute power. While they arrogantly regard themselves as the sole repository of truth and wisdom, they treat their students as a faceless, monolithic mass. To use Stevick's metaphor, teacher-despots wield a sword with three edges: *mystery, miracle,* and *authority.*

> 'Mystery is the substitute for independent thought, authority is what imposes and enforces mystery; miracle is what assures the follower that he has in fact trusted his destiny into the right hands' (1980: 284).

Educational philosophies which categorically assign the pride of place to the teacher are called *teacher-centred approaches.*

For many years, teacher-centred concepts of education have come in for sustained criticism and the pendulum seems to have swung to the other extreme. Advocates of so-called *learner-centred approaches* claim that the teacher's sole job in the classroom is

> 'to provide the best conditions for learning. The teacher is a means to an end: an instrument to see that learning takes place'(Byrne 1976: 1). ⊙⁵

⊙⁵ Watch Mitra's TED talk (2013) 'Build a school in the cloud'. Identify the main messages.

How did the children in his experiment learn English?

Do you think that the type of education Mitra recommends is the way forward?

Why (not)?

By giving up her time-honoured role as an authority figure, the teacher should behave as a 'human among humans' (Littlewood 1981), they insist (Chapter 6.5). Empathy, needs analysis, counselling skills, self-actualisation, integration, autonomy, creativity and growth are well-known buzzwords. Teachers should learn to show a low profile, and students should refuse to bow to her whims.

⊙⁶ A sceptic might say 'The more fervently you try to prove you're right, the less credible you become'. Do you (dis)agree? Why?

There is nothing wrong with any of these laudable principles. What is not acceptable is the missionary fervour displayed by some proponents of learner-centredness (Medgyes 1986). Firstly, they should not believe that they have invented the wheel – good teachers have always been learner-centred. Secondly, they should substantiate allegations such as 'nine out of ten [teachers] treat their students as full-time linguistic objects' (Stevick 1980: 127) – an accusation which I find exaggerated. Thirdly, and most importantly, zealots should practise what they preach. ⊙⁶ While emphasising the importance of needs analysis in ELT, for example, they should not ignore students' frequent objections to pairwork, groupwork, games, roleplays, simulations, projects and other similar activities. Simultaneously, pleas for more grammar, more L1 explanations, more drills, more translation exercises and more error-correction should be taken seriously.

Students in the classroom, just like children or adolescents in everyday life, are often more conservative than teachers (Nunan 1987). This attitude may be explained by a feeling of insecurity caused by their relative ignorance. Stevick himself warns that

> 'if we, in our zeal to be "humanistic", become too "learner-centred" with regard to "control", we undermine the learner's most basic need, which is for security. We may find that we have imposed our own half-naked anarchy on the class. Absence of structure, or of focus on the teacher, may be all right in certain kinds of psychological training, but not in our classrooms [...] The student's place is at the center of a space which the teacher has structured, with room left for him to grow into' (1980: 33). ◉⁷

A great challenge for almost everyone, including teachers, is how to strike the right balance between being the 'therapist' and the 'policeman' at appropriate times (Maslow 1968).

EXAMPLE

> As a teacher trainer, I have often seen trainees go through a typical form of identity crisis. They begin their teaching practice by holding the reins too loose, thus disrupting the long-established power relationships in the classroom. Their pupils thrust into the vacuum, which leads to neglect of study and discipline problems. Panic-stricken, the trainees suddenly pull the reins in. The pupils' reaction is a mixed feeling of incomprehension and disappointment.

In my experience, students generally demand far more security than teachers deem desirable. In many so-called learner-centred classes, communication between the teacher and the students is no less one-directional than in the class of the much-criticised authoritarian. Widdowson rightly points out that

> 'it is because these differences in the exercise of authority have not been properly recognized that the authoritative actions of the teacher have at times been discredited quite improperly as authoritarian impositions of power' (1990: 189).

3.3 The other side of the desk

In the quote above, Stevick refers to the 'absence (...) of focus on the teacher'. In another book (1976), he acknowledges that, while the learners can afford to be ignorant and insecure, the teacher should always look like a strong person, a source of stability. Dry wittily remarks that

> 'a sure recipe for low learner performance is to set up a situation where the learner pities the teacher, and then pities himself for being saddled with a pitiable teacher' (1977: 200).

But it is very difficult for the teacher to look confident when her authority is continually challenged, when she is constantly warned to withdraw, when she is perennially reminded of the numerous, and often conflicting, roles she is expected to play in the class. ◉⁸

◉⁷ Control and security. What happens if the teacher is not in control?

Supply examples from your own teaching or learning experiences.

◉⁸ How can teachers find the right balance and 'rise from the ashes' day after day (Antier 1976)?

Further reading: Dörnyei & Kubanyiova (2014)

> **EXAMPLE**
>
> *Hoyle (1969: 59-60) lists the following roles ascribed to the teacher in a general educational setting:*
>
> - *a representative of society (inculcates moral precepts);*
> - *a judge (gives marks and ratings);*
> - *a resource (possesses and conveys knowledge and skills);*
> - *a helper (provides guidance for student difficulties);*
> - *a referee (settles disputes among students);*
> - *a detective (discovers rule-breakers);*
> - *an object of identification (possesses traits which students imitate);*
> - *a limiter of anxiety (helps students to control impulses);*
> - *an ego-supporter (fosters students' self-confidence);*
> - *a group leader (establishes group climate);*
> - *a parent surrogate (acts as object of bids for attention.*

⊙⁹ After checking Hoyle's and Harmer's lists, can you think of any other functions?

Further reading:
Harmer (2007)

In the context of the foreign-language class, Harmer (1991) attributes to the teacher the role of the controller, assessor, organiser, prompter, participant, resource, tutor and investigator. ⊙⁹ Oddly enough, the role in which she could act as herself is not mentioned on either list or anywhere else.

Professional literature teems with books on the learner, but is very slim on the teacher. Seldom can we read about her fears and anxieties, which may culminate in what is sometimes called the *Battered Teacher Syndrome* (Chapter 5.3). Few studies have analysed the teacher as a person who hankers after self-actualisation and 'caring and sharing' just as much as her students. If it is the teacher who admittedly exerts the most immediate influence on the students' motivation, we ought to make sure that she herself is duly motivated.

> 'Not until we have taken a critical look at teachers' attitudes, both individual and professional, will we be ready to determine what obstacles still lie in the way of creating the kinds of learning environments that will be most helpful to our students' (Savignon 1976: 114).

To use Savignon's metaphor, it's time to attend to the other side of the desk, too! To be fair, the desire to understand ourselves is not motivated by sheer altruism – we wish to lead as full a life as our students. It is in this sense that I advocate a 'teacher-centred' approach. The rest of this book hopes to give assistance in understanding some of the linguistic and psychological aspects of our work as English teachers in general and non-NESTs in particular.

Summary

In this chapter, I have argued that classroom teaching should be embedded in an endless flow of two-way interaction between the teacher and the students. I have studied the delicate power relationship between teacher and student in terms of duties and responsibilities. Challenging current interpretations of learner-centredness, I have made the claim that students can only be motivated and helped after teachers have understood themselves.

From now on, my attention will be focused on ELT. As a lead-in, in Chapter 4 I shall revisit the native/non-native division in the context of ELT.

Further reading

- **Dörnyei, Z. & M. Kubanyiova** (2014) (Re-)igniting the flame of teacher vision. In Z. Dörnyei & M. Kubanyiova *Motivating Learners, Motivating Teachers: Building Vision in the Language Classroom* Cambridge University Press (pp. 123–144).

  The chapter is based on the premise that only those teachers can motivate learners who themselves are motivated professionals. The authors highlight the discrepancy between the language teacher's ideal self and her actual self, and offer vision-related strategies whereby her enthusiasm can be kindled – or re-kindled when it is waning.

- **Harmer, J.** (2007) Describing teachers. In J. Harmer, *The Practice of English Language Teaching* (4th edition) Pearson Education Limited (pp. 107–120).

  Chapter 4 in this highly acclaimed guide starts with a brief description of what teaching is, then moves on to discussing the teacher's multifarious roles in the classroom and her relationship with learners. The chapter ends by pointing out differences between NESTs and non-NESTs.

- **Underhill, A.** (2013) Mess and progress. In T. Pattison (Ed.), *IATEFL 2012 Glasgow Conference Selections* IATEFL (pp. 242–250).

  Based on a plenary lecture, Underhill's starting point is that 'the class you teach is a *mess*, and so is your school [...] It's OK to be in a *mess*. It's just a fact. If you're alive, that's what you're in.' He then discusses what leadership involves and how a learning organisation should operate.

CHAPTER 4

Natives and non-natives in opposite trenches

Focus points

- The development of 'Content and language integrated learning' (CLIL)
- Differences between the formalist and the activist teacher
- The role of fun and role-play in the foreign-language class
- The status of NESTs and non-NESTs

4.1 Learning content and carrier content

In effect, every teacher is a language teacher. In biology, maths or history, the teacher's primary job is to teach a way of talking and therefore seeing the world (Postman & Weingartner 1969). Language is the most direct way of conveying information about

> 'bodies of knowledge that have been consciously acquired by scientists over years of study and that can be transmitted by conscious and overt instruction of various sorts'
> (Gee 1988: 218-9).

For teachers of 'content-subjects', language is the means and knowledge is the end. But even in the case of 'skill-subjects', such as physical education, music or art, language is an important mediator.

The natural medium of instruction is the mother tongue. In a number of countries, however, teaching is conducted in a second language which has a privileged status in society (Chapter 1.2).⊙¹ The scope for instruction in a second language is determined by several factors, including the type of school, the age of learners, the nature of school subjects and so on. A special case in point is bilingual education or immersion programmes in which a second or a foreign language serves as the language of instruction in all, or some, of the school subjects. ⊙²

Foreign-language teachers, however, are a special lot, because for them the foreign language embodies both the means and the end. Typically, they teach knowledge *about* and skills *in* the foreign language mediated *by* the same foreign language in virtually all situations¹. ⊙³ Furthermore, foreign-language teachers have no direct body of knowledge available in the sense that physics or history teachers have. Or rather, they have two different sets of content to teach: the systems of the foreign language – the syntax, the vocabulary, the phonology – and the topics which serve to present specific items of those

⊙¹ Check the definition of 'Content and language Integrated Learning' (CLIL) on the internet.

Do you have any direct or indirect experience of it? If so, what are its pros and cons?

⊙² Broca (2016) maintains that it is usually the academically better student who can gain access to CLIL education. How true is this in your country?
Further reading

⊙³ Is teaching English through English an ideal and/ or a reality in your context?

---

¹ Classroom interaction is conducted in the foreign language, except when the teacher decides to call on the mother tongue for help in monolingual settings (Chapter 6.6).

systems; Littlejohn (1992) calls these two sets the *learning content* and the *carrier content*.

Roughly speaking, foreign-language teachers fall into two groups which may be termed formalists and activists (Chapter 6.3). The distinguishing feature between them is in the content that they prioritise.

The *formalist teacher* is preoccupied with the learning content, while the carrier content is merely a pretext for her to introduce and practise new language items.

EXAMPLE

A colleague told me the following story. She decided to present the 'what make?' structure to a group of 11-year-olds. The carrier content she chose was cars. Thus she asked the pupils: 'What make is your parents' car?', to which they answered: 'It's a Ford', 'It's a Volkswagen' and so on. During the break, a boy stopped her in the corridor to tell her, in L1 of course, that they had just changed their Skoda for a Nissan and how happy he was. It took the teacher quite a while to realise what he was getting at: he had apparently taken a pattern practice for a genuine inquiry.

The formalist constantly strips utterances of their contextual meaning by producing questions like: 'Where's John?' and expecting answers like: 'He's at the railway station'. Now if students naively (or maliciously) were to inquire who John was, which railway station he went to and what for, the bewildered teacher's reply could be that it didn't matter, the point was to practise question-and-answer.

EXAMPLE

A young colleague of mine was teaching two nine-year-olds, a girl and a boy. In one of the first lessons, he was presenting the prepositional phrases: in, on, under. To demonstrate the differences, he put a book alternately in, on and under the desk. The teacher then asked the class 'Where is the book?'. Before long, the boy began to chuckle. 'What's up?' the teacher asked. 'But teacher, can't you see where the book is?' The little girl snapped at him: 'Come on, of course he can! He's just trying to teach us the words'.

Unlike the boy, the girl had apparently understood the difference between the reality of the outside world and the artificiality of the classroom.

The activist teacher, on the other hand, claims that it is the carrier content that should stand in focus. Thus she takes every opportunity to use the foreign language in the classroom as a genuine means of communication, led by the commonsensical argument that one can best learn something by rehearsing it in life-like situations. Therefore, she sets up communicative activities.

EXAMPLE

Suppose you are observing an intermediate English lesson. After they have read an article about homeless people, the teacher initiates a discussion about the down-and-out in Britain versus their home country. In protest, some students say that they never talk about such issues, even in their mother tongue, and anyway they have come here to learn the grammar of English and not sociology or politics.

⊙⁴ Read the four statements below (Medgyes 1999a). What do you think? Formulate arguments to challenge these assumptions.

a) 'The carrier content is a mere excuse for highlighting the learning content.'

b) 'Learners have no real messages to convey in the classroom.'

c) 'The foreign language is not a genuine means of communication for learners.'

d) 'The foreign language lesson is not suitable for creating real-life situations.'

⊙⁵ I maintain that teachers and learners engage in role-play all the time, and this can only be endured if seasoned with humour (Medgyes 1999a).

What do you think?

Further reading:
Seidlhofer (1999)

⊙⁶ Watch these amusing TED talks:

Terry Moore (2011) 'How to tie your shoes'.

James Burchfield (2003) 'Playing invisible turntables'.

Joachim de Posada (2015) 'Don't eat the marshmallow'.

Which one(s) would you show your class?

Why?

It is likely that this teacher's attempt has failed, mainly because students have felt unable to express their thoughts and emotions in L2 at a level adequate to their maturity and L1 competence. But even if the conversation had come off, it would surely have been quasi-communication, fundamentally motivated by the aim of learning the formal properties of English.[2]

All foreign-language teachers, irrespective of their allegiance, face a paradox, which results from the inextricability of learning content and carrier content.[3] ⊙⁴ Consciously or unconsciously, all of us are keen to resolve this dilemma. Good teachers are ready to change their activist and formalist robes as the classroom situation requires, and the best teachers are able to slide from one role into the other quickly and with great dexterity.

Nevertheless, there is a catch. Soudek & Soudek (1985) found that foreign-language teachers complain about stress and exhaustion more often than teachers of other subjects. I assume that strain and fatigue are chiefly caused by the constant necessity to play a role. Indeed, foreign language teaching consists of *an endless series of role-plays*, in which the teacher, as well as the learners, engage in game-like activities which are not always fun (Berne 1964).

Role-play can have two meanings. In our everyday usage, it denotes a classroom activity: learners are placed in an imaginary situation in which they are expected to behave as though it were a real one. For example, two students are asked to act out a dialogue at the greengrocer's: 'Antonio is the greengrocer and Amanda is the customer'. Although role-play is a standard form of practice, many learners, in my experience, dislike it, because (a) they do not fancy acting in the persona of someone else, and (b) it is very tiring because it requires learners to use the foreign language and their imagination at the same time.

The other meaning of role-play is far more comprehensive: it refers to an *all-embracing mode of classroom behaviour*, resulting from the teacher's attempts to bridge the gap between the learning content and the carrier content.

But it is precisely the elusiveness of foreign language teaching that makes it a worthwhile pursuit. Many of us seem to enjoy our job, partly because of the effort of trying to climb up the crest of the waves coming from opposite directions. Antier (1976) goes so far as to suggest that the pleasure of dressing up is in fact one of the main driving forces that keep us going. Indeed, foreign-language teaching is a craft requiring a good deal of acting skills (Rives 1979). ⊙⁵ I shall return to the topic of role-playing in greater detail in Chapter 5.2. But now let me turn to the native/non-native division in the context of ELT. ⊙⁶

---

[2] Parenthetically, Gabelentz, a 19th century German scholar, once observed that 'the best language teacher, for beginners at least, is a talkative person with a limited range of ideas' (in Stevick 1984: 134). This seems a very apposite description of the activist, who is eager to communicate although she is aware that the students' L2 level does not allow for sophisticated interaction.

---

[3] This paradox is well represented by the ambivalence of the learning/carrier content dichotomy. After all, if we happen to be activists, we may well say that for us the topic of classroom interaction is the learning content while grammar is the carrier content in that grammar merely carries the message of genuine communication.

4.2 Revisiting the native/non-native speaker division: the three surveys

Within the constraints of the distinction discussed in Chapter 2, every teacher is either a NEST or a non-NEST. My basic assumption is that NESTs and non-NESTs are two different species. In this light, let me advance four hypotheses:

Hypothesis 1 They differ in terms of their language proficiency.
Hypothesis 2 They differ in terms of their teaching behaviour.
Hypothesis 3 The discrepancy in language proficiency accounts for most of the differences found in their teaching behaviour.
Hypothesis 4 They can be equally good teachers in their own terms. ☉[7]

As these four hypotheses constitute the fundamental tenets of my book, I shall take every opportunity to validate them, except for **Hypothesis 1** which I regard as confirmed by the arguments put forward in Chapter 2.

With regard to **Hypotheses 2–4**, I have had resort to two chief research methods: *questionnaires* and *interviews*. They include:

Survey 1 28 respondents from the US; then a follow-up interview with seven of them.
Survey 2 216 respondents from ten countries.
Survey 3 81 Hungarian non-NESTs, followed by ten interviews.

In the following, I shall briefly describe each survey and report on the respondents' background.

Survey 1 (the US survey)

In the spring of 1989, I circulated a questionnaire among colleagues at the American Language Institute (ALI) of the University of Southern California, Los Angeles (**Appendix A**). The 17–item questionnaire was completed by 28 respondents, all of whom were employed at ALI at the time of the study.

25 respondents were native speakers of English (including two British citizens) and three were bilinguals. Five respondents were aged 21–30, 11 respectively were 31–40 and 41–50 years of age, and one person was over 60. The woman–man ratio was 13 (46.4 per cent) to 15 (53.5 per cent).

The respondents were MA or PhD holders, or were currently studying for a postgraduate degree; six of them were studying for their MAs and thirteen preparing for their PhDs, mostly in the field of linguistics or applied linguistics. In return for free tuition and a modest stipend, the 19 postgraduate students worked as part-time 'teaching assistants', teaching English to international students. In addition, nine respondents were either part-time language instructors or full-time supervisors at ALI, whose job it was to inspect and support teaching assistants, to design materials, as well as to teach for a few hours per week.

The average length of ELT experience was 11.6 years, ranging between two and 34 years; a few respondents had also taught some other foreign language during their career. Somewhat surprisingly, 13 respondents were teaching English with no formal teaching qualifications. The teaching load of most respondents was moderate, averaging ten hours a week; part-timers had a

☉[7] Look at these four hypotheses. Do you expect the survey results to prove or to disprove them? Give your reasons.

⊙⁸ 'If English were the drug, expatriate teachers would be the dealers' (Barduhn 2014: 40).

Can you explain this statement?

Further reading:
Johnston (1999)

⊙⁹ How well are expatriate teachers paid compared to local teachers in your country? Why the differences?

⊙¹⁰ Do expats in your country generally (try to) learn the local language? Should they?

tougher load, exacerbated by long hours of driving from one school to the other (hence they were ironically called 'freeway teachers').

21 respondents had considerable overseas teaching experience as well, with an average of 4.6 years. The most frequently indicated motives for working abroad were, in this order: seeing the world, encountering different cultures, learning foreign languages, doing research or tertiary-level study and earning money. ⊙⁸ When asked whether they regarded teaching as their main professional interest, 17 people answered 'yes'; the ten colleagues who gave negative answers said that they had been motivated by the stipend, free tuition, and/or the sheer pleasure of teaching (one person skipped this item). ⊙⁹

It is a cliche to note that native speakers of English, on the whole, do not speak foreign languages. My group of respondents claimed to speak an average 1.2 foreign languages at low level, 0.9 at medium, 0.3 respectively at high and near-native level. 'No big deal!' some admitted. Considering the fact that they were all foreign-language teachers and had spent massive amounts of time abroad, they certainly could have done better. ⊙¹⁰ The data show, for example, that the length of their stay in the country whose native language they claimed to speak best was 2.8 years. Incidentally, they rated themselves with respect to 'gift for language learning'; on a five-point scale, they averaged 2.3 (5 was best).

Survey 2 (the international survey)

This fairly comprehensive survey was designed, administered and evaluated by Thea Reves and myself in the course of 1990-92 (Reves & Medgyes 1994.[4]) After the questionnaire had been drawn up, it was distributed with the help of local British Council offices in sixteen countries where English was a second or foreign language. The 23-item questionnaire was designed for both NESTs and non-NESTs (**Appendix B**).

A total of 216 respondents from ten countries returned the questionnaire completed.[5] The following countries were represented (**Table 1**):

Table 1: Distribution of respondents by countries in Survey 2 (N=216)

Country	Number of respondents	Country	Number of respondents
Hungary	51	Czechoslovakia	21
Zimbabwe	34	Yugoslavia	15
Nigeria	26	Russia	12
Israel	25	Sweden	6
Brazil	21	Mexico	5

Out of the 216 respondents, only 18 (8.3 per cent) claimed to be native speakers of English, and the remaining 198 (91.7 per cent) spoke one of 17 languages as their mother tongue. This implies that this sample, in contrast to the US sample, overwhelmingly consisted of non-NESTs. The woman–man ratio was 172 (79.6 per cent) to 44 (20.3 per cent).

---

[4] Emphatically, I would like to acknowledge Thea Reves's contribution. Without her dedication, **Survey 2** could not have been conducted.

[5] My thanks are due to George Kershaw for lending me his collection of questionnaires from Russian and Czechoslovak respondents in 1993.

With regard to the level of teacher training, 180 (83.3 per cent) respondents had at least one year's training, and only 36 (16.7 per cent) had less than one year. The length of training typically varied between three and six years. As for their EFL experience, 146 (66.7 per cent) teachers had more than five years, 53 (24.5 per cent) between one and five years, and only 17 (7.9 per cent) had less than one year of experience.

In terms of school allocation, 65 (30.1 per cent) teachers were employed in elementary schools, 93 (43.1 per cent) in secondary schools, 38 (17.6 per cent) in colleges or universities, and 19 (8.8 per cent) in private language schools.[6] One item revealed that a large number of teachers worked not only in their full-time job but at other institutions too – an indication of the economic necessity for 'moonlighting'. ⊙[11] The average teaching load was fairly high: close to 50 per cent taught more than 20 hours a week.

A few questions only related to non-NESTs. 86 respondents (43.7 per cent) had never been to an English-speaking country. 68 (34.6 per cent) had spent up to three months and only 43 (21.8 per cent) a period of over three months. ⊙[12] The answers to the question: 'How often do you speak with native speakers of English?' showed the following picture (**Table 2**):

Table 2: Frequency of contact with native speakers in Survey 2 (N=198)

Frequency	Number of teachers	Percentage
every day	42	21.2
once or twice a week	29	14.6
once or twice a month	14	7.0
a few times a year	38	19.1
rarely	58	29.2
never	12	6.0
missing	5	2.5 ⊙[13]

Finally, non-NEST respondents were asked to rate their command of English compared to other non-NESTs working in their home country. On a five-point scale, the average was 3.6 (5 was best).⊙[14]

Survey 3 (the Hungarian survey)

In the spring of 1992, I sent a questionnaire to non-NEST members of IATEFL-Hungary; 81 respondents returned the questionnaire completed (**Appendix C**).

All the respondents were native speakers of Hungarian with an average 12.7 years of experience; the length of experience ranged between 3 months and 40 years. The woman–man ratio was 71 (87.7 per cent) to 10 (12.3 per cent). The table below shows the distribution of respondents according to the age-group they were teaching. (They could indicate more than one age-group.) (See **Table 3** on page 32).

⊙[11] As a non-NEST, do you need to 'moonlight'? What kind of extra job(s) do you do?

⊙[12] Non-NESTs who have never, or hardly ever, visited English-speaking countries were found to regard the NEST as the ideal teacher (Llurda 2008).

Does your experience support this claim?

⊙[13] How much time have you spent in English-speaking countries so far? Have these stays helped you to become a better teacher? If so, in what way(s)?

⊙[14] How do you rate your English-language competence compared to that of your colleagues? Have you reached your plateau, or are you still improving?

---

[6] Several of the participants were teaching in more than one school, which affects the figures.

Table 3: Distribution of respondents according to the age of students in Survey 3 (N=81)

Age of students	Number of respondents
4-6	0
7-10	3
11-14	13
15-18	45
19-24	40
24+	36

The data seem to confirm the deplorable fact that Hungarian non-NESTs have to take on second and third jobs to make ends meet.

Survey questions relating to the native/non-native issue

In the table below (**Table 4**), there is a list of those items which are closely related to some aspect of the NEST/non-NEST issue.[7]

Table 4: Survey questions relating to the NEST/non-NEST issue (summary)

	Questions comparing NESTs and non-NESTs	Survey/Item	Chapter
1	Do you see any difference in teaching behaviour between NESTs and non-NESTs? Describe.	2/13 1/17	6.3
2	What is the NEST/non-NEST proportion in your school?	2/12	7.1
3	What would be the ideal proportion of NESTs and non-NESTs? Justify.	2/17 1/16	7.1
4	Who is better: the NEST or the non-NEST? Justify.	2/14	7.2
5	Do you know of any organised NEST/ non-NEST cooperation? Describe.	2/15 1/15	8.1
6	Suggest ways of strengthening cooperation.	2/16	8.1

	Questions concerning non-NESTs' command of English	Survey/Item	Chapter
7	What are your main difficulties using English?	2/23a 3/5b 3/7	5.1
8	Has your English become better or worse since graduation?	3/3	5.1
9	Can you still make any progress?	3/6	5.1
10	Do your language difficulties hinder you in your work? If so, be specific.	2/23b	6.1
11	Have students had any effect on your English? If so, describe this.	3/4a 3/5a	9.2
12	Specify areas where your English has improved.	3/4c	9.2
13	Suggest techniques to overcome your difficulties.	3/8	9.2
14	Outside the classroom, how can you improve your English?	1/8 3/4b	10.1 ⊙15

⊙15 Look at **Table 4** and give a brief answer to each question. Compare your answers with a colleague's.

---

[7] The text of the original questionnaire items has been reworded, simplified and collated to help the reader gain a better overview of the major issues (see **Appendices A-C**).

As the data obtained from the three surveys and the follow-up interviews have affected and supplemented my own views to a greater or lesser extent, I shall draw on them at appropriate places in the chapters indicated above.

At the same time, I have to emphasise that the findings should be treated with a great deal of caution for the following reasons:

- The samples are limited in size; there are only 11 countries represented in the three surveys.
- The representation of the countries involved is not proportionate.
- The data are not distributed according to the countries represented.
- As all the data are based on self-report, their validity cannot be confirmed (Seliger 1979).[8]

I can only take heart from Popper's (1968) argument: as hypotheses cannot be scientifically confirmed but at best be *disconfirmed*, the fundamental test of validity consists in competitive resistance to refutation.

Summary

In this chapter, I have put foreign-language teachers into two groups according to the relationship between learning and carrier content. I have demonstrated a major feature distinguishing them from teachers of other school subjects, namely the feature of assuming a role. I have brought the issue of the native/non-native dichotomy back within the framework of ELT and set up four basic hypotheses. To pave the way for substantiating these hypotheses, I have introduced three surveys I conducted, highlighting a number of questions they set out to address.

The next two chapters will analyse non-NESTs' teaching behaviour in contrast to NESTs'. Chapter 5 examines those aspects in which non-NESTs appear to be disadvantaged, whereas Chapter 6 displays the brighter side of being a non-NEST. Pulling the two strings together, Chapter 7 closes the debate by offering an answer to the question: 'Who is worth more: the NEST or the non-NEST?'.

---

[8] In Seliger's (1979) view, the data gained from self-reports are of dubious value.

Further reading

- **Broca, Á.** (2016) CLIL and non-CLIL: differences from the outset. *ELT Journal 70* (pp. 320–331).

  While acknowledging the merits of CLIL, the author argues that this type of education is selective by excluding students who are academically less able. She warns that more attention should be paid to ordinary, non-CLIL courses, in which the student cohort is more diverse.

- **Johnston, B.** (1999) The expatriate teacher as postmodern paladin. *Research in the Teaching of English 34* (pp. 255–289).

  Based on life-history interviews with three expatriate EFL teachers from Poland, the paper sheds light on the marginalised role they play in a marginalised occupation. Like medieval knights, they fight for a noble cause in a post-modern era rife with moral dilemmas and political tensions.

- **Seidlhofer, B.** (1999) Double standards: teacher education in the Expanding Circle. *World Englishes 18* (pp. 233–245).

  This paper argues that non-NESTs are double agents, who lead a double life, conforming to double standards, invariably engaging in double think and double talk. The central message is that these negative terms may be rendered positive connotations if interpreted correctly in teacher education.

CHAPTER 5

The dark side of being a non-native

Focus points

- Non-NESTs' persistent language deficiencies in English
- Teacher talking time in class
- The stress of being an English teacher
- Coping with misbehaving classes

5.1 The linguistic deficit ⊙¹

Provided the native/non-native distinction is accepted in general (Chapter 2), it must also be accepted that non-NESTs are less proficient users of English than NESTs.

On the whole, non-NESTs are well aware of their linguistic handicap and of its all-pervasive nature. In no area of English-language proficiency can we emulate NESTs: we are poorer listeners, speakers, readers and writers. True enough, long stays in English-speaking countries, hard work and dedication can help us narrow the gap between 'us' and 'them', but very few of us will ever be able to catch up. To achieve native-like proficiency is wishful thinking. ⊙²

At the same time, we seem to be able to identify our major weaknesses, both in relation to NESTs and our fellow non-NESTs. When asked to identify their difficulties in English, non-NESTs involved in **Surveys 2** and **3** pinpointed them with ease.[1]

Survey results
Question 7: What are your main difficulties using English?

In **Survey 2**, non-NESTs were asked to label their problem areas. In analysing them, I pulled the difficulties indicated into larger, and inevitably arbitrary, categories to produce the following table (**Table 5**):

⊙¹ Read the extract in **Appendix D**. Note Dracula's problem with English and any oddities in his language use.

⊙² The Englishman flattered Dracula for his excellent command of English.

Have you ever been flattered by a native speaker? If so, how did you feel?

---

[1] At this point, some readers may wish to stop me and say that all this is too obvious to ask for evidence. Far from it! Wherever I have presented my ideas about the NEST/non-NEST issue, there have always been people in the audience who challenged this assumption – all of them NESTs! In Chapter 7, I shall reflect upon their queries.

Table 5: Frequency of language difficulties as perceived by respondents in Survey 2 (N=198)

Difficulty	Frequency	Difficulty	Frequency
vocabulary	42	articles	7
fluency	33	phrasal verbs	7
speaking	28	colloquial English	6
pronunciation	27	slang	5
listening	20	tenses	5
grammar	17	synonyms	3
idioms	16	word order	3
appropriacy	10	fear of mistakes	3
intonation	9	writing	2
prepositions	9		

Survey results

Question 8: Has your English become better or worse since graduation?

One item in **Survey 3** asked the respondents to judge their overall command of English, compared to that at the time of graduation from university or college; there were three options supplied: *better, better in some respects/worse in others* and *worse*. To my delight, out of 81 respondents, nobody marked 'worse', 48 indicated 'better' (59.2 per cent) and 33 (40.7 per cent) the middle answer.

Survey results

Question 9: Can you still make any progress?

Here, the respondents of **Survey 3** were asked to say whether they believed that their proficiency had reached a plateau. 53 respondents (65.4 per cent) perceived that they were still making progress, as opposed to 28 (34.6 per cent) who felt that they were not. Subsequently, those who complained about fossilization had to name their major difficulties on the basis of eight options available. The following results were achieved (**Table 6**): ◉³

Table 6: Frequency of language difficulties as perceived by respondents in Survey 3 (N=28)

Difficulty	Frequency	Difficulty	Frequency
speaking	16	grammar	6
vocabulary	14	speech functions	4
pronunciation	11	listening	4
writing	9	reading	4

In the following section, I shall touch upon the major sources of difficulty indicated by the two samples.

◉³ Look at **Tables 5 and 6**.

Do the results correlate with your own experience of language difficulties?

Vocabulary

Vocabulary and speaking/fluency were considered to be the two most common problem areas. The frequency of vocabulary difficulties would, in fact, be even higher if some other labels in **Table 5**, such as idioms, appropriacy, phrasal verbs, slang and synonyms, had been added.

This came as no surprise. ☉⁴ Since the vocabulary of any language is an enormous set in that it contains any number of lexical items, all of which are used in myriads of contexts, vocabulary resists mastery. In addition, whereas there are plenty of dictionaries to show the correct use of vocabulary, there is not – because there cannot be – a dictionary to show whether or not a lexical item has been used appropriately in a given situation. It is no wonder that non-NESTs feel hopelessly insecure about their use of vocabulary, as a rule.

The problems are endless. We do not even know the English names for common objects in our immediate surroundings, let alone how to use them off the cuff when necessary.

EXAMPLE

Look around the room you're in at the moment. Do you know the English for all the objects that you can name in your mother tongue? Now look out of the window. How many trees and flowers can you name in L1? And in English?

Similar problems seem to arise with regard to idioms and appropriacy. ☉⁵

EXAMPLE

Is it all right if we use idioms, such as to keep body and soul together *or* to stick one's neck out*? Don't they sound like cliches? They do, according to a recent dictionary of cliches (Ammer 1992). In closing a letter, when do we write* Yours sincerely, Sincerely, Regards, With best regards, With warmest regards, Best wishes, Love, Yours, *etc.? Is* Yours faithfully *still 'in'? Is there any difference between* May I use your pen? *and* Can I use your pen? *Or between* What do you mean? What are you getting at? *and* What are you on about?

Similarly, most of us are in trouble with phrasal verbs, slang, and synonyms.

EXAMPLE

Do you prefer endure *and* tolerate *to* put up with*? Or* emerge *and* arise *to* crop up*? Doesn't slang sound odd when used by a non-NEST? Do you ever say* That's neat *or* cool *or* That's jolly good *or* bloody good *or (God forbid!)* f...ing good*? How about the phrase* You bet *or* You guys*? (Did you know that this latter one may refer to women as well as men?) Can you tell the difference between synonyms such as* prevent, hinder, hamper, impede, obstruct, thwart *and so on?*

The respondents did not, but could well have, referred to collocations and proverbs as perennial sources of difficulty. ☉⁶

☉⁴ Vocabulary occupies the top of the list. I am not surprised – are you? Why (not)?

Further reading:
Medgyes (1999a)

☉⁵ Do you use many idioms in English? How about colloquialism and slang?

☉⁶ The use of online corpora can now give an accurate view of typical collocations.

Since the late 1980s, a number of collocation dictionaries have been published, which help learners to see which word goes with which.

Do you ever consult such dictionaries?

⊙⁷ Which kind of mistakes do you tend to correct most often: lexical or grammatical? Why?

⊙⁸ Note the proportion of student versus teacher talking time in your next class. Consider not only the quantity, but also the quality of the teacher talk (Harmer 2007).

⊙⁹ Read this anecdote.

A few years ago, I went into a shop in London to buy a shirt. The assistant asked 'What size?' 'I don't know exactly,' I stammered. 'Men of your age should know what size they are,' he said and turned his back on me. Gobsmacked, my subtle English competence evaporated without a trace. I cursed in Hungarian instead.

Have you ever been in a similar situation? How did you cope?

⊙¹⁰ Here are some characteristics of ELF speakers (Jenkins 2000). *[p]*, *[t]* and *[k]* (as in *pin*, *tin* and *kin*) are not aspirated; the dark *[ɫ]* (as in *bull* or *table*) is pronounced lightly; the schwa *[ə]* (as in *nonsense* or *eloquent*) is uttered as a full vowel; *[ð]* and *[θ]* (as in *this* or *bathe* vs. *thin* or *bath*) are replaced by their closest consonants.

Do you find these features in your learners' or your own English too? If so, do they bother you?

Vocabulary is a morass for everyone, but non-native speakers, and hence non-NESTs, are more prone to get bogged down.

The non-NEST's uncertainty is apparent in her error correction techniques, too. In an empirical study, Sheorey (1986) found non-NESTs to be more heavy-handed in marking errors than NESTs – except for lexical errors, an attitude which Sheorey attributed to the non-NESTs' inability to grasp the lexical subtleties of English usage. Her findings are consistent with those of Hughes & Lascaratou (1982) and many others. ⊙⁷

Oral fluency

Speaking skills and fluency are the runners-up in the statistics. NESTs, on the whole, are more fluent speakers than non-NESTs. Oral fluency involves several aspects, such as speech rate, readiness to speak and the ability to speak coherently – it goes without saying that NESTs score higher on all counts.

This does not rule out the possibility of some non-NESTs speaking faster than NESTs. In my observation, there are some whose speech rate is even higher in English than in their mother tongue, possibly due to an unconscious strategy intended to impress the hearers and boost their own self-confidence.

Similarly, some non-NESTs are more talkative in English than in L1; in a classroom context, this may be conducive to increased teacher talking time – not always a virtue. 'Compulsive chatterboxes' may also be driven by compensatory strategies or perhaps by a desire to practise English under any circumstances. ⊙⁸

On the other hand, I have seldom come across non-NESTs who can use English as coherently and as lucidly as their mother tongue or as their NEST counterparts. Non-NEST speech tends to be redundant and clumsy, owing to difficulties in finding the appropriate structures or phrases on the spur of the moment. ⊙⁹

Pronunciation

Pronunciation was marked as the third most critical area in **Surveys 2** and **3**. We have all met non-NESTs whose pronunciation is hardly distinguishable from some native-speaker norm. As a rule, perfect imitators parrot British English or American English. It looks as though native speakers, up to a certain point, appreciate good pronunciation produced by non-natives.

Those non-NESTs who use the British variety generally speak with an RP (Received Pronunciation) accent. However, as RP is spoken by only a small fraction of British people, imitating it is not always considered to be an asset in Britain.[2] ⊙¹⁰

---

[2] The attitude to pronunciation has not always been as permissive as it is today. Stevick quotes Borden & Busse, 'speech correctionists' of the 1920s, who called their students 'patients' suffering from 'defects of foreign dialect' and recommended the following treatment: 'If the patient stubbornly persists in substituting T as in 'town' for TH as in 'thin' [...] hold the blade of his tongue forcibly down in its proper position by means of a wire form [called] a 'fricator'. If he persists [...] push his tongue back into its proper position with a forked metal brace' (in Stevick 1976: 93).

EXAMPLE

- *In an effort to get rid of this 'stigma', a Hungarian colleague remoulded his English into some kind of Liverpudlian accent.*
- *A student of mine, after spending six months in Scotland, came home speaking Scottish English and ever since he has been trying hard to perfect his Scots.*
- *Another colleague, after marrying an African, moved to Kenya for a few years. When her marriage broke up, she came back to teach in Hungary. On one occasion, I overheard colleagues who had visited her class complain about her 'poor English' – they apparently failed to recognise that she was in fact a near-native speaker speaking with a typical African English accent.*

Pronunciation that approximates to a native norm is, in some quarters, regarded as a primary indicator of success with English. Although there is some empirical evidence that non-standard pronunciation produced by non-native speakers can be a barrier to intelligibility (Mitchell & Brumfit 1991), this is an obviously exaggerated view – pronunciation should not be ascribed as important a role as some people would have us believe (Krashen & Terrell 1983). ⊙¹¹

EXAMPLE

Once I was invited to an international conference along with a fellow-Hungarian whom I had not met before. When she uttered her first sentences in English, she sounded so ridiculously Hungarian that I was hardly able to suppress a chuckle. But as she went on, I became stunned by her fluency and highly idiomatic use of English, so much so that I chose to keep silent whenever she was around.

Although they sometimes like to poke fun at foreigners speaking with a typical French, Russian or Japanese accent, native English speakers are generally tolerant of pronunciation differences, because some kind of foreign accent suits a foreigner's image. As I have mentioned earlier, some natives in fact resent 'accentless' speech saying, as it were, 'How dare you speak my mother tongue so well? It is *my* property if you haven't noticed!' (Corder 1973).

On the other hand, I do believe that non-NESTs should be sensitive to pronunciation, as indeed to any other aspects of language proficiency. We ought to be aware, for example, of our ingrained errors because, like folk-songs, such errors are passed down from generation to generation. I began to call this phenomenon 'the goose-effect' after a friend had related the following story.

EXAMPLE

'As my own teacher had pronounced goose *as* [guːz], *I used it that way. Then one day I suddenly discovered that it should in fact be* [guːs]. *The painful realisation that I had taught* goose *wrongly for so long urged me to systematically revise my vocabulary containing the minimal pair* [s/z]. *Subsequently I checked the pronunciation of virtually every word in my vocabulary.'* ⊙¹²

What I regard as far more important than 'perfect' pronunciation is the eagerness to make progress. It is precisely for the lack of eagerness that I find the story below agonising.

⊙¹¹ Despite the ELF movement, traditional views still hold. For example, read these words of Hermans, a Dutch teacher trainer.

'[...] when a non-native speaker of English is able to speak with a near-native accent, native speakers consider what is being said to be more credible than when the same sentences are uttered by someone speaking with a mild or heavy accent [...]. So if it matters, let's teach it!' (Hermans 2014: 44-45)

Do you think he is right or wrong?

Justify your opinion.

⊙¹² Can you recall any persistent pronunciation errors you used to make, but then got rid of? Compare experiences.

⊙¹³ Wrong pronunciation can lead to disasters. After watching this brief sketch on YouTube, explain what causes the misunderstanding.

German coastguard
http://www.youtube.com/watch?v=Nn9PL FM7lU

⊙¹⁴ VOICE (2013), an online databank of one million words, registers recurring features of ELF usage. Here are a few examples.

- Dropping the s in the third person singular.
- Confusing the relative pronouns who and which.
- Omitting or inserting a(n) and the.
- Using the generic isn't it? in tag questions.
- Substituting the that-clause for the infinitive.

Are you aware of any of these features in your own language use, or in that of your learners?

Do you correct such 'errors' in your students' speaking or writing?

⊙¹⁵ Do the activity in **Appendix E** (Medgyes 2001: 441-2).

Compare your scores.

EXAMPLE

'One day, as I was browsing the vocabulary list at the end of a coursebook,' a friend related, 'I discovered that I should pronounce front *as [frʌnt] and not [frɔnt] as I had believed. I ran up to a colleague to confess my sin. First she didn't understand what I was getting at and when she did, she just shrugged her shoulders and said, "So what?" ' ⊙¹³*

Grammar

Unlike vocabulary, grammar is the non-NESTs' favourite hunting ground. If there is one area where we claim to be at home, it is grammar. The reason is that it is far more concrete than vocabulary. Its gist can be compressed into a book of 200-300 pages and is therefore 'learnable'; indeed most non-NESTs successfully swotted up grammar during their college years.

This relative feeling of security, however, may be conducive to attaching more importance to grammar than it deserves. Studies on error correction show that non-NESTs tend to penalise grammatical errors with the utmost severity, including even the use of structures that have long come into everyday use, such as *if I was* in hypothetical sentences.[3]

The trouble is that non-NESTs usually learnt English grammar from coursebooks at school and subsequently from pedagogic grammar books at college. Hence, unless they come into everyday contact with native speakers, their grammatical knowledge remains 'bookish'. Apart from the fact that those books might have laid down rules that were outdated even at the time of publication, they inevitably present a more compartmentalised and defective picture of grammar than can be justified by actual use. In awareness of these dangers, conscientious non-NESTs constantly struggle to catch up with developments in language use. ⊙¹⁴

The surveys showed that respondents had numerous difficulties with prepositions and articles.

EXAMPLE

What is the difference between before, in front of *and* outside the house? *(Note:* difference *between and not* among, *though there are three elements to be distinguished.) Does* approve *go with or without of? Do we* agree to, on, with *a proposal? Can we* agree [0] *a proposal? Should I write* the respondents *or* [0] respondents *in the survey? Similarly,* [0] non-NESTs' *or the* non-NESTs' *attitude?*

Some non-NESTs are preoccupied with accuracy to the point of obsession.

EXAMPLE

Both as a participant and a trainer, I have attended numerous in-service training courses where, at the insistence of colleagues, discussion has often revolved around peripheral and nebulous issues, such as whether or not the sentence He has been being attacked *is a correct utterance, or the nuances between* going to *and* will *to express future time.* ⊙¹⁵

---

[3] Incidentally, non-NESTs were found to treat spelling errors even more harshly. Sheorey (1986) ascribes this attitude to the fact that non-NESTs feel most comfortable with spelling, as it consists of a set of rules even more finite than those of grammar.

Highly proficient non-NESTs seem to have a better sense of proportion. While recognising the pivotal role that grammar plays in language learning and language use, they are aware that it is just one area of study. In my experience, the more proficient the non-NEST is, the less grammar-centred she is!

Listening comprehension

Next down the line of blind spots come listening skills. Logically enough, those non-NESTs who are particularly hampered and annoyed by their incapacities are the ones who are ready to expose themselves to extended periods of concentrated listening, such as watching English-language films or listening to radio broadcasts. ⊙**16** I assume that the eagerness to undergo such tantalising experiences is in direct proportion to the degree of overall proficiency.

EXAMPLE

- *Many colleagues admit that it is all right as long as native speakers with some standard variety of English talk to them. The situation deteriorates when they happen to meet a regional dialect. And it is almost impossible to make out conversations overheard on the London tube or the New York subway.*
- *Watching TV is another challenge. TV news causes few problems. Western movies, documentaries and interviews cause much greater difficulties. But worst of all are sitcoms and comedy shows! We miss every other punchline, mostly because of the references and allusions that only people living in that country can appreciate.* ⊙**17**

Writing and reading skills

These two skills seem to pose relatively few problems. This may be due to the fact that non-NESTs are relatively satisfied with their ability to read and write, or rather that they attach less importance to them than to their oral skills. I suspect that this latter consideration carries more weight: since oral proficiency is a 'make or break' requirement and a good predictor of success in teaching (Britten 1985), flaws in reading and writing skills are easier to conceal.

5.2 'Schizophrenia' and 'inferiority complex'

In Chapter 4.1, I argued that foreign-language teachers are doomed to assume roles. I further contend that the non-NESTs' predicament is aggravated by the fact that we have to act in a foreign language, which is at least as fugitive as the learning content/carrier content dichotomy. To us, English is full of mystery, both from a linguistic and from a cultural point of view (Medgyes 1983). As has been shown in Chapter 5.1, by definition we have a less reliable knowledge of the English language than NESTs. In addition, we are likely to have relatively scanty information about the culture, or rather cultures, of English-speaking countries. Yet, in the classroom we have to appear to be well-informed sources in both respects.

The point is that we are at a junction between two languages and several cultures. By birth, we represent our native language and culture, but by profession we are obliged to represent a foreign language with its cultural load.

⊙**16** We can now use online resources such as YouTube for concentrated listening.

What similar sources and resources have you found most useful?

⊙**17** On YouTube, watch the sketch 'Four candles'(2006) with the Two Ronnies.

The British audience roared with laughter. Did you, too? Was there anything that made it difficult for you to understand the jokes?

Whilst being enriched by two sets of language and culture, in the classroom we are beset with problems caused by our double-barrelled nature. Having examined some of our language-related pitfalls, let me now mention a handful of difficulties of a linguistico-cultural or purely cultural nature.[4]

EXAMPLE

- *In the classroom, should I establish rules of conduct conforming to the code of certain English-speaking countries (for example, should I expect students to stand up to greet me when I enter the classroom)?*
- *Should my own behaviour also correspond to such rules (for example, should I give instructions in an indirect mode allegedly characteristic of British traditions: 'Would you come to the blackboard, Susan?' or 'Why don't we do one more task?').*
- *Should I use typical features of English discourse, such as euphemism, understatement or tongue-in-cheek remarks?*
- *Should I take over pedagogical techniques commonly applied in certain English-speaking countries (such as questioning techniques)?*
- *Should I create an 'English classroom' with posters, pictures, cut-outs, and so on?*
- *After the class, in my role as a 'counsellor' or 'parent-surrogate', should I talk to my students in English?*
- *In the school canteen, should I behave 'English-fashion', for example, by putting the napkin on my lap or loading the food on the back of my fork?*
- *In the staffroom, should I speak with other non-NESTs in English or in our mother tongue?*

All these issues relate to the question of role-playing. For if, true to my native identity, I deliberately speak with what is called a Hunglish accent or use the imperative to give instructions ('Susan, come to the blackboard!'), which is the standard form in Hungarian schools, I present an imperfect model of English.

If, on the other hand, I put on a distinct RP accent, I may sound pompous or ridiculous and, more importantly, convey a false idea of the way most native speakers speak. By the same token, if I use the indirect way of giving instructions, I may appear snobbish and alien in an otherwise genuinely un-English environment.

Non-NESTs are split between two patterns of behaviour. I say 'behaviour', because:

> 'speaking English does not merely imply producing the right sounds at the right moment. Speech is behaviour. In his intonation, his countenance, his gestures (or absence of gestures), the teacher of English almost literally sheds his [L1] personality during the four or five hours a day he is called upon to perform in front of his audience' (Antier 1976:3).

In my experience, the better the command of English, the more difficult it is for non-NESTs to keep their L1 and L2 behaviours separated. At a near-native level, we may in fact become so much imbued with the English language and the cultures it conveys that we tend to carry them over into our L1 behaviour as well. ⊙[18] With some exaggeration, I would say we behave in the classroom (and sometimes even in our private lives) like plasticine Brits or Americans. We have two characters, both of them sham; we display signs of 'schizophrenia'. ⊙[19]

⊙[18] This may not be true in all teaching cultures. What is your experience?

⊙[19] Bernat (2008) says that non-native teachers often feel like imposters, because they feel inadequate, fraudulent, full of self-doubt and anxiety.

What about you?

---

[4] In Kachru's (1977) view, a non-native RP speaker is incongruent if she is wearing this linguistic mask without combining it with the mannerisms and cultural features of a native RP speaker.

EXAMPLE

I have a few Hungarian colleagues who speak impeccable English. In addition, they wear tweed jackets, Clarks shoes and Marks & Spencer underwear. They buy English language calendars containing a plan of the London tube and the colleges of Oxford, subscribe to The Economist and have their radio tuned in to BBC 1 (and not BBC World Service). They eat a lot of chocolate, Cadbury's if possible. Their L1 utterances are interwoven with English phrases as if the Hungarian language were not subtle enough to express the meanings, or out of sheer sloppiness. Others prefer to 'go American'. ⊙[20]

It is little wonder that not all students are keen to follow such a model, and many would utterly refuse to put on the mask of a foreigner. 'Please no games, no songs, no role-plays, no intonation drills, no touching each other's hands – teach us the grammar!' Hidden behind their conservative attitude may lie a fear of identity crisis. The rejection of 'fooling around' is particularly characteristic of adult students, many of whom 'get into a state of 'psychic death' in the foreign language class as they feel they are losing the ego established with so much pain during their lives' (Bárdos 1984:116).

Getting back to teachers, few non-NESTs have reached a level of competence high enough to be worried about losing their native identity. On the contrary, most of us are doing our best to acquire a bit more 'Englishness'. Instead of schizophrenia, we suffer from an inferiority complex caused by glaring defects in our knowledge of English. We are in constant distress as we realise how little we know about the language we are supposed to teach. Indeed, most non-NESTs are all too aware that they are teachers *and* learners of the same subject.

EXAMPLE

This reminds me of a teachers' conference. At the end of his talk the lecturer – a native speaker of English – asked for comments. The awkward silence was broken at last by an elderly colleague, modestly proposing that non-native speakers had better not contaminate the air still resonant with the voice of a real native speaker. She seemed to entertain the belief that a non-NEST can have no pertinent ideas in the presence of a native speaker (Medgyes 1983).

Of course, every good teacher is an avid learner of the subject she teaches. Good physics teachers read science magazines and good PE teachers eagerly learn about new techniques in, say, high-jump and even try to reproduce them as much as they possibly can.

However, a basic difference between teachers of foreign languages and those of other subjects is that, whereas the latter have an equal chance to gain access to new horizons of knowledge and skills, foreign-language teachers do not. In terms of both English-language proficiency and familiarity with at least one English-speaking culture, NESTs are better off – and usually immeasurably better off! And for us non-NESTs, this thought is not an altogether encouraging one (if I may avail myself of British understatement). ⊙[21]

⊙[20] Rajagopalan remarks ironically: 'If you can't be a native, at least try to pass for one' (in Llurda 2005:286).

Do you know anyone who apes native speakers? How does this feature in their behaviour?

⊙[21] Ghanem (2015) notes the chief advantage he has over non-native teachers lies in the cultural knowledge he can provide, rather than in his better language skills.

Do you agree? Explain your reasons.

Further reading:
Lazaraton (2003)

5.3 The stress cycle

As I pointed out in Chapter 3.3, studies on the language learner are plentiful, while those on the language teacher are much less common. This also applies to research on stress in ELT: whereas books and articles on anxiety in language learning are in abundance, there is hardly anything written about *'the sickness from teaching'* foreign languages. This is a regrettable fact, considering that anxiety-ridden teachers are likely to raise the students' anxiety level too. Learning about how to alleviate our own stress is a precondition for being able to deal with learner stress. ⊙²² Jersild (1955) mentions that unless the teacher understands and accepts herself as a person, she is unable to help students understand and accept themselves. In a similar fashion, Maley (1984) remarks that we should in fact be more concerned with teacher stress than with learner stress. After all, whereas learners have several valves through which they can let off steam outside the classroom, teachers are more prone to take their worries home. In contrast, within the framework of general education, teacher stress does not seem to be a neglected research area.

⊙²² In your experience, how does stress affect language teachers – and non-NESTs in particular? What typical symptoms have you noticed?

In a highly illuminating book called *'Being a teacher'*, Claxton contends that

> 'the *vast* majority of teachers, particularly in secondary schools, are feeling overloaded, pushed around, confused, fed up and unappreciated' (1989: 1).

Stress affects teachers in every possible way: physically, mentally, behaviourally and emotionally alike. Surveying teacher stress in three English comprehensive schools, Dunham (1992) lists 31 different symptoms of stress, among which 'feelings of exhaustion', 'marked reduction of contacts with people outside school', 'frustration because there was little sense of achievement' and 'irritability' were the leaders. But 'large increase in consumption of alcohol', 'depression', 'loss of weight' or 'overeating", and 'marital and family conflicts' were also among the symptoms.

The symptoms of stress, however, are not to be mixed up with the causes of stress. ⊙²³ In the teaching profession, there are mounting concerns over the rate of changes and an ever stronger urgency to acquire new skills, in the face of a worldwide tendency to treat teachers more like workers and less like professionals. Extrapolating these worries into their own lives, people often moan: 'Well, no wonder there's so much stress and distress – such is our age!', to which Jersild pithily replied as long ago as the 1950s:

⊙²³ The causes of stress in the teaching profession are manifold (Medgyes 2004).

Can you supply a few examples?

Further reading:
Mousavi (2007)

> 'Ours is called an age of anxiety, and so it is. Each age is an age of anxiety' (1955: 20).

Claxton (1989) attributes stress to the incompatibility between duties and wishes. Roughly speaking, duties are laid down in our job description, whereas wishes include our professional aspirations and preferences. Problems begin to emerge when we are unable to carry out our duties as efficiently as we would wish, owing to all sorts of limitations, personal and external. The greater the disparity between what we *have to*, *want to* and *can do*, the greater the demands on us. If these demands are too pressing, we feel overloaded. However, this is not yet the stage of full-blown stress.

The critical stage sets in, says Claxton, when our injunctions, that is our ingrained views about personal worth, are undermined. Irrespective of whether these beliefs are clearly articulated or remain arcane, they set the standards we attempt to live up to: in effect they are personalised demands. If we repeatedly fall short of our expectations, we ultimately lose self-esteem, which is the fundamental component of psychological survival (Stevick 1980). Or as Claxton puts it:

> 'What started out as an objective assessment like "That lesson didn't go as well as I had expected" gets recast as "I made a mistake", which leads to "I'm a poor teacher" and even "I'm a failure (as a person)" '(1989:60).

As we experience chronic underachievement, we begin to feel threatened, and this feeling sets our defence mechanisms in motion. In an effort to hide our real and assumed inadequacies, we resort to various forms of avoidance strategies, such as eschewing human contact or projecting the blame onto others. The gradual increase of 'toxic waste' is conducive to accelerated tension, poorer performance and ultimately to the symptoms of stress described above.

Claxton illustrates this vicious circle like this (**Figure 5**):

Figure 5: The stress cycle ⊙²⁴

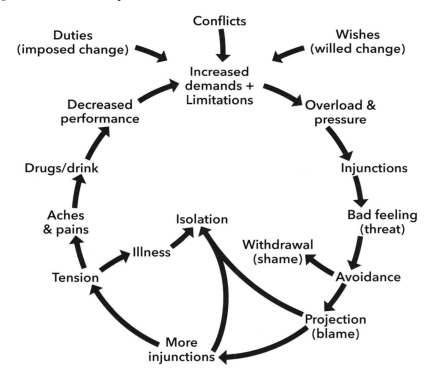

It appears that there are three alternatives open to the stressed teacher: to move (on to another profession), to improve (her situation as a teacher), or to suffer (from constant stress). As the second option promises to be the most viable and desirable, let me recommend a road to recovery from stress. The 'cure' for non-NESTs consists of seven steps.⁵ ⊙²⁵

⊙²⁴ Do you know any colleagues to whom the stress cycle in **Figure 5** applies?
Further reading:
Enyedi (2008)

⊙²⁵ In Maley's opinion (1992), teaching is a permeable job: easy to enter, easy to leave.

Do you know of any non-NEST colleagues who decided to quit teaching? Why was this?

---

⁵ Speaking of survival strategies, I found that two respondents in **Survey 3** had recently given up teaching. Although they both remarked, rather sarcastically, that the best way to improve one's command of English was to quit teaching, it turned out from their response that their career change had been motivated merely by financial gain. In fact, one of them admitted that he missed teaching a lot, while the other one warned that her example should not be followed.

5.4 Stress without distress[6]

Admit it

In order to break the vicious circle, first of all we have to admit to ourselves that we are in a state of stress. We may find comfort in the thought that everybody is stressed to a greater or lesser degree. Spock (1946) wrote that every child is an anxious child, but some children are more anxious than others – the same applies to adults, I presume.

Some teachers refuse to take this first step under the pretext that they do not feel stressed. Indeed, some of them are hyperactive and always on the go.

EXAMPLE

Once I worked with a 'workaholic' colleague. His obsession was that his students had poor writing skills – perhaps it was true. To remedy the situation, in every lesson he would give them a long essay assignment, which he would collect the next day and return meticulously corrected the day after, reminding everyone that this was just the first draft and he would now expect a second and, if necessary, a third draft. While this was dragging on, the new assignments kept piling up relentlessly. The drill came to an abrupt end one day when the students simply walked out. Strangely enough, the teacher gave in without a fuss and looked much relieved himself.

Compulsive work for this teacher, it seems, was nothing else but a technique to avoid facing his state of stress.

Be that as it may, if we feel vaguely depressed, edgy or defensive, or abused when mildly criticised, or, on the contrary, we begin to hurt people for no apparent reason – we may be in the initial stages of the stress syndrome (Jersild 1955). The reason why stress is hard to recognise is that it attacks in the most diverse forms. Thus, each one of us should seek individual treatment for the malaise.

Speak out

The trouble is that, under stress, people are reluctant to come out into the open. And the more desperately they try to hide, the more stressed they become. So they are back at square one.

As I have indicated several times, we non-NESTs are especially vulnerable because of our language deficiencies. For many of us, having these exposed in public is a recurrent nightmare.

EXAMPLE

In Chapter 8.3, I shall examine some forms of collaborative teaching. In anticipation, let me refer to a team-teaching programme run in Japan. The programme involves inexperienced native speakers and experienced Japanese non-NESTs teaching in tandem. Participation is obligatory, and quite a few Japanese teachers would wish to opt out. In Siriwardena's (1992) findings, the main reason for reluctant participation is the non-NESTs' fear that their 'poor command of English' may be revealed.

---

[6] This title is, in fact ,that of one of Hans Selye's books (1974). A Canadian of Hungarian extraction, Selye was the first researcher to explore stress in great detail.

Indeed, we may easily lose face before both our students and our fellow-teachers because of what we reckon to be inadequate knowledge of English. It is also true that in some cultures, and in a number of schools, this revelation may lead to serious consequences. This threat may partly explain the fact that most non-NESTs are not in the habit of observing each other's classes or discussing their professional qualms. ⊙26

EXAMPLE

> *A few colleagues have confided in me that they feel uneasy whenever they have to communicate in English in the presence of fellow-non-NESTs. 'Will I make a good impression on them?' they wonder. And whilst they cannot help making judgements about others, they are being simultaneously assessed by their fellow teachers.*

⊙26 Do you feel stressed when you have to speak in public? Are you more inhibited in the presence of native or non-native speakers? Why?

In a study by Horwitz *et al.* (1986), three components of foreign-language anxiety are distinguished. The first one, *communication apprehension*, is caused by the conflict between the learner's mature ideas and the immature linguistic resources available to express them. The second component of anxiety is called *fear of negative social evaluation*; this is the issue I have alluded to in the previous two examples. The third component is *test anxiety*, which in the context of non-NESTs translates into anxiety experienced whenever they have to perform before their advanced students.

In another study, Tobias (1986) points out that anxious learners tend to engage in what he calls *derogatory cognition*. This means that their limited cognitive capacity is so much preoccupied with anxiety that they cannot focus on performing the task itself; hence their L2 performance is bound to suffer.

These research data may look convincing, but unfortunately they do not bring us closer to curing the ills. All I can offer to those suffering from a fear of exposure is that there is no point in trying to hide, because we simply cannot hide in the long run. ⊙27 With English rapidly gaining ground, with the spread of mass media and with more and more imported NESTs encroaching on our erstwhile private property, it is hopeless to close the classroom door behind ourselves and hedge our bets. In view of the unfeasibility of keeping secrets these days, we had better take the initiative and speak out.

⊙27 Characteristically, Park (2012) gave her paper with this title: 'I am never afraid of being recognised as an NNES'. How about you?

Shift into mastery mode

There are various strategies we apply, mostly unconsciously, to cope with difficult situations in our personal and professional lives. Two patterns of behaviour, *mastery-mode* and *survival-mode*, represent the extremes of a complex continuum.

In mastery-mode, people are eager to obtain new information and master new skills. This implies confronting challenges and, at times, losing battles. In survival mode, people's overall desire is to play it safe, therefore they search for simple, reassuring and stable models. As Holt remarks (1971), fearful people choose to sleep on the floor so that they don't fall out of bed, and refrain from placing bets so that they don't lose any money.[7,8]

---

[7] This dichotomy is reminiscent of risk-taking and risk-avoiding strategies, in the context of language learning (Beebe 1983, Faerch & Kasper 1983).

[8] In his excellent book, *The Inner Game of Tennis* (1979), Gallwey arrives at similar conclusions in the world of sport. His matrix for the inner game involves four basic skills: letting go of judgement, the art of programming ('Trust thyself' being the major component), letting it happen, and concentration.

And yet, over and over again, people in survival mode are rudely awakened from their dream. What they regard as brutal attacks, people in mastery-mode consider to be exciting adventures. Referring to Pirsig's novel, *Zen and the Art of Motorcycle Maintenance*, Claxton asks:

> 'What happens when you are trying to take a motorbike engine to bits and you burr the head of a screw? In mastery-mode you sit down quietly with a cup of tea and chew over the alternatives (use a drill, ring someone up, take it to the garage, cut a new slot). In survival-mode you look around guiltily to see if anyone saw you, feel upset and angry, kick the stupid bike, knocking it over, breaking an indicator and stubbing your toe into the bargain, and become sulky and withdrawn for the rest of the day' (1989: 186).

Non-NESTs under stress work in survival-mode. Such is the attitude of the teacher who lashes out against learner errors, while she herself is scared of speaking lest she should also commit errors. Krashen (1981) calls hesitant and excessively slow L2 speakers *monitor-overusers*, as opposed to *monitor-underusers* who happily chat away in any situation.

EXAMPLE

András is a Hungarian with a brilliant command of English. Highly cultured and quick-witted, he is the star guest at any party. That is, when Hungarian is the language of communication. In sharp contrast, when conversation switches into English, András becomes reticent and self-conscious.

Nowadays he does not attend parties to which native speakers of English are also invited. The main reason, he admits, is that he feels unable to communicate in English as effectively as his English interlocutors. He is less fluent, his utterances are clumsy and un-English. His charisma just won't get across.

'Speaking English is like wearing an uncomfortable costume,' he says. 'Too tight, 100 per cent polyester. It's all sham and artificial. If scratched beneath the surface, his utterances are hollow, unsuitable for carrying personal messages. Well practised holophrases tied together on a string. And whenever he lets go of them for a second, he begins to sink, as in a marsh.'

'No more English, thank you,' András concludes sarcastically. 'I've arrived home. All I want to enjoy for the rest of my life is the warmth and comfort ensured by my mother tongue.' ☉²⁸

⊙²⁸ How do you feel when you have to socialise in English outside the classroom? Anxious? Relaxed? Anything else?

The final solution András has arrived at would be difficult to condone and is, fortunately, very rare. On the other hand, I cannot deny that his arguments sound sadly convincing. In spite of my pleas for mastery-mode and unravelling stress...

Open the safety valves

Society at large expects teachers to convey positive values and set a good example. Affected by the same vices and weaknesses as anyone else, however, most of us cannot live up to such high expectations. The conflict between social demands and our incapacity to meet them may cause a guilty conscience and contribute to the development of stress.

In foreign-language education, learner-centred and humanistic approaches proclaim particularly noble ideas (Chapter 6.5). One of their slogans, 'caring and sharing', is borrowed from Moskowitz's famous book, *Caring and Sharing in the Foreign Language Class* (1978).

EXAMPLE

The vocabulary of this collection of humanistic techniques for language teaching only contains words with a positive meaning. Thus we can find beautiful *and* love, *but not* ugly *and* hate, *the rationale being that the foreign language class should serve as a podium for promulgating positive notions and sentiments only.*

The snag is that we often feel life is treating us badly and our students are a nuisance. And then along comes the humanist holding his magnifying mirror close to our face. We look in it and what stares back is far less attractive than we would like it to be.

My advice is that we should not look into mirrors or step on the weighing scales too frequently. But if we must, let the anger erupt. Letting our frustrations and hatred break loose is sure to have a prompt and soothing effect. Thus relieved, let us try to have a good laugh.

EXAMPLE

An elderly colleague told me the following two stories. He used to have a wooden ruler to tap the teacher's desk with whenever the noise exceeded a certain decibel limit. Once, as he was tapping away with no apparent effect, he angrily hit the desk with such strength that the ruler broke into two. The next day each pupil presented him with a ruler – forty-two in all.

On another occasion, the same temperamental teacher pounded on the desk with his fist, for a change. The smash was so precise that it caught the edge of his pocket watch sitting innocently on the desk. The watch shot out like a bullet, hitting against the head of one of the most unruly boys. It (the watch) broke into smithereens on the floor. This time, the teacher was given no replacements... ◉²⁹

Of course, besides exploding, there are numerous other ways of relieving stress. Sleeping in at the weekend, frequenting a masseur or masseuse, stroking pets, working out, doing relaxation exercises, having a good cry – we should all search for our own ways of letting off steam and once found, indulge in them as often as we possibly can.

Don't Sweat the Small Stuff

As I was writing this chapter, I found a book with this strange title: *Don't Sweat the Small Stuff – P.S. It's All Small Stuff* (Mantell 1996)

This somewhat cynical epigram may serve as a warning to those who believe that teaching English is, in essence, some kind of humble service for mankind.

◉²⁹ Speaking of unruly kids, Cowley notes: 'It is a war out there, and we need to use every single weapon we have at our disposal' (2001: 46).

Do you agree?

Further reading: Ur (2012)

⊙30 Teaching is often labelled with one of these synonyms: *job, profession, calling, mission, vocation, duty, business, pursuit, career, occupation, work.*

Which one(s) are most suitable? Why?

EXAMPLE

A few years ago, English teachers in Hungary invited a well-known teacher trainer from Britain to give a workshop. He was the sort of 'animateur' who would get participants into pairs, stand them up with their backs closely pressed against each other, and then ask one person in each pair to breathe in and out calmly while the other one would be feeling for his or her heartbeats. My job was to recruit a sizable audience for his workshop. Hearing the visitor's name, an English colleague impatiently turned down my invitation. When I asked what the matter was, he blurted out: 'Look, this guy is a crusader. He's convinced that ELT is a mission. It isn't. It's simply a job like any other.' [9] ⊙30

In similar vein, Maley warns against straining too hard in the name of 'high ideals':

'I am saying that there are more important things in life than language teaching and that anyone who becomes too closely bound up with it risks adding an emotive supercharge to what is only one part of the life experience' (1984: 80).

It seems to me that people with messianic faith spread the same stress that they themselves are victims of. Referring to a magazine article, Claxton quotes a school teacher describing her self-awakening process:

EXAMPLE

'As the years passed, I discovered that I had developed a special school "personality" which was a distortion of myself. I had built it up, at first quite unconsciously, but later it became a deliberately assumed mask. The "personality" had to conceal my natural impatience, my moods, my fatigue and make me appear endlessly dynamic and reassuring. With it, I wooed the children to learn by setting out to entertain them. It became increasingly difficult to switch off, without my crumbling into a disintegrated heap. I discovered that I had become a "character" and was fast becoming a caricature of myself' (1989: 33).

Another scary account is given by a teacher who had just quit the teaching profession.

EXAMPLE

'I decided that I had to get out of teaching when, walking down the corridor, I heard myself screaming "Tie!" at some kid I didn't even know. I suddenly realized that I wasn't myself any more: I didn't give a damn whether he was wearing a tie or not' (Claxton 1989: 33).

In the foreign-language class, too, there are teachers who will make a mountain out of a molehill in their stressed state of mind.

EXAMPLE

A friend told me that she had an English teacher at school who was obsessed with errors. Once she called on a boy to read out a homework exercise, warning him that she would give him as many bad marks as he made mistakes. In five minutes the boy ended up with fifteen mistakes – and fifteen bad marks!

---

[9] Widdowson (1990) warns that 'caring and sharing and linking hands' may work in Southern California, but not in other parts of the world. He adds that individuals who are forced to reveal their private life in public during psychotherapeutic learning tasks may 'disengage' from learning altogether.

Given this, it is no wonder that students sometimes find the foreign-language class a threatening place. Horwitz *et al* (1986) found, for example, that 38 per cent of their survey respondents endorsed the item 'I feel more tense and nervous in my language class than in my other classes'.

Enjoy yourself

I believe that the *sine qua non* of good teaching is for the teacher to feel confident and relaxed in the classroom. It all starts with physical appearance. Some teachers like to dress up smartly, others prefer jeans. Some male colleagues shave every day – others, perhaps, ought to...

To return to my hobbyhorse, teaching is a bit like acting. We need relaxation and meditation before we step on the stage.

EXAMPLE

- *A friend of mine, a leading actor in Hungary, tells me that every night he arrives at the theatre well before anyone else. He retreats into his dressing-room and takes his time dressing and making up. Preparation lasts for a good hour and a half. Meanwhile, he is not to be disturbed. By the time the curtain rises, he is in full control of himself.*

- *This reminds me of sports divers. At the very edge of the jumping board, they stand still and concentrate for what seems to be long minutes before they jump off. In an interview, a diver said that in those few seconds, they perform the jump in their mind's eye in the minutest detail.*

'Stop it, man! Come down to earth!', I hear you exclaim. 'What teacher can afford these luxuries?' All right, but if we can't afford to enjoy our profession, what's the point of doing it? Why remain a teacher, then?

It is not only our right, but our top professional duty to feel good about ourselves. I should come first. I should find pleasure in the classroom before anyone else. After all, I spend one third of my life there. I should do what pleases me – and if it pleases my students too, so much the better. ⊙³¹

Find the right balance

Although in everyday usage anxiety has negative connotations, we can also speak about positive anxiety, which is stimulating, energising and focusing.

Adapting Hebb's (1972) curve representing people's general behaviour for the teaching profession, Dunham (1992) demonstrates that increasing demands can raise the teacher's efficiency up to a certain point, but beyond that point they will lead to reduced job effectiveness (**Figure 6**).

⊙³¹ To some, this might appear a rather egotistical claim. Shouldn't the students come first? What do you think?

Figure 6: The relationship between increasing demands and teacher performance

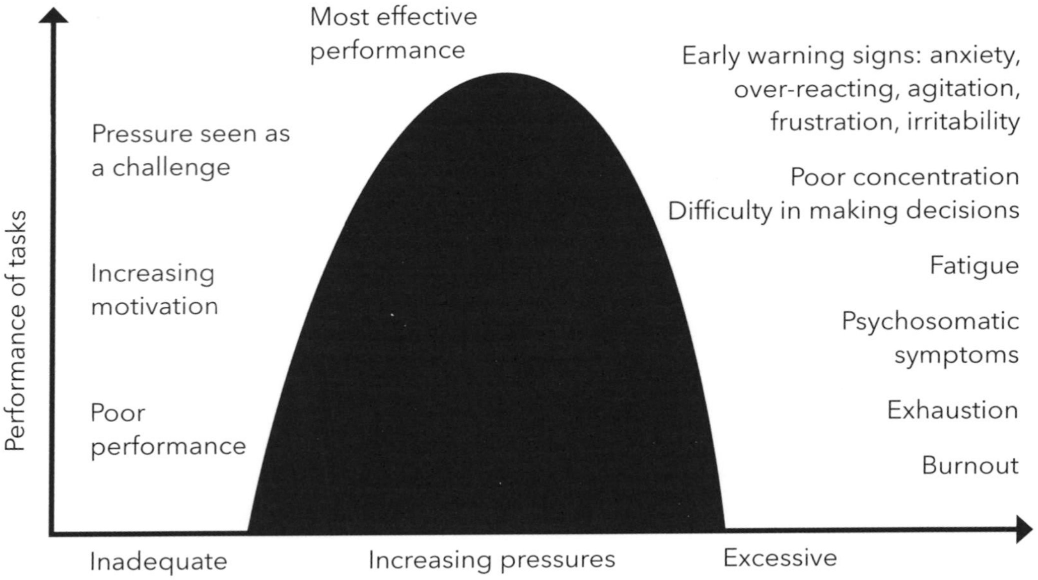

With reference to language learning, Scovel (1978) makes a distinction between *debilitating anxiety* and *facilitating anxiety*, the former being detrimental, whereas the latter is an asset to L2 performance. A staunch believer in lowering the *affective filter*, Krashen himself admits that a moderate degree of anxiety may be helpful for learning (1981).

We need to brace ourselves for the formidable task of teaching, too. The question is how to strike the right balance. For if our tension drops below a certain level, we are likely to be too drowsy to provide sufficient stimuli, whereas if we are too hyped up, we tend to be over-demanding. ⦿³²

Finally, let me refer to a study yielding paradoxical results. According to a combined rating supplied by pupils, parents, colleagues and head teachers, Claxton found that good teachers were more stressed than poorer ones.

> 'This, at first surprising, finding is interpreted as showing that the "better" teachers have the professional confidence to admit openly to the stress they experience. They are more able, because of their stable self-esteem, to tolerate being thought of as weak by others' (1989: 142).

Or as the adage says: 'To be not good enough is good enough'. If we have the guts to admit our weaknesses, we are sure to have set out on the right path to overcoming our stress. ⦿³³

Summary

In this chapter, I have evaluated items in my surveys which related to non-NESTs' language deficiencies. I have examined major problem areas in some detail. I have studied the possible causes of two typical non-NEST attitudes, *schizophrenia* and *inferiority complex*. Having described various stages of the stress cycle, I have recommended a seven-step cure for stressed non-NESTs.

After this gloomy picture, it is time for the sky to clear up. So let us quickly move on to Chapter 6.

⦿³² On TED.com, watch McGonigal's lecture (2013) entitled 'How to make stress your friend'.

What are its main messages? How could her advice be used for your own and your students' benefit?

⦿³³ Adapting the Marxist rallying cry, Rajagopalan demands 'NNSTs of the world wake up, you have nothing to lose but your nagging inferiority complex' (2005:300).

Do you agree? Why (not)?

Further reading

- **Enyedi, Á.** (2008) The rather well-fed caterpillar and the very hungry butterfly. In B. Beaven (Ed.) *IATEFL 2007: Aberdeen Conference Selections* IATEFL. (pp. 38–47).

  This lecture-turned-paper uses a children's story as an allegory to describe the life cycles of ELT teachers from pre-service training until they become fully-fledged professionals and mentors of younger generations. It portrays the kinds of clashes teachers are bound to face throughout their career.

- **Lazaraton, A.** (2003) Incidental displays of cultural knowledge in the non-native-English-speaking teacher's classroom. *TESOL Quarterly 37* (pp. 213–245).

  The article investigates the cultural knowledge of non-NESTs through a discourse analysis of interactions with their students. It focuses on instances which are not planned but emerge at random in the course of other pedagogical activities.

- **Medgyes, P.** (1999a) Language training: a neglected area in teacher education. In G. Braine (Ed.) *Non-native Educators in English Language Teaching* Lawrence Erlbaum (pp. 177–195).

  The main argument of this lecture-turned-paper is that for non-NESTs to be effective and self-confident professionals, they have to be near-native speakers of English. The example through which this assumption is demonstrated is a vocabulary course for trainee teachers at a Hungarian university.

- **Mousavi, E. S.** (2007) Exploring 'teacher stress' in non-native and native teachers of EFL. *ELTED 10* (pp. 33–41).

  The paper investigates differences between NESTs and non-NESTs in terms of the levels and causes of stress. Non-NESTs were found to be more vulnerable to stress, mainly due to their perceived English-language deficiencies.

- **Ur, P.** (2012) Classroom discipline. In P. Ur, *A Course in English Language Teaching* Cambridge University Press (pp. 244–255).

  After defining classroom discipline, the author suggests ways of creating a disciplined classroom and of dealing with discipline problems if need be. The five episodes at the end of the chapter are accompanied by her insightful comments.

CHAPTER 6

The bright side of being a non-native

Focus points

- The making of 'good' teachers
- The role of language learning strategies (LLS)
- Differences in teaching behaviour between NESTs and non-NESTs
- Correcting mistakes in oral communication
- The roles of self-awareness and empathy in the teaching-learning process
- The pros and cons of using L1 in the English class

⊙¹ Do you disagree with any of these six hypotheses?

If so, which one(s)?

What are your reasons?

In this chapter, I intend to study the positive aspects of being a non-NEST. For this purpose, I shall set up the following hypotheses. Non-NESTs can:⊙¹

- provide a good learner model for imitation;
- teach language learning strategies more effectively;
- supply learners with more information about the English language;
- better anticipate and prevent language difficulties;
- be more empathetic to the needs and problems of learners;
- make use of the learners' mother tongue.

6.1 Providing a good model

Proficient speakers and successful learners

My starting point is that not all successful language learners are proficient language users. 'Come on, this is absurd!' I hear you say. 'How can you claim to be a successful learner if your English is poor?' Of course, I am also aware that there are thousands of non-NESTs whose command of English leaves a lot to be desired. But whose English does not? Is there a yardstick against which we can objectively measure the level of English proficiency?

The concept of 'the proficient speaker' is an abstraction. In the absence of reliable measurement tools, it is left to our discretion to consider one teacher to be more proficient than another. The trouble is that our subjective judgment might occasionally mislead us.

EXAMPLE

Compare two non-NESTs, Mr Antoglio and Ms Lin. Mr Antoglio is undoubtedly a more fluent speaker, but is he a better writer too? Has anyone compared their written production? ⊙²

For the sake of argument, let us suppose that Mr Antoglio *is* more proficient in all four skills. But does that imply that he is a more successful learner too? Are proficiency and success synonyms? My answer is *no*. While proficiency is relatively measurable, success is less tangible in that it is a potential which may or may not feature at a high level of proficiency.

I ought to add, however, that Mr Antoglio spends one month in England every summer, whereas Ms Lin has never set foot in an English-speaking country. Isn't it possible that if the two teachers had had equal chances, Ms Lin would be a more proficient user of English on all counts? Considering the circumstances, isn't she a more successful, albeit less proficient, user of English?

Although I set greater store by success than by proficiency, I need to exercise caution.

EXAMPLE

Mrs Belova[1] had never been able to travel, but what further aggravated her situation as a teacher was that she was a mother of four, therefore she had to tutor private students in the afternoon before doing the housework and looking after the children. As she had no time to attend in-service training courses or energy for regular self-study, she felt that her command of English, which had never been particularly good, was deteriorating.

In a professional sense, Mrs Belova was seriously disadvantaged – little wonder her English was poor. But was she a successful learner? She may well have had the potential, but as it was not manifested in a relatively high degree of proficiency, there is no point of speaking of success in her case.

Do linguistic problems impair teaching effectiveness?

The next question I want to examine is the relationship between the teacher's language proficiency and teaching effectiveness.

Survey results

Question 10: Do your language difficulties hinder you in your work? If so, be specific.

In Chapter 5.1, I analysed various sources of difficulties the respondents in my surveys had specified. As a follow-up, I examined to what extent non-NEST respondents felt gaps in their knowledge of English hindered them in their teaching practice. **Table 7** summarises the results: ⊙³

---

[1] In the early 1950s Russian was made the compulsory foreign language in primary and secondary schools in several Central and Eastern European countries. As there was an acute shortage of teachers of Russian teachers, teachers of other foreign languages were turned into Russian teachers in crash courses. For several decades people living behind the Iron Curtain in Eastern Europe had little opportunity to meet English speakers, let alone travel to English-speaking countries. Nevertheless, quite a few teachers had an amazingly good command of English.

⊙² A former president of Hungary, Árpád Göncz, had learned English in prison while a political prisoner. Later, he became a superb translator, but couldn't speak English.

Can you think of any similar examples?

⊙³ Look at **Table 7** and choose the item that applies most to you. Specify the language difficulties that you feel hinder your work.

Table 7: The perceived influence of language difficulties on the effectiveness of teaching in Survey 2 (N=156)

Degree	Number of respondents	Percentage
not at all	49	31.4
a little	59	37.8
quite a bit	39	25.0
very much	7	4.5
extremely	2	1.3

According to the figures, a comfortable majority claimed they were not very much hindered by their language difficulties. To tell the truth, this is not quite what I had anticipated. I would have expected them to believe that their command of English played a more considerable role in the success of the teaching operation. Three possible interpretations spring to my mind to explain the respondents' attitude. Firstly, it may be that this majority speak English at a level high enough not to encounter a lot of linguistic problems; however, in view of the long list of language difficulties claimed by the respondents, this does not appear to be a plausible argument. Secondly, they may not have reflected upon the possible harm caused by deficient knowledge of English. Thirdly, they may have assumed that language proficiency was not a cardinal factor in terms of teaching efficacy. ⊙[4]

⊙[4] Can you suggest any other possible reasons for this?

Incidentally, in comparing these results with the respondents' teaching qualifications, I found that the better qualified teachers felt less hampered by linguistic issues. This may simply be explained by the fact that university education provided them with a better command of English. Another reason may be that a more substantial amount of teacher training raised their awareness of the complex nature of the teaching profession, in which language proficiency was just one condition for effective teaching. Conversely, the less training a teacher received, the more anxious she might be about the harm her poor language proficiency might cause.

Successful learners and successful teachers

In trying to address this issue, I pose two questions. The first one is: 'Do you have to be a successful learner in order to become a successful teacher?'

My answer is *yes*. I believe that a successful teacher is, by definition, a successful learner of English: poor learners do not make good teachers. Some might counter this view, however, with the opinion that unsuccessful learners may well be in possession of outstanding teaching qualities which are capable of offsetting their language handicap. This may occasionally be the case, and indeed I have also seen teachers, especially in primary schools, whose teaching abilities have far exceeded their command of English.

EXAMPLE

Once I visited a lesson where a group of secondary-school students role-played a court trial. Their speaking skills were incredibly good. Throughout the lesson, the teacher was standing at the back of the classroom, keeping silent – if I hadn't known that he spoke English far worse than his students, I would have thought that his reticence had only been motivated by wise pedagogical considerations.

Or I could also allude to esoteric situations where the non-NEST is just two lessons ahead of her students . For all that, I claim that the cases above are exceptions to the rule and success in learning is a prerequisite of success in teaching.

Another interesting point to consider is whether teachers with a better command of English should teach more advanced groups and leave beginners' groups to their less proficient colleagues. ⊙[5] This may appear to be an academic question, as most schools follow this practice anyhow, but I cannot help voicing my concern in this respect.

Let me take two examples. Firstly, poor proficiency usually includes poor pronunciation too. Now, if a teacher with non-standard pronunciation sets out to teach beginners, she is likely to ruin her students' budding pronunciation system. If she is a well-trained teacher, she may provide opportunities for the class to listen to native speakers, but this will only reduce the damage done. Secondly, those teachers who are content with teaching only beginners are in danger of leaving their own English to rust (if it ever was any good), because they are not being forced to improve it. Ideally, teachers should alternate between high- and low-level groups.

The second question is this: 'Does every successful learner become a successful teacher?' Here I do not hesitate to give a negative answer. It is common experience that many successful learners are lousy teachers.[2] This may be explained by several factors, among which poor training must be the major one. But there appears to be a less obvious aspect, too, which concerns some non-NESTs with a flair for learning languages. In their complacency, they tend to be oblivious of the fact that not everybody is as gifted as they are, and even fewer people are as keen to learn English as English teachers are!

To sum up, there seems to be a one-way relationship between the successful learner and the successful teacher, but it is a more indirect one than some might believe. It appears that success in learning English is a necessary, but not a sufficient, condition for success in ELT.

Language models and learner models

By arguing that non-NESTs are good models for imitation, I implicitly suggest that NESTs cannot be imitated. But this is only partly true.

A non-NEST can set two models before her students: a language model and a learner model. As a language model, she is a deficient one, insofar as she is a learner of English just like her students, albeit at a higher level. The closer she is to native-speaker proficiency, the better a language model she is. But non-NESTs, by definition, cannot be 'perfect' models (Chapter 2).

On the other hand, a non-NEST can aspire to be a 'perfect' learner model. Let me refer back to the relationship between proficiency and success. I pointed out there that, although they are related concepts, they are not the same. Thus Mr Antoglio serves as a good language model, but he is not much of a learner model, owing to his propitious learning background. In contrast, Ms Lin, who is less proficient, but has learnt everything through her own efforts, is a more credible learner model.

⊙[5] 'The teachers with a better command of English should teach the more advanced groups.'

Do you agree? Is this standard practice in your country?

---

[2] The same applies to other areas of study. Good physicists do not always make good physics teachers, nor do good pianists necessarily become good piano teachers.

Robert, a university lecturer, has become a living legend in Hungary thanks to his phenomenal command of English. In fact he is often taken for a native speaker; he regularly lends his voice to dubbing studios for English-language versions of Hungarian films. But Robert is more than a perfect imitator: he is an excellent translator of Hungarian fiction.

His students are usually baffled when they hear that he started to learn English at the age of 16 and was 30 at the time of his first trip to England. All in all, he has spent just one year of his life in English-speaking countries.

Mind you, Robert is not a 'model' teacher. He often goes to class unprepared and is generally impatient with slow or listless students. Yet, the fact that such a high level of proficiency is within a non-native speaker's reach has an inspiring effect on his students. Students generally set greater store by attracting his attention than by attaining the highest grade.

⊙⁶ Have you ever been taught by a 'born teacher'? What was she/he like?

⊙⁷ A long time ago, Dewey (1929) said that born teachers do exist, but their successes tend to be born and die with them.
Has the situation changed? If so, explain how.

⊙⁸ Many NESTs may, of course, have learned other languages and may have developed learning strategies which can usefully be shared.
Can any NESTs provide examples from their own experience?

Let me sidetrack for a moment. Lately, a lot has been written about the importance of careful lesson preparation, effective teaching techniques, ways to develop abilities of reflection and empathy and the like. 'Good teachers are not born, but trained', we often hear. In partial disagreement, I claim that the best teachers *are* born, though they may need proper training to bring forth their inborn capacities. ⊙⁶ ⊙⁷

A less abrupt variation of the adage is that 'There may be a *few* teachers who are born, but *many* teachers are needed'. I am quite prepared to accept this view, as well as the one that stresses the crucial role teacher education plays. I also readily acknowledge that we can and do learn a lot from 'made' teachers. However, I claim that the best model is the one who has undergone proper training *and* is endowed with certain 'extra qualities'. If this is the case, why does the professional literature keep quiet about the nature of such personal traits, whatever they may be? My complaint is that teacher education today seems to advocate the pedestrian and pedantic teacher instead of the bright and ingenious one.

By the same token, shouldn't the issue of the non-NEST as a successful language learner deserve more attention than it gets in teacher education programmes? The message I want to get across is this: only those non-NESTs should be set as models who are successful learners of English themselves. Anything less is a compromise.

On the other hand, NESTs cannot be imitated as learners, because they are not learners of English. ⊙⁸ Since they have acquired English as their mother tongue, just as we non-NESTs have acquired our L1, they can give us little advice about the basic process of language learning. In compensation, as it were, they can obviously claim to be far better *language* models.

6.2 Teaching language-learning strategies

Functions and types of language-learning strategies

It is a truism that some people pick up languages more quickly and effectively than others. There are huge differences between non-NESTs, too, in terms of success with English. Success depends on several factors, such as: background, motivation, age, intelligence, aptitude, level of education and knowledge of other foreign languages. An additional factor which has a bearing on success is called *language-learning strategies* (LLS).

LLS are specific actions employed to facilitate the learning and recall of one or several components of proficiency (Wenden & Rubin 1987). Facilitation does not only imply making the process easier, but also making it

'faster, more enjoyable, more self-directed, more effective, and more transferrable to new situations' (Oxford 1990: 8).

LLS can be grouped in several ways; a classification with a pragmatic rationale has been proposed by Oxford, who puts LLS into two major groups, each including three sub-groups (**Figure 7**).

Figure 7: Interrelationships between direct and indirect strategies ⊙⁹

⊙⁹ Identify the LLSs that have worked for you. Or did you learn languages by 'instinct' (Oxford 2011)?

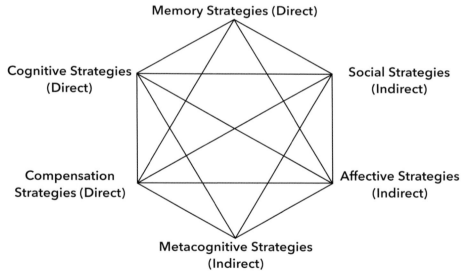

Memory Strategies (Direct)

Cognitive Strategies (Direct)

Social Strategies (Indirect)

Compensation Strategies (Direct)

Affective Strategies (Indirect)

Metacognitive Strategies (Indirect)

Direct strategies consist of memory strategies (how to memorise and retrieve new information), cognitive strategies (how to understand and produce the language) and compensation strategies (how to use the language despite limited knowledge). *Indirect strategies* include metacognitive strategies (how to coordinate the learning process), affective strategies (how to regulate emotions), and social strategies (how to learn with other people).

Oxford likens the relationship between direct and indirect strategies to that between the actor and the director in the theatre. The 'actor' deals with the language itself, whilst the 'director' ensures the suitable background for the 'actor' to learn as well as possible. In subsequent chapters of her book, Oxford supplies a number of specific LLS to demonstrate their use and significance.

All language learners employ LLS. Success with learning largely depends upon the ability to select the most appropriate strategy for dealing with a specific learning task. Having interviewed seven extremely successful language learners, Stevick concludes that there is not a common pattern emerging: everyone seems to learn in their own ways. ⊙[10] What works for some learners, utterly fails for others:

> 'Hardly a clear model for an aspiring language student who wants to profit from their example!' (1990: 138).

⊙[10] Given that everybody learns in their own way, is it at all worthwhile teaching LLSs? Why (not)?

EXAMPLE

It is a standard listening comprehension exercise to have students listen to the audio with their books shut before they look at the printed text. Some students are happy with this procedure, others prefer to listen and read at the same time, yet others insist that they be allowed to scan the text before they listen.

With regard to grammar, many students expect the new structure to be explained before they are asked to use it. Others like to experiment with the new item first and then infer the rule, on the basis of some kind of reinforcement.

Or have you met learners who are prepared to cram their memories with uncontextualised words belonging to the same semantic field, such as species of trees or pieces of clothing? I have. (I know at least one: myself.)

In Chapters 9 and 10, I shall recommend a number of strategies and techniques for self-improvement.

Can language-learning strategies be taught?

Although both teaching experience and research studies show enormous differences in learning style, the quest for the secrets of good language learners has never ceased. Research has been motivated by the assumption that, if we managed to find out more about them, we might be able to convey the strategies that worked for more successful learners to less successful ones. Books and articles written about 'the good learner' abound and the findings show a great deal of overlap (Rubin 1975, Stern 1975, Naiman *et al.* 1978, Wesche 1979, Rubin & Thompson 1982). The list supplied by Omaggio (1978) offers a good synthesis of the work done in this field. She claims that good learners: ⊙[11]

⊙[11] Are you a good language learner? Look at the seven bullet points. Which of these features fit your learning style?

- have insight into their own LLS;
- are actively involved in the learning task;
- are willing to run the risk of making mistakes;
- are good guessers;
- are prepared to attend to form as well as meaning;
- use the target language as early as possible;
- are tolerant to ambiguities inherent in the target language.[3]

---

[3] These findings should be treated with caution, however, because it is possible that the LLS employed by good learners are also employed by bad learners and that their failure is caused by some other factors (Skehan 1989).

Good learners are capable, then, of gleaning a repertoire of LLS which suits their personality as well as the particular learning environment. The majority of learners, however, seem to grope in the dark and move along on a hit-or-miss basis, unless they are fortunate enough to receive tailor-made support from knowledgeable teachers. The question is to what extent LLS are teachable – an issue that has produced hardly any tangible results so far (O'Malley *et al.* 1985).

Nevertheless, the idea of sensitising learners to LLS has gained popularity; there are books and articles in abundance dealing with this subject. Many researchers entertain the hope that, if we make students more responsible for their own learning, they will gradually reach partial and, eventually, full autonomy (Chapter 3.1).

Supposing that LLS can be developed, teacher education ought to take more notice of them. ⊙¹² Specifically , provision should be made for trainees to:

- become familiar with the LLS that they and other successful learners employ;
- acquire techniques to develop new strategies that are likely to suit their individual potential and the learning context;
- learn how to raise their prospective students' awareness of the LLS they themselves are using.

Manuals dealing with LLS in teacher education are already accessible; one of the most widely-used practice books is *Learning to Learn English* (Ellis & Sinclair 1989) (see more about learner-autonomy in Chapter 9.1). ⊙¹³

By virtue of being conscious learners of English, non-NESTs stand a better chance of sensitising their students to LLS In Chapter 6.1, I argued that not all successful learners become good teachers. An additional cause of failure may be unnecessary insistence that students employ the same LLS that have helped the teachers to achieve success in English.

Let me make two remarks on the plight of NESTs. Firstly, in spite of their lack of personal experience of learning English, their training programme should also include information about the role of LLS. Secondly, it should not be forgotten that NESTs have also pursued LLS in their contact with foreign languages. This experience may well have been short-lived, negative or distant, yet it could perhaps be taken advantage of in their job as teachers of English. ⊙¹⁴

6.3 Supplying information about the English language

Language proficiency and language awareness

A language teacher's expertise consists of three components: (a) language proficiency, (b) language awareness, and (c) pedagogic skills. While *language proficiency* implies skills in the target language, *language awareness* involves explicit knowledge about the language, which does not necessarily assume a high level of language proficiency. In her role as an instructor, the teacher exhibits varying degrees of *pedagogic skills*.

⊙¹² On YouTube, watch Sid Efromovich's TEDx talk '5 techniques to speak any language' (2013).
Is this the way you learn languages? Would you recommend these techniques to your students?

⊙¹³ Sharle & Szabó (2000) define autonomy 'as the freedom and ability to manage one's own affairs, which entails the right to make decisions as well'.
In this sense, do you consider yourself an autonomous language learner? How would this feature in practice? In what ways do you encourage your learners to take more responsibility for their own learning?

⊙¹⁴ '[N]ative speakers know the destination, but not the terrain that has to be crossed to get there; they themselves have not travelled the same route' (Seidlhofer 1999: 238).
Explain this statement.

⊙**15** The concept of method 'has had a magical hold on us' for a long time (Kumaravadivelu 2001: 557) but this is no longer true.

What is the situation today?

Further reading:
Kumaravadivelu (2001),

⊙**16** Before you look at **Table 8**, collect as many differences in teaching behaviour between NESTs and Non-NESTs as possible. Use your own and your colleagues' teaching experience.

Throughout the history of language teaching, great importance has been attached to the teacher's pedagogic skills, although this concept lends itself to diverse interpretations. In Chapter 4.1, I introduced two opposite attitudes, which Rivers (1981) calls the *activist–formalist dichotomy*. As I pointed out, the essential difference between them lies in what they place in the centre of their attention: the carrier content (teaching the language itself) or the learning content (teaching *about* the language). Activists prefer to develop language skills, whereas the formalists' endeavour is to develop language awareness. The pendulum has swung from one end to the other at regular intervals.

Today most researchers would agree that language pedagogy has broken away from the single-method conceptual framework and the constraints of bipolarity (Stern 1983).[4] ⊙**15** We have at last realised that language teaching is far too complex an operation to bear any form of stringent codification. Incidentally, I like to think that the best teachers have never worn such straitjackets.

Differences in teaching behaviour between natives and non-natives

Be that as it may, I suspect that individual teaching style is largely determined by whether a teacher happens to be a native or a non-native speaker. In my view, NESTs and non-NESTs can be distinctly separated along the activist-formalist faultline, even if the antagonism has been officially declared defunct. Although several studies have confirmed this assumption (Roberts 1982, Chaudron 1988, Politzer & Weiss 1969), I turn to my own research findings for corroboration.

Survey results

Question 1: Do you see any difference in teaching behaviour between NESTs and non-NESTs? Describe.

Out of a total of 216 respondents in **Survey 2**, 146 (67.6 per cent) gave a positive answer, and only 32 (14.8 per cent) said they perceived no differences. 38 teachers (17.6 per cent) left this question unanswered.

Next, the respondents with 'yes' responses had to identify those differences; **Survey 1** respondents were asked the same question. Since this question in both surveys was open-ended, I had to collate the data under comprehensive headings, a method which inevitably led to simplifications. ⊙**16** **Table 8** gives a summary report of the responses.

---

[4] Incidentally, the last method whose basic tenets were 'carved in stone' was the Communicative Approach. Not long after its conception in the 1970s, however, its maxims, suggestive of an activist allegiance (Chapter 6.3), were felt to be so stifling that the label was first pluralised and decapitalised ('communicative approaches'), and then diluted into 'communicative language teaching', a term so general as to be almost meaningless. Since it had an apparently humanistic ring, large numbers of teachers allegedly 'went communicative'. To what extent they were truly loyal to this bland label after the classroom door had closed behind them remains a mystery.

Table 8: Perceived differences in teaching behaviour between NESTs and non-NESTs in Survey 1 and 2 (N=216+28) ⊙¹⁷

NESTs	non-NESTs
own use of English	
speak better English	speak poorer English
use real language	use 'bookish' language
use English more confidently	use English less confidently
general attitude	
adopt a more flexible approach	adopt a more guided approach
are more innovative	are more cautious
are less empathetic	are more empathetic
attend to perceived needs	attend to real needs
have far-fetched expectations	have realistic expectations
are more casual	are more strict
are less committed	are more committed
attitude to teaching the language	
are less insightful	are more insightful

focus on:
  fluency
  meaning
  language in use
  oral skills
  colloquial registers
	focus on:
	  accuracy
	  form
	  grammar rules
	  printed word
	  formal register

teach items in context	teach items in isolation
prefer free activities	prefer controlled activities
favour groupwork/pairwork	favour frontal work
use a variety of materials	use a single textbook
tolerate errors	correct/punish errors
set fewer tests	set more tests
use no/less L1	use more L1
resort to no/less translation	resort to more translation
assign less homework	assign more homework
attitude to teaching culture	
supply more cultural information	supply less cultural information⊙¹⁸

Table 8 demonstrates that NESTs and non-NESTs are seen as showing a great many differences in basic aspects of teaching behaviour. Thus my second hypothesis set forth in Chapter 4.2, namely that *NESTs and non-NESTs appear to differ in terms of their teaching behaviour*, seems to have been supported by the survey results.

Not surprisingly, there was general agreement that NESTs have a better overall proficiency in English. Among other things, the NEST's superiority in this respect features in more real language use and a higher degree of self-confidence in using the language in general, and in the classroom in particular.

⊙¹⁷ Check the list in **Table 8** and identify the differences between your list and the one in the table.

As a learner and/or a teacher, which items would you challenge?

⊙¹⁸ Since the first edition of this book, the list of differences has been supplemented with a few more items: inaccurate pronunciation and grammar, traditional teaching style, efficient work, awareness of negative transfer in learners' interlanguage.

(Butler 2007, Ma 2012, Samimy & Brutt-Griffler 1999).

If you are a non-NEST, are these features characteristic of you?

Afterwards, I summarised various components of teaching behaviour under three general headings: general attitude, attitude to teaching the language and attitude to teaching culture. In explaining their answers, the respondents reiterated that, on the whole, *the discrepancy in language proficiency between NESTs and non-NESTs accounts for most of the differences found in their teaching behaviour*. Thus the respondents seem to support the third hypothesis I advanced in Chapter 4.2.

At this point, I do not wish to engage in a detailed analysis of all the divergences found between NESTs and non-NESTs. Let me dwell briefly on some of those which relate to their attitude to teaching English, and then deal with the other issues in subsequent chapters.

Explaining the differences in attitude

The respondents frequently expressed the view that non-NESTs are usually preoccupied with accuracy, the formal features of English, the nuts and bolts of grammar, the printed word and formal registers. Many lack fluency, have a limited insight into the intricacies of meaning[5] , are often in doubt about appropriate language use, have poor listening and speaking skills, and are not familiar with colloquial English. It is only reasonable to suppose, then, that they place the emphasis on those aspects of the language that they have a better grasp of.

The respondents indicated that the same applies to other components of teaching behaviour. If non-NESTs have a restricted knowledge of context, they tend to teach unfamiliar language elements in a context-poor environment, or in isolation. If they are engrossed in fighting their own language difficulties, they cannot afford to loosen their grip over the class. Or as one respondent put it:

> 'Non-native speakers fear the chaotic landscape one encounters when stepping away from a rule-oriented world.'

As groupwork and pairwork often create unpredictable situations full of linguistic traps, non-NESTs favour more secure forms of classwork, such as lock-step activities. Similar reasons are claimed to account for the non-NEST's preference for standard coursebooks, which by their very nature provide security. On a general plane, the same motives encourage the non-NEST's more controlled and cautious pedagogic approach.

At this point, some may say that, contrary to what I promised in the title 'The bright side of being a non-native', I am still trying to rub in the non-NEST's weaknesses. This is not true; to my mind, most of the items in **Table 8** do not carry value judgments. Some of them imply equal values (such as focus on fluency versus accuracy, or flexibility versus cautiousness). Others are ambivalent in nature. For example, the statement that non-NESTs pay more attention to reading and writing should not necessarily be regarded as a criticism. Writing skills, as such, are no less valuable than oral skills. An order of priority among various skills can only be set up in accordance with the general aims of English-language teaching valid for a specific teaching environment. If these aims should (as in many countries they do) set greater store by the printed word, then the non-NEST's preoccupation with reading and writing is fully justified. ☉¹⁹

☉¹⁹ In the light of your own curriculum goals, what priorities are teachers of English expected to adopt? Check against **Table 8** and identify a few general patterns.

---

[5] Form and meaning rhyme well with learning content and carrier content (Chapter 4.1).

On an unequivocally positive note, non-NESTs were found to be more insightful than NESTs. This follows from the differences in the process of mastering the English language. Acquisition being largely unconscious, NESTs are not aware of the internal mechanisms operating language use and therefore are unable to give their students relevant information about language learning. On the other hand, during their own learning process, non-NESTs have amassed a wealth of knowledge about the English language. Their antennae can intercept even the minutest item as a possible source of problems, of which NESTs are likely to take no notice.

EXAMPLE

Have NESTs ever realised the magnitude of the difficulty that the there is *structure causes to speakers of certain languages? Are they aware of the confusion about prepositional phrases:* She sat on it *cannot be* She sat it on. *Conversely,* He put it on *cannot be* He put on it. *However,* Polly put the kettle on *is just as correct as* Polly put on the kettle *(except in the nursery rhyme). Have they thought about the small difference between* I hate it that you... *and* I know [it] that you...? *Or the one between* Will you come? *and* Will you be coming?

Of course, NESTs are also capable of refining their language awareness. In their own terms, they are just as capable as non-NESTs, supposing that they avail themselves of the opportunities provided by teacher education, foreign language learning and, above all, by experience. Those NESTs who have spent an extended period of time in the host country and have even taken pains to learn the students' mother tongue should be incomparably more perceptive than those who have not. ⊙[20]

6.4 Anticipating and preventing language difficulties

Monolingual classes and the role of culture

Non-NESTs sharing the learners' mother tongue are in a particularly favourable position. Since we have jumped off the same springboard as our students, both in a linguistic and cultural sense, we are intrinsically more sensitive to their difficulties than NESTs. Discovering trouble spots requires little energy and time; messages can be exchanged merely by winking an eye. Let me illustrate this point with a few examples from Hungarian.

EXAMPLE

To the surprise of NESTs who have recently arrived in Hungary, basic structures such as have got *and* there is *do not exist in Hungarian. Nor do we have genders; hence even near-native Hungarian speakers of English inevitably mix up* he *and* she.

Interestingly, the English don't have a generic term for the Hungarian szekrény *– the equivalent of* Schrank *in German and* shkaf *in Russian. (*Cupboard *does not cover a* wardrobe, *surely?)*

⊙[20] In terms of their professional behaviour, Ellis (2006) recognises a subtle distinction between monolingual and bilingual NESTs.

How are they different?

Further reading: Ellis (2006)

⊙²¹ Read this example and note the problems of using *enough*.

- *My car is big enough.*

- *There are more than enough cars on the roads in Budapest.*

- *My Volkswagen isn't a big enough car for our family.*

- *This should be explanation enough for why the mayor is considering introducing a toll in the city centre.*

Would *enough* be a difficult item for your students as well? Would NESTs understand the reason(s)?

Choose a chronic language problem which your students wrestle with, but NESTs are usually unaware of (McNeill 2005). Give your reasons.

⊙²² Which is it more important to teach: source culture (L1) or target culture (L2) (McKay 2002)?

Which target culture, British, American, or another one? Or international culture, perhaps?

Give your reasons.

And this is just the tip of the iceberg. Without wishing to discourage the enthusiastic NEST from trying her hand in Hungarian (or any other language, for that matter), it has to be admitted that she would have to spend a whole lifetime to fathom all the subtleties of the language. Better born a Hungarian... **⊙²¹**

Obviously, those expatriate NESTs who stay put in one country manage to gather far more experience about their students' specific language problems than those who drift on every other year. And since language is a major carrier of a people's culture, familiarity with the language brings NESTs closer to their students' cultural roots, too. Discovering divergences in cultural patterns may shed light on why students are unable to comprehend a specific language element.[6]

While we are on the subject, **Table 8** indicates that NESTs and non-NESTs also differ in terms of their attitude to teaching culture. By virtue of coming from an English-speaking country, NESTs are able to provide more information about its culture. However, the more the English language spreads and diversifies in the world, the less it will remain the privilege of NESTs. In our days, there is a pronounced tendency for culture to become less language-specific and more country-specific. **⊙²²**

EXAMPLE

Recently, I spent some time in England. At a party, I talked to an American colleague about the linguistic and cultural deficit of non-NESTs. She said that, despite being a native speaker, she would also frequently feel excluded in the company of Brits. As fate would have it, a few minutes later conversation took a sudden turn around the dinner-table. I was rapidly losing my bearings. Catching my eye, the American whispered to me: 'This is it. I don't have the faintest idea what they're talking about, either!'

Two more comforting thoughts. Firstly, although NESTs are genuine specimens of their culture, they often have stunningly little factual knowledge about it. With the spread of various channels of mass media and travel, devoted non-NESTs can become just as well-informed as their average native counterparts. Secondly, in a monolingual class we certainly have far more background information about the students than even the most well-informed NEST. Indirectly, this knowledge is likely to enhance our capacity to anticipate and prevent the students' learning difficulties.

Errors and error correction

As I have argued above, linguistic and cultural awareness can help non-NESTs anticipate students' difficulties. Most of us have developed a 'sixth sense', which becomes more and more subtle with the accumulation of teaching experience. Those of us who have been teaching long enough can, with a fair degree of accuracy, predict what is likely to go wrong before the student opens his mouth. By analogy with the oft-mentioned (and oft-challenged) notion of 'native speaker's intuition', this might be called 'non-native speaker's intuition'.

In possession of this anticipatory device, non-NESTs stand a good chance of preventing problems which often materialise in deviant usage or, for want of a better word, errors.

---

[6] Even extremely proficient non-native speakers are frequently bewildered by headlines in the popular press.

EXAMPLE

I mentioned above that the English have got *structure is hard for Hungarians to crack, because the notion of possession is expressed by means of a different structure. The literal translation of* I have a book *is roughly* Is a book to me (Van egy könyvem). *The similarly perplexed Russian learners may produce* At me book, *which correctly is* U menia kniega. *On the other hand, the German and French learner will easily pick up the* have got *structure:* Ich habe ein Buch *and* J'ai un livre.

Teacher training can, of course, suggest ways of dealing with error prevention. To stay with the above example, trainees should be:

- reminded that the English *have got* structure is a source of difficulty;
- shown a few wrong sentences which are likely to come up;
- advised about teaching techniques to prevent wrong sentences;
- offered ways of correcting errors once they have been committed.

The study of error analysis and error correction has come a long way. There is plenty of literature available on the subject and even inexperienced teachers have a host of techniques up their sleeve to deal with (which is not to say that they are effective ones, too). Dulay, Burt and Krashen must be right in claiming that

> 'if a popularity contest were held among the various aspects of verbal performance, errors would surely make off with the first prize' (1982: 139).

Errors can be of two types: overt and covert errors (Medgyes 1989). *Overt errors* can typically be related to achievement strategies employed for the purpose of effective communication even at the risk of producing incorrect utterances (Corder 1983). Errors resulting from success-oriented efforts are easily detectable and palpably present. Many learners, however, prefer to play it safe by resorting to reduction strategies. This implies using only well-oiled structures and words, or, in extreme cases, avoiding topics where communication is likely to lead to errors. Reduction strategies may well be conducive to 'error-free' performance, but as they entail curtailing the desired message, the production is less than optimal; I call these invisible errors *covert errors*. ◉23

It follows from my logic that, while overt errors are conspicuous signs of learning taking place, covert errors actually impede the development of communicative skills. Covert errors are all the more pernicious as they typically produce this effect under the disguise of well-formed utterances.

While techniques for the correction of overt errors have been worked out in great detail, covert errors generally pass ignored, partly because by definition they are reluctant to exhibit themselves. I argue, however, that by adopting appropriate error correction strategies, we may cut down on covert errors, too. Since reduction strategies are adopted in an effort to avoid committing errors, teachers should stop stigmatising overt errors and, simultaneously, should reward students who are brave enough to take risks.

As **Table 8** shows, NESTs and non-NESTs are thought to behave differently with regard to error correction too. Since native speakers generally regard language as a means of achieving some communicative goal, they do not make a fuss about errors unless they hinder communication. ◉24 In contrast, we non-NESTs are notorious for penalising overt errors (and grammatical errors in particular),

◉23 How did your own teachers try to prevent errors? What happened when a mistake persisted? Did they penalise the learners for 'covert errors', too?

Would you? Why (not)?

Further reading: Ur (2012)

◉24 As a non-NEST, do you ask/expect native speakers to correct your mistakes? Do they? Why (not)?

⊙²⁵ On YouTube, watch this amusing sketch:

Grammar police interrogation www.youtube.com/watch?v= 3X4qi7AwDQl&feature=share

Note the errors which the interrogator keeps correcting. Would you also correct them if your students made them?

⊙²⁶ A student who was being taught by a non-native teacher of American English wrote in her diary: 'I am happy. You are like us. You understand my feelings about English' (Thomas 1999: 12).

What do you think she meant by this?

probably because we regard English primarily as a school subject to be learned and only secondarily as a communicative medium to be used. But the main reason for our heavy-handed attitude must lie in our deficient knowledge of English.[7] **⊙²⁵**

To step out of this vicious circle, I suggest that we place more trust in our 'sixth sense' to understand, anticipate, and prevent students' difficulties, a quality NESTs cannot claim to possess.

6.5 Showing empathy

Hot and cold education

A term borrowed from psychology, *empathy* means the power to understand and enter into another person's feelings. In the terse definition of Guiora *et al.* (1972), empathy is the ability to put oneself in another person's shoes.

In my view, empathy is one of the most characteristic features of the successful teacher. Studying the emotional implications of student/teacher relationships, Salzberger-Wittenberg *et al.* (1990) write that students expect the teacher, among her other roles, to act as a 'provider and comforter'. This role may imply expectations ranging from realistic ones to the most far-fetched (Chapter 3.3). **⊙²⁶**

In education, the term 'empathy' received wide currency in the wake of Rogers' highly influential book, *Freedom to Learn* (1983). This book also gave a strong impetus to the birth of what is commonly called the *humanistic movement*. In this context, Bowers (1986) makes a distinction between 'hot' and 'cold' education. *Hot education* harbours such concepts as learner-centredness (Chapter 3.2), equal roles in the classroom, two-way interaction (Chapter 3.1), problem solving, simulation activities and so on. In contrast, *cold education* incorporates such notions as teacher control, one-way interaction, guided programmes of instruction and so on. Needless to say, the humanistic philosophy of education is a typical case of hot education.

The humanistic movement soon reached the shores of foreign language education. Moskowitz coined the slogan: 'Affective education is effective education' (1978:14), with the implication that the foreign language class should, in its own ways, contribute to the learners' emotional growth and facilitate the process of self-actualisation (Chapter 5.4). In similar vein, Stevick claimed that

> 'a teacher must be willing and able to share the most important aspects of life, to give freely of self' (1980: 294).

In compliance with the new philosophy, alternative terms to replace the word teacher were offered, such as *facilitator, counsellor* or *mentor*, all of which were supposed to reflect basic changes in the teacher's role. None of them have stood the test of time in foreign-language education.

---

[7] It is no mere chance that many non-NESTs beg native speakers to correct them – even in situations where native speakers find their insistence a nuisance and do not understand the underlying motives.

In the 1970s and 1980s, 'teaching with a human face' was the name of the day, as though empathy, for example, had not been a quality all good teachers had shared, implicitly or explicitly, over the centuries (Medgyes 1986). The movement also admitted a number of zealots into its ranks, who impatiently rejected any other way of thinking. Such fanatics ought to have been restrained by the tolerance Rogers himself advocated:

> 'Some teachers raise the question, "But what if I am *not* feeling empathetic, do *not*, at this moment, prize or accept or like my students? What then?" My response is that realness is the most important of the attitudes [...]. So if one has little understanding of the student's inner world and a dislike for the students or their behavior, it is almost certainly more constructive to be *real* than to be pseudoempathic or to put on a facade of caring' (1969: 126). ⊙²⁷

Empathy and self-awareness

It may well be true that some people are endowed with a higher degree of empathy than others. Teacher education, however, can contribute to the relative development of this quality. In this regard, Szesztay stresses the importance of the relationship between empathy and self-awareness. She suggests that

> 'the more self-aware someone is, the more capable he is of understanding and appreciating other perspectives. In turn, being open and receptive to other perspectives has great potential for learning more about yourself' (1992: 71).

Translating this into the teaching/learning relationship, more self-aware learners are supposed to be more able to get in touch with their own future learners. By the way, research findings seem to confirm that highly empathetic learners do better in foreign languages than less empathetic ones (Guiora *et al.* 1972, Schumann 1978).

Thus two relationships are assumed to strengthen each other: the one between empathy and self-awareness in general, and the other one between self-aware learning and empathetic teaching. Now let me try to apply these relationships to the NEST/non-NEST context.

Earlier on, I argued that non-NESTs are more self-aware, by virtue of being learners of English themselves (Chapter 6.2). Supposing that the two assumptions above are true, non-NESTs are more empathetic than NESTs who have acquired English.

These speculations seem to have been confirmed by the findings of **Surveys 1 and 2**. As **Table 8** demonstrates, non-NESTs are perceived as more empathetic on all counts.

Firstly, they can attend to the students' real needs to a greater extent; I suppose that this applies with particular force to monolingual settings. In contrast, NESTs, either working with linguistically heterogeneous groups in an English-speaking country, or with monolingual groups overseas, probably have a less clear picture of their students' givens and aspirations. They hardly ever have the facilities to run a proper programme of needs analysis, but even if they do, the results will probably be less reliable than the non-NEST's gut feelings based on her comprehensive familiarity with the students' linguistic, cultural and personal background.

⊙²⁷ Have you ever been disliked by a teacher? What were the signs of her negative feelings? As a teacher, how would you treat a student you don't like?

Secondly, thanks to the basis of their familiarity with the teaching/learning context, non-NESTs are more able to set realistic aims for the students by matching their individual potential with social demands. For example, in mainstream education, non-NESTs are more cognisant of the constraints of the national curriculum, the teaching materials available and the examinations the students are expected to take. Similarly, they are in a position to gauge realistically the level of motivation that students studying in a particular type of school normally have.

Thirdly, the respondents were of the opinion that non-NESTs tend to be more strict than their non-native counterparts. This may partly be due to their deeper understanding of the prevalent circumstances. If they know, for instance, that it is in the students' interest to take a state examination, they are obliged to adapt their teaching methods to the stringent examination requirements; this involves being more demanding in terms of home assignments as well. Very often, non-NESTs simply cannot afford to be as casual as NESTs, whose involvement with the target country is far less thorough (Chapter 6.6). ⊙28

Having said that, it must be noted that a higher degree of empathy is merely a potential which not all have available. I have come across quite a few non-NESTs who have shown precious little empathy towards their students, as well as many NESTs whom I have found amazingly understanding. It goes without saying that, in addition to teacher education, the best training for NESTs to enhance their capacity of empathy is to learn the language of the host country. I would advise non-NESTs, too, to take up a new foreign language (time permitting), because this experience may deepen our understanding of the students' plight (Schumann & Schumann 1977, Lowe 1987, Waters *et al.* 1990).

⊙28 I mention three reasons why non-NESTs are potentially more empathetic than NESTs.

Can you give any examples from your own experience to support these claims?

6.6 Benefiting from the mother tongue

The monolingual principle

'To use or not to use the mother tongue?' – this has been one of the greatest issues in the foreign-language class for nearly a century. Prior to that, the Grammar-Translation Method did not only allow the use of L1, but made it an integral part of the teaching/learning process. On the one hand, it was one of its main goals to teach the subtle uses of the mother tongue, inasmuch as the learner was expected to translate literary texts from and into the mother tongue. On the other hand, L1 was an indispensable teaching device for explaining structures and vocabulary, giving instructions, doing various kinds of exercises and so on.

It was around the beginning of the 20th century that a monolingual approach spread in language pedagogy, as a result of the Reform Movement led by such eminent scholars as Sweet, Jespersen, Palmer and others (Howatt 1984). Essentially, their message was that the target language should be the sole medium of communication, with the underlying rationale that a focus on L2 would maximise the effectiveness of learning. 'The more you use the target language, the better you will master it' – this tenet sounded so obvious that it did not demand empirical evidence. And indeed, its protagonists did not offer any.

It is quite probable that the Reform Movement and its pedagogical offspring, the Direct Method and subsequently the Audio-Lingual Method, would never have made such a strong impact on ELT if they had not been supported and, in fact, coerced by the profound and growing influence of English-speaking countries and of monolingual NEST teachers (Chapter 1).

However, the advocates of the monolingual principle were always aware of the role L1 played in foreign language learning. Palmer's (1921/1964) approach, for example, rested on basically contrastive assumptions, and Lado, a chief architect of the Audio-Lingual Method, even wrote an influential book under the revealing title: *Linguistics Across Cultures* (1957). As usual, it was the disciples who claimed exclusive rights for the 'truth'. They not only encouraged L2 use in the classroom, but made it obligatory and ubiquitous. The most fanatical went as far as to persecute the deviants. Pupils caught using their mother tongue during the foreign language class in Kenya or the French colonies, for example, risked corporal punishment (Phillipson 1992a), while dissident teachers put their jobs in jeopardy. ◎²⁹

EXAMPLE

> *I remember a class I visited in the heyday of the Audio-Lingual Method. After presenting new vocabulary in English in the most laborious fashion, the teacher eventually supplied the Hungarian equivalent for each item – in a whisper.*

As this example reveals too, the monolingual principle has seldom been carried through.

Towards the late 1960s, it became clear that the monolingual orthodoxy was untenable on any grounds, be they psychological, linguistic or pedagogical. To refer only to pedagogical qualms, how can teachers and students be expected to use English exclusively, when both of them are non-native speakers of English and share the same mother tongue? How can anyone be forced to engage in a pretentious game where the number one rule is: 'Behave like someone you are not'?

Returning to the NEST/non-NEST distinction, the monolingual principle made non-NESTs feel

> 'either defensive or guilty at their inability to "match up" to native speakers in terms of conducting a class entirely in English' (Harboard 1992: 350).

But I suspect that a rigorous application of the monolingual principle harmed NESTs in particular, since they may have harboured the belief that they could do well without learning the language of the host country (Phillipson 1992a). The only people who could possibly gain from this dogma are those unqualified native speakers of English who regard ELT as a casual career.

Incidentally, there are thousands of unqualified or underqualified native speakers teaching English in all corners of the world. Most of them are adventurous youngsters with backpacks, who are impelled by a desire to see the world, meet interesting people, learn foreign languages and meanwhile make a bit of money out of ELT (Chapter 4.2). While sympathising with their stamina and goodwill, I must admit that they are doing considerable disservice to ELT by decreasing the level of professionalism.

◎²⁹ Did your English teachers use a lot of L1 during their classes? If so, was this mostly due to:

a) a principled decision to do so?

b) their poor command of English?

c) sheer laziness?

Share your experiences (Ma 2012, Macaro 2005).

71

A more recent development is for unemployed people from the Centre to seek an ELT job in the Periphery (Phillipson 1992a), and I have even met a few senior citizens trying to prolong their active years by means of ELT employment overseas. But these sporadic initiatives pose a far smaller threat than large-scale operations, whereby unqualified people from all ranks invade countries like swarms of locusts (Chapter 7.1).

Why is L1 use still spurned?

Monolingualism is obviously past its prime. Nevertheless, while granting the restricted use of L1, standard training manuals make but a few passing remarks on this complex issue, with no attempt to determine the desirable extent of L1 use, to specify the pedagogical situations which call for it, or to suggest activities which draw upon the learners' L1 command; nor do syllabuses and teaching materials like to dwell upon this issue.

Atkinson (1987) offers four possible explanations for this neglect:

1 The fact that professional thinking is still haunted by the failure of the Grammar-Translation Method. These sceptics should consider, however, that the Grammar-Translation Method, at its best, was probably no less successful than any other method in achieving the goals it had set. The inapplicability of the Grammar-Translation Method today is simply due to the radical changes in the general aims of language teaching, in compliance with the dictates of present-day needs.

2 The influence of applied linguists, notably that of Krashen and his associates, who argue that foreign languages are acquired in basically the same way as the mother tongue, hence the role of L1 in the classroom should be minimal (Atkinson 1987 Dulay, Burt & Krashen 1982, Krashen & Terrell 1983). One must not forget, however, that Krashen's hypotheses are far from conclusive and have in fact been under fierce attack ever since they were advanced (McLaughlin 1978, Gregg 1984).

3 The axiom that one learns the foreign language through constant practice, a fact which, in my view, does not preclude the applicability of L1 as a teaching device.

4 The backwash effect resulting from the hegemony that native speakers generally enjoy in ELT.

From my perspective, this fourth argument seems to be the most crucial, but before I elaborate on it, let me mention just two arguments for the judicious use of the mother tongue. Firstly, if learners like translation, there is no point in depriving them of this learning tool. Bear in mind that they are likely to achieve better results if they trust the teaching method whereby they are taught. In any case, knowledge about the psychological processes that take place during language learning is so scanty that the confident assertion that any technique should be banned as 'wrong' is, to say the least, unwise. Secondly, and perhaps more importantly, moderate use of the mother tongue in certain situations can save a lot of class time. ⊙30

⊙30 In **Appendix F**, there is a list of situations in which L1 may be used in the English class. Put an X on the rubric of your choice. Compare results and discuss the causes of any differences.

Further reading:
Littlewood & Yu (2011)

The Centre and the Periphery

Now let me return to the issue of the backwash effect mentioned under 4 above.

When discussing the unfeasibility of putting countries into neat groups on either side of the native/non-native borderline, I referred to Phillipson's (1992a) distinction between the Centre (that is, core-English countries where English is the indigenous native language) and the Periphery (that is, countries where English is a second or foreign language) (Chapter 1.2). In his passionate book entitled 'Linguistic Imperialism', Phillipson is of the opinion that the Centre attempts to consolidate and strengthen its influence over the Periphery through, among other things, the spread the English language.

Thus the hub of ELT is in the Centre: it is from British and US headquarters that the massive ELT operation is directed. ⊙**31** Namely , the Centre provides an unrivalled base for:

- pursuing academic research activities relating to ELT;
- storing and retrieving ELT information and experience gathered anywhere in the world;
- running commercial ELT schools in and outside the Centre;
- training EFL/ESL teachers and teacher trainers for employment in the Periphery;
- running in-service courses in the Centre and abroad;
- offering MA programmes in applied linguistics and EFL/ESL;
- setting standards and examinations with international recognition;
- publishing ELT materials and teacher-resource books and journals;
- extending consultancy support and, quite often, financial aid.

The high level of expertise of British and US professionals is only parallelled by the degree of their interests in holding a firm grip on the menagerie. Thousands of native English speakers make a living out of ELT, in one way or another. A few become quite wealthy, the majority do not, and least of all do teachers at the chalkface – but all of them can make ends meet. Today, ELT should not be regarded primarily as an educational mission – it is a huge industry regulated by strict laws of market economy.

No wonder that some ELT specialists, working in, or coming from, the Centre, treat the English language as their exclusive prerogative. Some of them reject the contribution of L1 out of hand, others reluctantly acknowledge its limited scope.

In all fairness, I do not blame them for this attitude. After all, publishing houses in the Centre cannot possibly cater for the specific needs of each periphery-country where English is being taught. Similarly, teacher trainers working in the Centre are unable to attend to individual demands within multilingual groups representing diverse linguistic and cultural backgrounds. Nor is it feasible to devise examinations with international currency which take into account the diverse circumstances of all the candidates.

As the Centre cannot be expected to cope with this issue, ELT experts in the periphery countries should take steps. If we non-NESTs claim to be capable of producing more suitable teaching materials for our students, let's write them. ⊙**32** If local trainers have an allegedly better knowledge of trainees' needs, let them run the courses on their own. If we reject the idea of employing unqualified native speakers, let's not employ them. And if we believe that the mother tongue can facilitate the learning process, let's work out an appropriate methodology in detail.

⊙**31** Is this still true (if it ever was)? Is it really an organised operation from the Centre?

What about local controls and initiatives?

Compare your different experiences.

⊙**32** What kind of course materials do you use: those produced in the UK or the US, or ones produced locally? In this respect, is there a difference between private sector language schools and mainstream schools? What are the pros and cons of 'homegrown' materials?

⊙³³ In Holliday's (2013) view, it is time for teachers in the Periphery to take centre-stage.

What do you think he means by this? Is it happening?

Be that as it may, the scores of books and papers written about and by non-NESTs cited in this new edition are just a small fragment of all the works published in the last quarter century. It is a welcome development that non-NESTs are no longer the voiceless majority in the ELT world and that the study of the NEST/non-NEST issue has come into its own (Kamhi-Stein 2016).

Unfortunately, none of these problems can be resolved by means of sheer goodwill and determination. There are huge obstacles in the way: psychological (lack of self-confidence), political (lack of clout) as well as economic (lack of resources) – let alone the language barrier. ⊙³³

Summary

This chapter was meant to be the most uplifting part of my book. I have analysed six assumptions, each with the purpose of shedding light on the brighter side of our job as non-NESTs. Namely, we are more able to provide our learners with a good learner model for imitation, to teach them effective language learning strategies, to supply them with information about the English language, to anticipate and prevent their language difficulties, to show empathy, and finally to benefit from the shared mother tongue. I have concluded the chapter by contending that if we wish to become more independent as non-NESTs, we have to take more initiatives.

The previous three chapters aimed to examine the role that NESTs and non-NESTs, respectively, play in the ELT operation. By relying upon my own research findings, I tried to validate two hypotheses I had advanced concerning the relationships between *language proficiency* and *teaching behaviour*.

All the preceding chapters were haunted by a question, which I have deliberately left unanswered – 'Who's worth more: the NEST or the non-NEST?' - until I had completed an in-depth analysis of all the relevant aspects of this issue. In Chapter 7, I shall risk taking sides in this question.

Further reading

- **Ellis, E. M.** (2006) Language learning experience as a contributor to ESOL teacher cognition. *TESL-EJ 10(1)* (pp. 1–20).

  This online paper challenges the widespread belief that monolingual teachers of English can understand their students' linguistic development without having learned a L2 themselves. Insights into learning and communication strategies can reveal the role learning experience plays in forming teachers' professional knowledge and belief systems.

- **Kumaravadivelu, B.** (2001) Toward a postmethod pedagogy. *TESOL Quarterly 35* (pp. 537–560).

  Following up on Prabhu's (1990) contention that there is no best method, Kumaravadivelu conceptualises a three-dimensional system consisting of three pedagogic parameters: *particularity, practicality* and *possibility*. He puts this system in practice in terms of the respective roles that learners, teachers and teacher educators are expected to play.

- **Littlewood, W. & B. Yu.** (2011) First language and target language in the foreign language classroom. *Language Teaching 44* (pp. 64–77).

  The paper exhibits the discrepancy between what official documents recommend and what teachers actually do in the classroom in using L1. While warning about the dangers of overuse of L1, it creates a framework for its integration into classroom practice to facilitate student learning.

- **Ur, P.** (2012) Error correction. In P. Ur, *A Course in English Language Teaching* Cambridge University Press (pp. 88–100).

  This chapter begins by identifying arguments for and against error correction, and then highlights potential dangers of correcting mistakes. After examining student preferences, Ur offers strategies to cope with errors committed in oral versus written productions.

CHAPTER 7

Who's worth more: the native or the non-native?

Focus points

- NESTs in state education, universities and language schools
- Prejudices against non-NESTs in employment policies
- Contrasting features of the 'ideal' NEST and non-NEST

7.1 Dreams and reality
'Suppose you were the principal of a language school.'

I gave two talks about the NEST/non-NEST issue: one in London and one in Paris (Medgyes 1992). In each audience there were about fifty highly sophisticated teachers, teacher trainers, applied linguists and publishers. The two groups only differed in that the London audience consisted mostly of native speakers of English, the Paris one mostly of native speakers of French.

At one point during my talk, I asked the following question:

'Suppose you were the principal of a commercial ELT school in Britain. Who would you employ?' ⊙¹

a) 'I would employ only native speakers even if they were not qualified teachers.'

b) 'I would prefer to employ NESTs, but if hard pressed I would choose a qualified non-NEST rather than a native without ELT qualifications.'

c) 'The native/non-native issue would not be a selection criterion (provided the non-NEST was a highly proficient speaker of English).'

Subsequently, I took a straw poll to find out the distribution of responses. Neither in London, nor in Paris did anyone vote for alternative a). With regard to the other two options, in London about two thirds of the respondents went for b) and one third for c), while the ratio in Paris was just the opposite. In Paris, I asked a follow-up question as well:

'Suppose you were the principal of a commercial ELT school *in France*. Who would you employ?'

While the alternatives were the same as before, the proportion of responses was even more slanted towards c); a) still received no votes.[1]

⊙¹ If you were the principal of a language school in your own country today, to whom would you give the preference, NESTs or non-NESTs?

Justify your decision.

---

[1] Both in London and in Paris I had toyed with, then abandoned, the idea of asking an even more provocative question:
  'Once you had decided to employ a non-NEST, would you:
  a) ask the teacher to conceal his/her non-native identity and pretend to be a native speaker of English?
  b) leave it to the teacher to resolve this dilemma at his or her discretion?
  c) insist that the teacher should reveal his or her 'non-nativeness'?'

Lack of time prevented me from asking for justification, but it is easy to suggest factors that may have influenced the respondents' decision. Those whose choice was b) must have heeded both *business and professional considerations*. ⊙²
With regard to the former, presumably they were aware that international students studying in Britain preferred to be taught by NESTs. This demand would have to be satisfied by the school principal – but not at all costs. On the other hand, their answers implied less homogeneity in terms of professional considerations. While they all agreed that NESTs and non-NESTs were worth more than native speakers without ELT qualifications, they may have held divergent views about who would make a better teacher, a NEST or a non-NEST.

In contrast to pragmatists, those choosing c) seem to have taken notice of professional considerations only – and thus might run the risk of losing their clientele. The fact that no one selected a) was a reassuring sign that principals who are led by short-term business interests, or by the delusion that native speakers are superior to non-native speakers under any terms, are not welcome at professional gatherings! ⊙³

But I wonder what accounts for the difference between London and Paris. What caused the London sample to show a more business-like attitude, so to speak? There are two possible explanations. On the one hand, NESTs may have empathised with the pragmatism of the 'school principal' because, as British employers or employees, they have encountered similar dilemmas. On the other hand, it may well be the case that non-NESTs attach more importance to professional considerations as a matter of course. Despite the tentativeness of these observations, the reaction of the two samples seems to indicate that:

- the ELT profession acknowledges the native/non-native division, or at least uses the concept in everyday communication;
- the NEST/non-NEST issue is controversial;
- there are several categories of consideration involved (business, professional, sociolinguistic, moral, political and others).

Why do principals reject non-natives?

In an issue of 'ELT Journal', Illés reported the following case:

EXAMPLE ⊙⁴

A highly qualified and experienced non-NEST, who had been living in English-speaking countries for the past six years, was doing research into the Teaching of English to Speakers of Other Languages. In an effort to combine theory with practice, he tried to find a teaching post in a language school in (I suppose) London. However, his applications were consistently turned down and he was not even short-listed. One letter of rejection from a principal clarified the real reason for his failure to get a job: 'I am afraid we have to insist that all our teachers are native speakers of English. Our students do not travel half-way round the world only to be taught by a non-native speaker (however good that person's English may be)'. (1991: 87).

⊙² Apart from professional considerations, what other aspects are, or should be, taken into account when making recruitment decisions?

⊙³ The story below was told by a native speaker of Indian English, who had recently found a job in the US. Why is her story not only amusing, but also illuminating?

'A 95-year-old neighbour of mine, a dear sweet old lady, recently introduced me to her daughter as a college teacher and quickly added "Guess what she teaches?" "What?", her daughter asked. "English, imagine someone coming from India to teach English here", replied my neighbor with a slight chuckle' (Thomas 1999: 5).

⊙⁴ What do you think of the job ad in this example? How does it fit in with the following observation?

'Teaching English as a second language is not rocket science! Anyone with a positive attitude, a willingness to succeed and the ability to communicate can be an excellent ESL instructor' (Ruecker & Ives: 744).

See the article by Rueckert and Ives (2015) in **Further reading**.

Note its title: is this ironic, or a reflection of fact?

⊙⁵ Prejudices against employing non-NESTs are generally justified by 'customer demand'.

In your experience, is the 'native speaker card' a legitimate one? Why (not)?

⊙⁶ Preference for hiring NESTs is a widespread policy (Clark & Paran 2007, Mahboob *et al.* 2004, Selvi 2010).

Look up a few *local* recruitment ads on the web. What typical features can you discover in them?

Further reading:
Ruecker & Ives)

⊙⁷ Actions against 'native speakerism' (Holliday 2006), such as the TESOL policy statements (1991 **Appendix G** and 2001 **Appendix H**), are getting stronger (Kamhi-Stein 2016).

Are similar initiatives promoted in your country?

⊙⁸ As a non-NEST, have you ever considered publishing in English? What difficulties do you think you might face (Flowerdew 2001)?

In my experience, too, many language schools advertise themselves as employing native English speakers only, because NESTs are 'better public relations items' and have 'a better business draw', as an American respondent in **Survey 1** put it. ⊙⁵ Others may decide against making their views public, but still refuse to employ non-NESTs. I quite agree with Illés's conclusion that the above was a typical case where commercial interests and educational principles were at loggerheads.

As part of his all-out war against the native/non-native division, Paikeday sarcastically notes:

> 'Sometimes you begin to wonder, when people start recruiting "native speakers" of English, for example, whether they don't really mean "White Anglo-Saxon protestants; Scots, maybe, but no Irish need apply"'(1985: 33).

Today, recruitment practices in private language schools in the two ELT strongholds, the US and Britain, are in a state of transition. ⊙⁶ In the past, major organisations involved in ELT, albeit never officially endorsing it, shut their eyes to discrimination against non-NESTs. In the wake of political changes, however, important ELT bodies have come under pressure to make clear and progressive policy statements . The most important resolution has been the one passed by the Executive Board of TESOL and made public in 'TESOL Matters' (1992) (**Appendix G**). ⊙⁷ In this document the Executive Board not only expressed its disapproval of discriminatory hiring policies, but also decided to take steps to abolish all forms of restriction based on the applicant's native language. Thus those who still employ EFL/ESL teachers on the basis of language origin have been declared outcasts, as it were.

However, as always, there is the other side of the fence. In response to someone who had given her full support to the TESOL resolution (Forhan 1992), another teacher from the US said that a school's primary duty is to satisfy its clients' expectations. In the case of newly-arrived immigrants, for example, anxious to enter the workforce, we should

> 'worry that a teacher's lack of native instincts about American English usage and cultural expectations could be detrimental to [the immigrants'] chances in job interviews' (Safadi 1992). ⊙⁸

Or let me give an example from my own experience:

EXAMPLE

An exasperated Hungarian friend of mine told me the following story. Last summer, she sent her son to England. As she could afford it, she enrolled him at a well-known language-school which employed non-NESTs too. On the first day, the boy bumped into a teacher from his school in Hungary, who was teaching in England for the summer. In all fairness, I have to state that the boy was not assigned this teacher – he got a Polish one instead.

'Suppose you were the principal of an ordinary state school'

Whether we like it or not, commercial language schools in Britain and the US have relatively well-defined hiring practices, partly because their customers arrive with fairly predictable expectations. To be sure, their needs are more specific than those of the learners who study English as a school subject. Furthermore, since language schools are relatively better-off than state schools, they often have the opportunity to choose between a NEST and a non-NEST – unlike most state-sector schools. ☉[9]

Survey results

Question 2: What is the NEST/non-NEST proportion in your school?

The assumption that ordinary schools cannot afford to employ NESTs has been borne out by the data provided by the 216 respondents of **Survey 2** (Chapter 4). The results show that almost two thirds of the schools do not employ any native speakers of English (64.3 per cent), while only about one third do (32.4 per cent). A negligible number of respondents claimed to work within an all-native-English staff (1.8 per cent); 1.4 per cent did not answer this question.

Table 9 shows the distribution of those respondents who worked within a staff with mixed language backgrounds.

Table 9: The proportion of native and non-native speakers of English in schools with a mixed native/non-native staff in Survey 2 (N=70)

Percentage of natives in the staff	Percentage of respondents
1-10	31.4
11-20	41.4
21-30	10.0
31-40	4.3
41-50	8.6
51-60	1.4
61-70	0
71-80	2.9
81-90	0
91-100	0

It should be mentioned that, even in schools with a mixed ELT staff, the proportion of natives typically ranged between 1 and 30 per cent. An aggravating factor is that this number probably included unqualified teachers too.

☉[9] Non-NESTs seldom look for a job outside their own countries, let alone in English-speaking ones. What are the reasons?

Further reading: Hayes (2009)

If you applied, do you think you would stand a chance? Why (not)?

Survey results

Question 3: What would be the ideal proportion of NESTs and non-NESTs? Justify.

After surveying the real situation, I decided to peep into the world of 'dreams'. Therefore, the respondents in **Survey 1** and **Survey 2** were asked to indicate whether they would prefer to hire a) more NESTs, b) an equal number of NESTs and non-NESTs, or c) more non-NESTs. The responses show great variability (**Table 10**).

Table 10: Preferences for native or non-native majority in Surveys 1 and 2 (N=24+187)

Preference	Survey 1		Survey 2	
	number of respondents	per cent	number of respondents	per cent
more NESTs	10	41.6	26	13.9
an equal number	10	41.6	100	53.5
more non-NESTs	4	16.6	61	32.6 ⊙10

As a reminder, **Survey 1** only included native/bilingual speakers of English, while in **Survey 2** there was an overwhelming non-NEST majority. In the light of the data, it seems that both samples would prefer a majority of their own language-group in the staff. In addition, the **Survey 2** respondents were more in favour of an equal number of natives and non-natives. However, if the data supplied for **Question 3** and **Question 2** are compared, the differences between dreams and reality are quite striking – not surprisingly, the international group of respondents would like to see far more NESTs in the staffroom than they can under the present circumstances (Chapter 8.1).[2]

Incidentally, this question produced strong correlations with two other variables in **Survey 2**. On the one hand, it turned out that the longer time a non-NEST had spent in an English-speaking country, the more she would favour a NEST majority. Furthermore, non-NESTs with higher qualifications proved to value the presence of NESTs to a greater extent than their less qualified colleagues.

7.2 Arguments for and against

Throughout the book, my discussion has revolved around comparing NESTs and non-NESTs from various perspectives. Now is the time to discuss who is worth more, the NEST or the non-NEST. Before I myself take sides in the debate, let me reveal my respondents' preferences.

⊙10 Explore the discrepancy between dreams and reality in your home environment. How do your data compare to those in **Table 9** and **Table 10**?

---

[2] Since the justifications in **Question 3** and **Question 4** are very similar, I shall disclose them together, when discussing **Question 4** (see page 81).

Survey results

Question 4: Who is better: the NEST or the non-NEST? Justify.

In **Survey 2**, the number of votes for NESTs and non-NESTs was almost the same: 54 respondents chose NESTs (25.0 per cent) and 57 favoured non-NESTs (26.4 per cent). Far more surprisingly, 87 respondents went for 'both' (40.3 per cent), an alternative that had not been supplied in the questionnaire. Had this option been added, I suspect it would have won even more votes. 18 respondents did not take sides in the debate (8.3 per cent). In view of the data, it is no exaggeration to suggest that the respondents (mostly non-NESTs) did not overestimate the role NESTs played in an EFL/ESL environment.

In justifying their choices, the respondents echoed most of the arguments forwarded in **Question 1** (Chapter 6.3) and added a few more. Those who called for a preponderance of NESTs chiefly attributed their superiority to a better overall command of English, especially featuring in the appropriate use of colloquial and idiomatic English. 'Native speakers are living the language, rather than adopting it', one respondent said. The students had more trust in NESTs, because of their confident use of English. Several respondents argued that, with a NEST at the helm, English had genuine relevance in the classroom, because it was the only form of verbal communication between the teacher and the students. NESTs were more capable of creating motivation and an 'English' environment in the school. Furthermore, they taught *the* language rather than *about* the language, and applied more effective and innovative teaching techniques; only seldom would a NEST slavishly follow the textbook like a non-NEST (Chapter 11.3). Others warned, however, that NESTs were more successful only with advanced learners, and a few protagonists cautiously remarked that the NESTs' superiority applied, but only with the proviso that they had been properly trained as EFL/ESL teachers (Chapter 6.6).

In favour of non-NESTs, ⊙[11] by far the most frequently mentioned argument was their ability to estimate the learners' potential, read their minds and predict their difficulties. Non-NESTs were said to be more sensitive, due to the linguistic, cultural and educational heritage they shared with their students. As one respondent put it, 'they were better able to satisfy their clients' expectations'. In monolingual classes, L1 proved to be an effective tool for explaining new material and drawing attention to differences between the two languages. In contrast, NESTs would elaborate on language items that were basically the same in L1 and L2. Non-NESTs usually imitated some standard norm, while NESTs often spoke a non-standard variety. Some respondents charged NESTs with hampering, albeit unwillingly, the spread of a recognised local variety of English. Interestingly, several respondents were of the opinion that the non-NESTs' speech was easier to understand, thanks to features of a non-linguistic nature as well. Others argued for non-NESTs on the grounds that they prepared their lessons more thoroughly and, as a rule, had fewer discipline problems. It was generally agreed that non-NESTs stood a better chance with lower-level students and children. A pragmatist noted that there would always be a majority of non-NESTs, simply because they were cheaper labour.[3]

⊙[11] Most students say that NESTs and non-NESTs can be equally good teachers (Mahboob 2004, Moussu 2010, Samimy & Brutt-Griffler 1999).

Who would you prefer to be taught by, and why? Be honest!

---

[3] This is not always the case, though. I suspect that within EU countries NESTs and non-NESTs earn approximately equal salaries.

⊙¹² Students' initial negative attitudes towards non-NESTs often change into positivity towards the end of their course (Pacek 2005).

Does your experience uphold or run counter to this observation? In what way(s)?

⊙¹³ Students such as the one quoted here may adopt an ambivalent attitude. Explain this contradiction.

'I came upon one evaluation that responded positively to the question "What did you like about the course, the instructor and the instructional style?" The response was "She was very kind, so I can learn English comfortably". However, the response to the question "What did you dislike?" was rather different. This read "We need native speaker teacher. It will be better."' (Thomas 1999: 10).

However, as I mentioned above, the majority of respondents would assign NESTs and non-NESTs an equal chance of success. Moderates agreed that since each group had their strengths and weaknesses, they would nicely complement each other. A proportionate number of natives and non-natives within the staff had the further advantage of offering a wider variety of ideas and teaching methods. Some respondents referred to the desirability of native/non-native interaction and cooperation: 'There is a lot to learn from each other!' one respondent remarked (Chapter 8). ⊙¹² Others warned that teachers should be hired solely on the basis of their professional skills, regardless of their language background (Chapter 7.1).

Finally, it is my turn to make a clean breast of my own preferences. If I were to determine the desirable proportion of NESTs and non-NESTs, I would definitely go along with the moderates, for almost the same reasons that they set out. I would have but one reservation, namely that I would not play down the importance of language background. On the contrary, I would consider it a top selection criterion, because of its far-reaching effect on teaching practice.

Let me reiterate: NESTs and non-NESTs teach differently in several respects. I firmly believe that the non-NEST is (more or less) disadvantaged in terms of a command of English. Paradoxically, this shortcoming is her most valuable asset, quite capable of offsetting the fact of limited proficiency. It is precisely this weakness that helps her develop capacities that a NEST can never aspire to acquire. I contend that NESTs and non-NESTs are potentially equally effective teachers, because in the final analysis their respective strengths and weaknesses balance each other out. *Different does not imply better or worse!* Therefore, the question 'Who's worth more: the native or the non-native?' does not make sense and is conducive to drawing wrong conclusions from the differences observed in their teaching behaviour. ⊙¹³ Hopefully, the data and the arguments provided in this and the earlier chapters have sufficiently validated my fourth hypothesis, namely that *NESTs and non-NESTs can be equally good teachers on their own terms*. Granted this, all four hypotheses formulated in Chapter 4.2 seem to be supported.

7.3 The 'ideal teacher'[4]

In recent literature, the concept of the ideal teacher has gained some notoriety, especially in relation to the native/non-native dichotomy. It appears that the glory attached to the NEST has faded and the number of ELT experts who contend that the 'ideal teacher' is no longer a label reserved for NESTs is on the increase.

As a matter of fact, this is no great revelation. As early as around the beginning of the twentieth century, the famous phonetician Sweet said:

> 'For teaching Germans English, a phonetically trained German is far superior to an untrained Englishman, the latter being quite unable to communicate his knowledge' (quoted in Howatt 1984: 182–183).

---

[4] Needless to say, the term 'ideal' is an abstraction – there is no such creature as an ideal teacher.

Almost a century later, O'Neill noted:

'I believe that as models fluent non-native speakers can be just as good as native-speakers are and, at least in some important respects, even better. Fluent non-native speakers reveal strategies (including the retention of clear but distinct foreign accents) that can help other non-native learners to cope better with the target language. Also non-native teachers have one inestimable advantage over native speakers, particularly those who have never learned a foreign language. They have actually learned the target language as foreigners and have *direct insight into and experience of the processes involved* for other non-native speakers' (1991: 304).

Edge, a well-known advocate of the non-NEST, reported on his experiences abroad:

'When I stood in front of a class of Turkish schoolchildren, there was clearly only a very restricted sense in which I could act as a model for them in social, cultural, emotional, or experiential terms, with regard either to their past or their future. The person who could act as such a model would be a Turkish teacher; and, if we believe that reference to the social, cultural, and emotional experiences, awareness, and aspirations of our pupils is important in learning, then this is the ideal model' (1988: 155).

These quotations – and there could be many others – hark back to the arguments for the non-NEST presented in Chapter 6.

On closer inspection, it turns out that ideal teachers cannot be squeezed into any one pigeonhole: each ideal teacher is ideal in her own way, and as such is different from all the rest. The concept resists clear-cut definitions, because there are too many variables to consider in the language teaching operation.

Nevertheless, in order to get a better grasp of the ideal teacher, let us suppose that all the variables are momentarily kept constant, except for the language proficiency component. So the question arises: Does the teacher with a better command of English stand a better chance of becoming an ideal teacher? In other words: *Is it true that the more proficient speaker is a more efficient teacher?* ⊙¹⁴ Let me briefly study this question in three possible dimensions.

The native/non-native dimension

My earlier assumption was that NESTs and non-NESTs can most conspicuously be detected by the significant differences in their command of English. But I also suggested that, from the non-NEST's perspective, proficiency resembles a coin. If we look on one side, we see the language deficit. But if we look on the other, we notice the benefits deriving from a non-native command of English. I further assumed that the advantages and disadvantages relating to non-native proficiency balance each other out in the final analysis. Thus in a NEST/non-NEST relation, 'The more proficient, the more efficient' is a false statement, incapable of bringing us closer to understanding the essence of the ideal teacher.

⊙¹⁴ There is general agreement that language proficiency is a make-or-break requirement for a non-NEST (Liu 1999, McNeill 2005, Tatar & Yildiz 2010).

Explain why.

⊙¹⁵ Have you been taught by any non-NESTs with a poor command of English who were nevertheless great teachers?

If you have, what compensated for their language weaknesses?

⊙¹⁶ What do you feel about this modified statement in relation to the original one? What are your reasons?

⊙¹⁷ Although the concept of the 'ideal' teacher is an abstraction, the debate between Yoo and Ren helps you to understand the complexity of this conundrum. Whose reasoning do you favour? Why?

Further reading:
Yoo (2014) vs. Ren (2014)

⊙¹⁸ Watch Silvana Richardson's IATEFL 2016 plenary entitled 'The "native factor", the haves and the have-nots' at http://iatefl.britishcouncil. org/2016/session/plenary-silvana-richardson.

Discuss the major issues she touches on. Which of her statements do you agree (or disagree) with?

The non-native/non-native dimension

All other variables being equal, a non-NEST's superiority over a fellow non-NEST can only be ascribed to her superior English-language proficiency. ⊙¹⁵ If we peruse the credit side of the account, it turns out that a more accomplished user of English, provided that she is also a more successful learner, tends to enjoy a larger share of the advantages. In a purely non-native context, therefore, it looks as though 'The more proficient, the more efficient' is a valid statement.

The native/native dimension

Here, 'The more proficient, the more efficient' is an absurd assertion, because in a linguistic sense there can be no differences between native speakers in their L1 competence even though in their actual performance the differences may be huge. The question, therefore, is whether or not NESTs can acquire the attributes of which non-NESTs are claimed to be the sole or, at least, the superior repositories.

My answer is yes – with certain reservations. With regard to all six points studied in Chapter 6, the NEST is a loser, just as the non-NEST is a loser with regard to her shortcomings in English. However, neither statement should be regarded as absolute. On the one hand, some non-natives are nearly as accomplished users of English as natives. On the other hand, those natives who are successful learners of foreign languages can counterbalance some of their drawbacks. This applies with particular force to those who have reached a certain level of proficiency in the learners' mother tongue.

Thus, from a NEST/NEST perspective, the original statement 'The more proficient in English, the more efficient in the classroom' should be modified like this: 'The more proficient in the learners' mother tongue, the more efficient in the classroom '. ⊙¹⁶

'How can I become an ideal teacher?'

As stated above, we can only become ideal teachers on our own terms. All other variables being equal, the *ideal non-NEST* is, then, the one who has achieved near-native proficiency in English. ⊙¹⁷ Given this, one of the most important professional duties non-NESTs have to perform is to improve their command of English; in Chapters 9 and 10, I shall supply a number of ideas about possible self-study techniques, mostly on the basis of the data obtained from **Survey 3** respondents.

On the other hand, the *ideal NEST* is the one who has achieved a fair degree of proficiency in the learners' mother tongue. All NESTs should take great pains to learn foreign languages, and those working in a monolingual setting for an extended period of time should try to learn the vernacular of the host country. Simultaneously, they should strive to increase their awareness of the grammar of English.

The ideal NEST and the ideal non-NEST arrive from different directions but eventually stand quite close to each other. Contrary to certain contemporary views, however, I contend that they will seldom become indistinguishable (Chapter 2.2). Nor would it be desirable, either! Both groups of teachers serve equally useful purposes in their own ways. In an ideal school, there should be a good balance of NESTs and non-NESTs, who complement each other in their strengths and weaknesses. Given a favourable mix, various forms of collaboration are possible.[5] ⊙¹⁸

---

[5] A favourable mix, to my mind, also implies a fair distribution of males and females, more and less experienced teachers as well as teachers with different teaching philosophies.

Summary

In this chapter, I have examined various contexts in which the question of selection between a NEST and a non-NEST might emerge. Respondents were interviewed about their preferences and the arguments underlying them. I have contended that the vague concept of the 'ideal teacher' should no longer be reserved for NESTs. Having studied the implications in three different dimensions, I have offered a tentative definition of the ideal NEST and the ideal non-NEST.

In Chapter 8, I shall take stock of opportunities for NESTs and non-NESTs to co-operate in and outside school.

Further reading

- **Hayes, D.** (2009) Non-native English-speaking teachers, context and English language teaching. *System 37* (pp. 1–11).

  Recent articles are often concerned either with the difficulties encountered by immigrant non-NESTs, or with the privileges NEST expatriates enjoy in foreign lands. In contrast, this paper reports on the situation of experienced Thai school teachers who are permanently employed at home. The interviews are centred around two issues: the teachers' classroom practice and their commitment to teaching.

- **Lowe, R. J. & M. Kiczkowiak** (2016) Native-speakerism and the complexity of personal experience: A duoethnographic study. *Cogent Education 3(1)*.

  In this dialogue the authors discuss stereotypical beliefs about NESTs and non-NESTs, how they became aware of native-speakerism and how various forms of discrimination affected their career paths and self-confidence.

- **Ruecker, T. & L. Ives** (2015) White native English speakers needed: the rhetorical construction of privilege in online teacher recruitment spaces. *TESOL Quarterly 49* (pp. 733–756).

  This paper reveals 'native speakerism' as manifested in the discourse of professional websites which recruit native English speakers for employment in language schools located in Southeast Asia. Jobs are advertised for white youngsters from a closed circle of native English-speaking countries, who are primarily driven by the desire to make money and get a taste for exotic cultures.

- **Yoo, I. W.** (2014) Nonnative teachers in the Expanding Circle and the ownership of English. *Applied Linguistics 35* (pp. 82–86).
- **Ren, W.** (2014) Can the Expanding Circle own English? Comments on Yoo's 'Nonnative teachers in the Expanding Circle and the ownership of English'. *Applied Linguistics 35* (pp. 208–212).

  Yoo's core argument is that while non-NESTs in the Expanding Circle cannot claim ownership of the English language, they are by default the ideal teachers, because only they can experience what it takes to learn English. Ren counters Yoo's view contending that ownership belongs to whoever uses English in their daily lives. He claims that it is time for the traditional *EFL* paradigm to be replaced with an *ELF* paradigm.

CHAPTER 8

Collaboration between natives and non-natives

> **Focus points**
> - Models of NEST and non-NEST collaboration
> - The difficulties of launching team-teaching projects

8.1 Collaboration outside the school

In the previous chapter, I pointed out that the desirable goal in all schools should be to achieve a fair balance of NESTs and non-NESTs – a desire which is clearly unattainable in the foreseeable future. Logically enough, the next question is what forms of organised collaboration are possible between NESTs and non-NESTs. First let me draw upon the data supplied by my respondents, which mostly refer to non-NESTs collaborating with NESTs outside the school. Afterwards, I shall mention several forms of NEST/non-NEST cooperation in the school and, more specifically, in the classroom.

Survey results

Question 5: Do you know of any organised NEST/non-NEST cooperation? Describe.

In **Survey 1**, out of the 21 respondents with considerable teaching experience abroad, only eight gave a positive answer, whereas in **Survey 2**, 91 respondents (42.1 per cent) answered in the affirmative, as opposed to 86 'no' answers (39.8 per cent); 39 respondents (18.0 per cent) left this question unanswered.

Collating the data of the two surveys, I found that the most frequently listed items were various forms of in-service training courses, workshops, seminars and conferences, usually organised under the aegis of national and local educational authorities, or agents from the 'Centre'. Mention was also made of professional gatherings run by local English teachers' associations and by branches and affiliates of IATEFL and TESOL. The British Council was also acknowledged for its role in recruiting NESTs from Britain and functioning as a 'culture centre'. Some respondents expressed their appreciation of the support provided by the American Peace Corps, while others included professional journals and bilingual schools among available opportunities. ⊙[1]

There are two observations I wish to make in this respect. One is that hardly anybody mentioned the possibility of NEST/non-NEST collaboration at school level. The other point is that collaboration was usually regarded as a one-way relationship, with the NEST being the benefactor and the non-NEST the beneficiary. Both aspects may be explained by the scarcity of NESTs. ⊙[2]

⊙[1] Is your local or national ELT association affiliated to a larger international organisation such as IATEFL or TESOL?

Further reading:
Braine (2010)

⊙[2] Generally speaking, are plenary speakers at local conferences NESTs or non-NESTs?

Incidentally, **Question 5** showed a significant correlation with other variables in **Survey 2**. For example, respondents teaching relatively small-size groups reported on collaborative activities more frequently than those who were working with larger groups. This discovery is not particularly surprising if we consider that small groups are the privilege of teachers from well-off schools who can afford to employ NESTs as well. The same explanation may apply to the strong correlation found between the length of time spent by non-NESTs in an English-speaking country and the frequency of native/non-native collaboration.

A significant positive correlation was discovered between this question and **Question 1**; that is to say, those who had experience of NEST/non-NEST collaborative efforts appeared to be more conscious of the differences in teaching behaviour between 'us' and 'them'. Finally, and perhaps most interestingly, those who participated in some kind of NEST/non-NEST collaboration (and hence were more likely to be more proficient speakers of English) turned out to be very perceptive of the effects that their L2 weaknesses might exert on their teaching behaviour (**Question 10**: see page 55). By the same token, those non-NESTs who claimed to be sensitive to maintaining and improving their linguistic skills solicited more NEST support than those who did not.

Survey results

Question 6: Suggest ways of strengthening cooperation.

While the former question investigated reality, **Question 6** elicited ideas about desirable types of NEST/non-NEST collaboration. More than two thirds of the respondents in **Survey 2** presented their 'wish lists'.

Nearly all the areas mentioned previously recurred here. Special emphasis was placed on the necessity of professional visits to English-speaking countries and running in-service training courses. 'Each school should have at least one NEST!' – was advocated as a minimal requirement, but views on how NESTs could be best employed ranged from using them as mere language consultants to partners in team-teaching. A few respondents would like to have English-language clubs set up, where they could chat with native speakers in informal circumstances.

Whilst, in most people's minds, collaboration was an exclusively one-way process, some respondents hinted at its cross-fertilising effect. Exchanging information on cultural issues was considered to be an obvious area of mutual benefit. On the more directly professional side, non-NEST respondents whose mother tongue had international currency wished to have a wider scope for teacher exchange programmes.

8.2 Collaboration in the school

At fortunate institutions with a mixture of NESTs and non-NESTs, the mutual benefits are patently visible. The profit non-NESTs can derive from daily encounters with NESTs is obvious. The language of communication is bound to be English in both professional and personal interactions within the English Department. It goes without saying that this permanent 'language bath' may dramatically improve the non-NESTs' English-language proficiency.

More concretely, the non-NEST can turn to her native colleague with questions that have cropped up during the planning or conduct of lessons. Although the idea that the NEST should be regarded as the ultimate arbiter in deciding what is correct and what is not has often been called into question (Preston 1984), it is clear that the linguistic judgements and intuitions of sophisticated native speakers, let alone qualified NESTs, are worth taking into account. In addition, a NEST can serve as a genuine carrier of the culture of an English-speaking country.

In my view, however, this relationship is not unilateral. ◎³ Non-NESTs can also supply NESTs with a lot of support. Provided that the NEST is keen on learning the host language and dipping into the culture of the host community, non-NESTs can help her with these endeavours. On the more informal side, they can help the newly-arrived native-speaker colleagues who have difficulty settling in.

NESTs and non-NESTs can collaborate on a less directly professional basis as well. The very existence of a multinational and multicultural staff inevitably contributes to a better understanding of each other's traditions, customs and mentality, helps get rid of prejudices, cliches and stereotypes, and engenders a higher degree of tolerance to each other – an attitude that will ultimately be conveyed to the students. Out-of-school gatherings and parties enable us to see the world through a new pair of spectacles and enjoy ourselves in the company of people who think in a different manner and speak a different language. ◎⁴

8.3 Team-teaching – the most intensive form of collaboration

When designing the timetable for the next school year, principals strive to make the best of the few NESTs available in the school. On the grounds of their native proficiency in English, they are often assigned advanced-level groups and conversation classes. Elsewhere, in order to make them accessible to everybody, they are torn into as many small bits as there are groups in the school. Needless to say, NESTs are not always pleased with this task allocation – some complain that they are regarded as 'rare animals in a zoo'.

A far less frequent form of harnessing the NEST is team-teaching. Whether or not in the context of NEST/non-NEST collaboration, team-teaching is a system whereby a group of teachers jointly undertake a programme of work with a group of students. ◎⁵ An umbrella term, team-teaching may range from two teachers engaging in some kind of loose relationship, such as planning a lesson together, to tighter forms of collaboration, such as team-teaching a series of lessons.

◎³ When NESTs and non-NESTs collaborate at school or university level, is the playing field level? Who can contribute, with what, to the 'common good'?

◎⁴ Lortie (1975) calls traditional schools 'egg carton-like institutions' employing 'lone rangers' (Medgyes 1995).

Are these metaphors appropriate to describe your past or present school?

◎⁵ Have you ever taught, or considered teaching, with a partner? Why (not)?

On the basis of the scanty literature available, the majority of those who have been involved in team-teaching are in favour of this pedagogical practice (Bodóczky & Malderez 1993, Brumby & Wada 1990, Schaefer & Chase 1991, Siriwardena 1992). They claim, for example, that collaborative relationships:

- encourage the partners to enter into an endless series of negotiating, listening and exchanging feedback sessions;
- foster a growth in mutual trust, openness, tolerance and responsibility;
- make the partners more reflective about their own teaching philosophies;
- enhance their familiarity with another value system and culture;
- decrease anxiety, loneliness and teacher burnout;
- stimulate better concentration. ⊙⁶

If team-teaching also involves upfront teaching, there are further benefits to be reaped:

- periods of intense concentration and relaxation alternate;
- students learn more effectively at the juncture of different teaching styles;
- motivation is higher than in the traditional classroom. ⊙⁷

It must be admitted, however, that team-teaching is fraught with potential drawbacks as well. For example:

- it is extremely time-consuming and expensive;
- some teachers do not like to work in close partnership;
- others refrain from team-teaching, because they feel vulnerable (Chapter 5.4).

I suppose that time and money are the major stumbling blocks which prevent teachers not only from trying their hand at team-teaching, but even from observing each other's classes on a regular basis.

Let me stress that team-teaching, with or without NESTs, is a useful form of further education, too. Its effectiveness results from two factors:

- the participants' language proficiency, language awareness and pedagogical skills are enhanced in the process of uncontrived interaction and negotiation;
- team-teaching, by its nature, is a prolonged activity in contrast to other forms of in-service training, which typically range from two hours to two weeks in duration. ⊙⁸

⊙⁶ Luo specifies different models of collaborative (EFL) teaching. Discuss elements of these models.
Further reading: Luo (2010).

⊙⁷ Choose one of these three papers: de Oliveira & Richardson (2004), Matsuda & Matsuda (2004), or Snow *et al.* (2004).

Present its arguments and discuss which of the three papers best suits your own school environment.

⊙⁸ On the basis of the three articles above, make a note of the many benefits and possible drawbacks of collaboration.

Compare these findings with those described here.

Summary

In this chapter, I have examined possible types of organised collaboration between NESTs and non-NESTs. On the basis of my surveys I found that cooperation depended, among other things, on the availability of NESTs in the school. After pointing out that collaboration need not be regarded as a one-way activity, I have elaborated on team-teaching, highlighting both its pros and cons.

Further reading

- **Braine, G.** (2010) *Non-native Speaker English Teachers: Research, Pedagogy, and Professional Growth* Routledge.

  A staunch supporter of the 'non-native speaker movement', the author gives a thorough overview of recent research on non-NESTs, exemplifying it through two case studies. He advocates that non-NESTs engage in collaborative efforts, enhance their language proficiency and make the most of professional organisations. His book ends with demonstrating the challenges faced by non-NESTs and ways to tackle them.

- **Luo, W-H.** (2010) Collaborative teaching of EFL by native and non-native English-speaking teachers in Taiwan. In A. Mahboob (Ed.) *The NNEST Lens: Non-native English Speakers in TESOL* (pp. 263–284) Cambridge Scholars Publishing.

  Based on an elementary school project in Taiwan, the paper presents collaborative models of teaching between 'imported' NESTs and local non-NESTs. The author specifies the components of R.E.F.L.E.C.T. and ways in which these elements can be incorporated into teacher education.

CHAPTER 9

When the learner is teaching

Focus points

- Being a permanent learner
- The language improvement component in pre-service and in-service courses
- The use of coursebooks by NESTs and non-NESTs

9.1 The non-native as a special kind of learner

Why is it important for teachers to learn?

In spite of their different perspectives, philosophers, educationalists, researchers and teachers all seem to agree that a fundamental condition for successful teaching is that the teacher should be a *permanent learner*. Heidegger, one of the most influential philosophers of the 20th century, argues that

> 'The teacher must be capable of being more teachable than the apprentices' (1968: 75).

Jersild, an educationalist I referred to earlier, formulates a similar view:

> 'A teacher cannot make much headway in understanding others or in helping others to understand themselves unless he is endeavouring to understand himself. [...] The process of gaining knowledge of self and the struggle for self-fulfilment and self-acceptance is not something an instructor *teaches* others. It is not something he does *to* or *for* them. It is something in which he himself must be involved' (1955: 13-14). ⊙¹

In trying to clarify why teachers need to learn to be good learners, Claxton (1989) presents three compelling reasons with reference to British education. Firstly, they need to learn to overcome the depression caused by the realisation that schools do not accomplish their task in present-day society. Therefore, teachers simply have to address certain basic questions: 'Why isn't it nearly good enough?' 'What needs doing?' 'What should I do?' 'How should I do it?', and so on. Whoever seeks an answer to such questions *is* a learner.

Secondly, education needs to be saved. Since besides teachers and learners, few people care about schools and even fewer know much about them, it is up to teachers to search for ways to bring about radical changes in the educational system. ⊙²

Thirdly, teachers have to learn for their students' sake. Claxton (1989) argues that the final aim of education is to teach learners how to learn, but this effort can only be facilitated by teachers who are examples of good learners themselves. We must adopt a learning stance to life, he says, if we want to help young people to adopt it themselves.

⊙¹ People often put the blame on others for their failures. However, the comic strip hero Pogo warns us 'we have met the enemy and he is us' (cited in Pajares, 1992: 319).

What does he mean? Does this apply to you as a teacher?

⊙² Watch Ken Robinson's TED talk 'Bring on the learning revolution!' (2010). Explain the meaning of these phrases and decide if you agree with his call for action – and why.

The phrases are:
- *revolution of education*
- *tyranny of common sense*
- *linearity in education*
- *diversity of talent*
- *fast-food model of education*
- *personalised curriculum*
- *treading on children's dreams*

Thus it is not a luxury for teachers to pursue learning, but an absolute necessity. If they are not prepared to make such efforts, no teachers should be allowed into the classroom. And doomed is the country which does not give enough leeway for its teachers to learn.

Pre-service and in-service teacher training

Teachers can engage in two kinds of learning activity: *organised* and *autonomous* learning.

Organised learning equals teacher training, which generally consists of two stages: *pre-service* (or initial) training and *in-service* training. Although the length and content of pre-service training courses for non-native speakers vary greatly from college to college, the primary aim of instruction is generally to provide the trainees with an adequate knowledge and awareness of English and certain pedagogical skills. In addition, the curriculum includes subjects of a general nature, such as education, psychology, literature, cultural studies, linguistics and so on. ⊙³ Pre-service training normally ends with some form of practice teaching. ⊙⁴

In-service training shows a far more varied picture. It may be more or less regular, last for two hours or two weeks, take place inside or outside the school, involve NEST support and/or participation, and so on. Any form of organised training is largely determined by the circumstances, including the educational authorities at national, local and university or college levels, economic and financial constraints, tradition, personal motivations and many other factors. A common intrinsic feature of pre- and in-service training is that both are fixed in scope and duration, have clear-cut objectives and follow a prescribed framework.

Several respondents in my surveys were of the opinion that non-NESTs were generally better qualified and were therefore better teachers than NESTs (Chapter 6.6). The direct causal link between better training and teaching success looks very plausible although, to my knowledge, no research has been done to confirm the validity of this relationship. ⊙⁵

Autonomous learning

It is a truism that learning is a lifelong experience and concerns people in all walks of life.

EXAMPLE

- *A national survey conducted in 1978 established that 80 per cent of all adults in the US were involved in some kind of learning and 75 per cent even planned their learning process (Wenden & Rubin 1987: 9).*

- *American adults have been found to spend an average 700 hours a year on learning projects. 'Although 700 hours constitutes only 10 per cent of an adult's waking time, surely this small percentage affects his life nearly as much as the other 90 per cent,' Tough says. 'He resembles an organization that maintains and increases its effectiveness by devoting 10 per cent of its resources to research and development' (Tough 1971: 4).*

- *Furthermore, Tough (1971) states that 70 per cent of all learning projects are planned and carried out by the learner himself, without outside human or non-human resources.*

⊙³ What is your own experience of pre-service training? Did it meet your expectations? What did you miss?

(Anderson 2016, Liu 1999)
Further reading

⊙⁴ Describe the practice teaching you had to do for your teaching qualification. What were the major challenges?

⊙⁵ In your experience, are non-NESTs generally better qualified than NESTs? If so, are they therefore also better teachers? Explain your reasons.

Teachers are probably no less involved in autonomous learning projects than other people. Pre-service training surely gave us a great deal, but it stopped when we became fully-fledged teachers. In-service training may also offer magnificent learning opportunities, but those opportunities are sporadic, constrained and compartmentalised.

Autonomous learning (or self-study), on the other hand, is non-stop, self-generated and wholesome. And it is highly flexible, in that the teacher-learner can adapt her activity to her individual needs, whims and time schedule. In addition, autonomy means that she carries full responsibility for her learning process (Dickinson 1987).

Self-directed learners have to be highly conscious individuals, capable not only of making decisions about their learning activity, but also of monitoring and evaluating it. As a result of continuous self-assessment, the successful teacher-learner alters her learning strategies from time to time. Incidentally, one of the leading goals of research on language learning strategies is to find the chief components of the processes that take place during effective self-study, thereby helping the learner towards autonomy (Wenden & Rubin 1987) (Chapter 6.2). ◎⁶

Autonomous learning may be pursued in several ways. In certain cases, the teacher-learner works out a detailed self-study programme with clearly designed aims, objectives, syllabus, procedures and timescale, and then sets out to follow her plans. At other times, she combines in-service training with self-study. Most frequently, however, self-study is largely *ad hoc* and does not necessarily entail systematic planning.

◎⁶ Are you a systematic or a spontaneous type of learner? How do you develop your own language learning and teaching competences?

9.2 Language fossilization and language improvement

The non-NEST's learning activity is pursued in three major directions: language proficiency, language awareness and pedagogical skills. Needless to say, these three fields are closely intertwined: no matter which of them she is dealing with at a given moment, her efforts will have a knock-on effect on the other two areas. Although the activities recommended below are aimed at language improvement, they will hopefully help non-NESTs to become more aware users of the English language and thus technically more skilled professionals as well.

As I argued in Chapter 2, with a few notable exceptions, non-native speakers do not achieve full mastery of the target language. Most of us seem to undergo a process called *fossilization*, during which incorrect linguistic features become a permanent part of the way we speak and write the target language (Richards *et al.* 1985). Selinker & Lamendella (1978) attribute fossilization to low motivation, the passage of 'critical age' and/or a limited range of target language input. Schumann (1978) contends that, within the group of second language learners, the degree of fossilization is determined by the extent of the social and psychological distance separating the learner and the target language culture.

Fossilization may also refer to a stage of 'frozen competence' beyond which no progress is feasible. Klein (1986) argues that every learner is bound to come to a halt at some point of proficiency, although it is far from clear, at the present state of our understanding of learning processes, what causes us to become arrested at a certain level of interlanguage (Stern 1983). Marton (1988) remarks that certain strategies adopted by communicative approaches, such as the avoidance of error correction and the enforcement of fluency activities, may be conducive to fossilized or even 'pidginised' competence, the latter referring to fossilization at an elementary level.

Although fossilization obviously catches up with non-NESTs as well, I contend that, with a few weary and cynical exceptions, we are generally all too eager to combat this process. With the purpose of validating this assumption, let me refer back to some of the findings of **Survey 3** (Chapter 5.1).

Question 8 asked the respondents whether their English had become better or worse since graduation. While nobody reported regression, nearly 60 per cent of the answers were 'better' and 40 per cent 'better in some respects/worse in others'. When asked whether they thought they were still making progress (**Question 9**), close to two thirds gave a positive and only one third a negative answer.

Now let me turn to three further questions in **Survey 3**, which I have not yet analysed in the previous chapters.

Survey results

Question 11: Have students had any effect on your English? If so, describe this.

The question-and-answer frame was designed like this:

> For most of us, it is in the classroom that we use English most frequently. Our primary communicative partners are the students, whose English is far poorer than ours. On the whole, how does this affect your command of English?
>
> It does ….. damage to my English.

⊙⁷ With reference to Table 11, how much damage (if any) do your students do to your own command of English? What are your most vulnerable areas?

Table 11: Damage caused to respondents' proficiency by their students in Survey 3 (N=81) ⊙⁷

Variable	Frequency	Percentage
no	22	27.2
hardly any	25	30.9
some	31	38.3
considerable	3	3.7
a lot of	0	0

As the results in **Table 11** show, the range of responses is evenly spread out between 'no' and 'some'. Since the proportion of responses is slanted towards positive values, I have examined only those areas where the respondents perceived improvement.

Survey results

Question 12: Specify areas where your English has improved.

The respondents had a menu consisting of eight alternatives and were free to indicate more than one area. The results are provided in **Table 12**.

Table 12: Areas in which respondents in Survey 3 perceived progress (N=81).⊙[8]

Variable	Frequency
Vocabulary	58
Listening skills	51
Speaking skills	51
Grammar	30
Reading skills	30
Speech functions	27
Writing skills	26
Pronunciation	21

⊙[8] Which areas of your English-language competence have improved over the years?

The table above reveals that the most considerable development was perceived in vocabulary, an area where progress can most noticeably be felt because it can to some extent be quantified (Chapter 5.1). The development in oral performance may be explained by the fact that language classes in Hungary have an oral emphasis. The low score recorded for pronunciation shows the respondents' realisation that fossilization in pronunciation is probably the most difficult problem to overcome.

Another item in **Survey 3** asked the respondents to list activities that had helped them to prevent or slow down the process of fossilization or, to put it positively, to make progress in English.

Survey results

Question 13: Suggest techniques to overcome your difficulties.

The 81 Hungarian colleagues supplied a rich collection of ideas and techniques – too rich, in fact, to be described in full.

As I pointed out in Chapter 5.2, non-NESTs are victims of two psychological disorders, which I have labelled: 'schizophrenia' and 'inferiority complex'. While schizophrenia is caused by the double act of having to change our 'English' and L1 personas in quick succession, an inferiority complex evolves because of the conflict between our teaching and learning roles.

Most of us non-NESTs are well aware of our double-faced nature: when we are in class, the learner's face is hidden; when we are out of class, the teacher's face is hidden. Not surprisingly, those who admitted to being aware of, and acquiesced in, this ambivalent role seemed to employ the most original techniques and supplied the most innovative ideas.

I have put the activities into two groups. The first group contains activities related to the non-NEST acting as a teacher; I call these *professional activities*. To the second group belong activities carried out with the non-NEST wearing her civilian clothes; these are called *non-professional activities*. ⊙[9] In the rest of this chapter I present a summary of the respondents' ideas about how the classroom might serve as a podium for improving our own language proficiency, while in Chapter 10 I shall list a few non-professional activities to be used in our private lives as ordinary, albeit highly motivated, learners of English.

⊙[9] How do you strive to overcome your language difficulties and combat the process of fossilization? Discuss various strategies and techniques.

Further reading:
Nemtchinova (2005)

9.3 Professional activities

The teacher's life oscillates between periods of preparation and teaching proper. Hence I distinguish between *before-the-class* and *in-the-class* activities.

Before-the-class activities

While preparing our lesson, we are beset with all sorts of problems. Apart from methodological issues, we must be capable of coping with the new language, making sure that, upon entering the classroom, we know it all thoroughly.

Lesson preparation is a less hurried activity than classroom teaching. We can afford to stop, think, check and rehearse. As an implicit goal of planning, we can make conscious efforts to improve our own language skills. In fact, most respondents agreed that this stage is a time for more effective self-study than the teaching stage itself.

Here is a list of some of the ideas that the respondents suggested for consideration:

- Make sure you know every new language item throughout the lesson.
- When you meet an unfamiliar item, try to infer its meaning from the context – then check your guess.
- Rehearse the new words and phrases in different contexts.
- Hunt for synonyms and antonyms.
- Most words have more than one meaning – look for polysemy.
- Have a couple of good monolingual dictionaries at hand.
- Check new grammar points – don't use old reference books.
- Consult the teacher's manual for the coursebook – if it is a good one, it will offer reliable, contextualised and down-to-earth information.
- Rehearse how to get across the new grammar and vocabulary items in a simple and clear way – a good example is worth more than anything.
- Listen to the audio and repeat the sentences one by one – this is the best way of practising pronunciation, intonation and sentence rhythm.
- If you don't have the recorded texts, read them aloud several times.
- Do all the exercises and activities planned for classwork.
- Check the right answers in the Key.
- Practise the drills until you can do them automatically.
- Should there be a dialogue, a poem or a song for the students to memorise, you memorise it too.
- Include communicative activities in your lesson – they need far more careful preparation than routine tasks.
- Look for ideas from other sources – even if your coursebook happens to be an inventive one.
- Add appropriate items to your home-made resource pack from time to time.
- Check, correct and grade every written assignment – adding written comments improves your own writing abilities.
- If you plan to set your students a test, try it out in advance.

And finally:

- Make your lessons challenging by providing challenging language input! ⊙¹⁰

⊙¹⁰ Which of the before-the-class activities in this list:

a) do you do regularly?

b) should you do more often?

c) do you decline to do?

In-the-class activities

In the class, there is no time to waste. The success of the lesson is largely determined by the thoroughness of preparation. However, a good lesson is more than the mere implementation of plans. If our aims do not go beyond that, there is a good chance that the lesson will be boring.

As I mentioned in Chapter 3.1, effective teaching is the result of two-way interaction between the teacher and the students. Therefore, the teacher often has to change her original plans according to feedback from the students; that is, she has to improvise.

Improvisation confronts the teacher with a real challenge in terms of language use. No wonder that teachers with a poor command of English nip attempts at spontaneity in the bud by adhering rigidly to their lesson plans. This is a pity, because unpredictable language use is the essence of genuine communication.

The language class produces countless situations which can elicit lifelike utterances. For example, when the teacher feels there is a draught, she asks a student to shut the window. When a student writing on the blackboard blocks the view, the teacher asks him to move aside a bit. When a latecomer arrives, the teacher inquires about the reason for his lateness. And so on. Dealing with situations which have not been planned is called *class management*. ⊙**11** The language of class management is closer to real life than even the most cleverly contrived communicative activities. Its genuineness lies in its spontaneity.

Thus class management is not only meritable, but offers unique opportunities for authentic L2 communication as well. Yet many of us try to avoid such situations or, failing that, switch into L1, simply because we cannot handle them as efficiently as we should. The reason for our insecurity lies in the fact that we did not attend school in an English-speaking country where we could have acquired this kind of language in real-life situations. Nor did pre-service training, it seems, pay sufficient attention to this difficult area. Thus we have to catch up on our own.[1]

Another important question relates to teacher-talking time (TTT) and student talking time (STT). Arguments against the unjustified amount of teacher talk are too obvious to list. We have to distinguish, however, between NESTs and highly proficient non-NESTs, on the one hand, who talk glibly because of a lack of self-discipline or a false methodological conviction and, on the other hand, non-NESTs with a poor command of English, whose increased TTT results from the sad fact that they too often get entangled in circumlocution and other forms of redundant language use. Others draw our attention to the dangers inherent in the belief that teacher-talk is always wasteful.

⊙**11** Which language do you prefer to use for class management, English or your native language?

What does your choice depend on (Hughes & Moate 2007)?

EXAMPLE

> *Some years ago, a teacher trainer from International House gave an in-service course for Hungarian non-NESTs which involved a great deal of demonstration teaching. In his view, our greatest fault was that we overused TTT at the expense of STT. When challenged, he volunteered to give a lesson to a group of 16-year-olds. To his credit, he practised what he preached – he spoke very little during the lesson. So little, in fact, that his initiatives were often met with utter incomprehension.*

---

[1] Fortunately, there are a few handbooks specifically designed to meet such needs. Let me recommend two of them in particular: Hughes's *A Handbook of Classroom English* (1981) and Willis's *Teaching English through English* (1981).

O'Neill (1991) described a lesson he had observed, where a NEST, in an effort to be very 'student-centred' and 'communicative', hardly opened her mouth during the lesson. He was probably right in saying that what he had seen was characteristic of 'student-neglect' rather than 'student-centredness' and the teacher's philosophy might lead to LEP (Limited English Proficiency) rather than advanced communicative capabilities.[2]

Non-NESTs often complain that their fluency suffers unless they have the regular opportunity to talk to native speakers. Lacking that, I would go as far as encouraging them to increase TTT, even at the students' expense.

EXAMPLE

One technique I recommend for occasional use is to steal 10 or 15 minutes of class time for teacher monologue, such as telling a story or reviewing a film. In modest doses, this seemingly egotistical trick may in fact foster rapport between the students and the teacher.

A final area of concern is the use of *teaching materials*. As I pointed out in Chapter 6.3, non-NESTs tend to cling to a single coursebook, as opposed to NESTs who prefer to use it as a jumping-off point, if at all. Some non-NESTs are, admittedly, the slaves of commercially available materials. They do not dare delete, change or insert anything. They drag on from task to task, from unit to unit. If they finished Unit 3 yesterday, today it's Unit 4. Exercise 1 is followed by Exercise 2, next comes Exercise 3 – and so on, *ad infinitum*. ⊙[12] They regard the coursebook as though it was the musical score of a Beethoven symphony.

EXAMPLE

Louis Alexander, the most popular textbook writer of the 60s and 70s, likened the relationship of the materials writer and the teacher to that of the composer and the conductor. The textbook should be regarded as the 'musical score', Alexander argued, which the teacher should use to elicit a performance from the class, that is the 'orchestra' or 'choir'. As teachers, we should be less concerned with how the score was put together and more concerned with the interpretation (Alexander et al. 1972).

I hope few teachers would share Alexander's view on this.

⊙[12] What classroom situations make you deviate from your lesson plan and the coursebook material? What causes this?

---

[2] In defence of reduced TTT, learner-centredness and communicative language teaching, Harmer (1992) responded to O'Neill's article. Essentially, he pointed out that the incriminated lesson had not discredited the underlying concepts, but only the bad teacher.

Summary

This chapter has explained why teachers need to keep learning throughout their professional career. Having dwelt briefly on pre- and in-service training as the two standard forms of organised learning, I then moved on to a discussion of self-study and fossilization in the light of survey findings. In the end, I suggested some self-study activities for the stages of lesson preparation and lesson conduct.

In Chapter 10, I shall present a list of activities the non-NEST can use to improve her knowledge of English at off-duty times.

Further reading

- **Liu, D.** (1999) Training non-native TESOL students: challenges for TESOL teacher education in the West. In G. Braine (Ed.) *Non-native Educators in English Language Teaching* Lawrence Erlbaum (pp. 197–210).

  Born in China ,but teaching in the US, the author argues that the needs of non-NESTs in teacher education programmes are not accommodated, mainly due to a lack of sensitivity towards the trainees' educational traditions. He offers remedies for improvements, especially with a view to enhancing their language development.

- **Nemtchinova, E.** (2005) Host teachers' evaluations of non-native-English-speaking teacher trainees – a perspective from the classroom. *TESOL Quarterly 39* (pp. 235–261).

  Based on a survey with NESTs and students in the US, this paper examines the classroom practice of non-NEST trainees. While acknowledging their strengths in various aspects of their work, it argues that only non-NESTs with a superb command of English can serve as role models for their students.

CHAPTER 10

When the teacher is learning

Focus points
- Ways of developing specific language skills
- The potential benefits of IT developments for ELT

10.1 Non-professional activities

Although non-professional activities are not pursued with the direct purpose of facilitating teaching, their contribution to the success of the teaching/learning process is fundamental. Ultimately, our own command of English is the most important tool we have to help students learn English.

A non-NEST's life is haunted by the English language, even at off-duty times. English is built into the fabric of our life and it stays with us even at home. We cannot help listening to, speaking, reading and writing in English around the clock.

As the respondents in **Survey 3** demonstrate, for the majority of us, the English language is not only a professional tool. For some, it is even more than a means for conveying messages – it is an end in itself. The process of tackling newer and newer aspects of the English language is a rewarding job for its own sake. The desire to reveal the intricacies of English is a hobby for many and a passion for a few. ☉**1** The way some respondents express their longing to possess the English language has an almost sensuous overtone. The love-hate relationship is expressed vividly by this respondent:

EXAMPLE

'I build up a dream-world where, in the end, you only talk to yourself. So instead of communication, you make language into the main isolation tool. You dream, you live in English, you think, you create in English – and you make up an "autistic" world driven by its own rules.'

In concrete terms of self-study, we all have a number of well-tried techniques up our sleeve. But surely our repertoire is limited – others use other techniques. So why don't we swop?

Survey results

Question 14: Outside the classroom, how can you improve your English?

Hundreds of good ideas were suggested by the 81 respondents in **Survey 3**, some of them general in nature, others more specific. In the following pages, I shall present a handful of them under the heading of the four major skills. I am sadly aware that some of them will not appeal to you, while others will be 'old hat'. ('I don't think my methods are unique!' said a respondent – and indeed they weren't...) But hopefully you will find a few worth trying. ☉**2**

☉**1** For millions of non-NESTs, English is not simply a tool for making a living, but also a hobby and a passion. Does this apply to you?

☉**2** Think of techniques that work for you to practise English. Suggest one for each of the four language skills.

10.2 Developing listening skills ☉³

Active and passive listening

First it was the radio. Then it was the tape recorder. Then came television, video, satellite TV. ☉⁴

One respondent relates that the 'Voice of America' laid the foundations of his English knowledge in the 1950s; he found a perverse pleasure in trying to catch the news over the jamming.[1] For another, BBC soccer broadcasts played a similar role: Arsenal, Manchester United and Chelsea opened the first windows on the English-speaking world. Radio Luxembourg with its rock music in the 1960s, and subsequently off-air recordings on bulky open-reel tape recorders during the period of Beatlemania, kindled the love of the English language in many of us. One teacher mentions how, as a young man, he learned hundreds of pop songs with 'perfect pronunciation' without being able to understand a word of English; it was only years later that he set about deciphering the meaning of the lyrics.

- In the survey, many teachers admit that they have their radio or their TV on, tuned to English-language programmes, round the clock. From time to time, they stop short when crossing the room, just to take a cursory glance at the television. Unconscious and conscious listening and watching periods follow each other at irregular intervals.

- On the other hand, we all have favourite programmes which we like to watch from the armchair (or while doing the hula-hoop in order to combine pleasure with losing weight, as one respondent admitted). Whether it be a soap opera or an MTV video clip, our eyes are hooked on the screen and for long minutes we forget that what we are watching is, in fact, not in our mother tongue.

Voice-over

Since the 1950s, it has been a standard ear-and-tongue training activity to stop the recording and repeat the sentences one by one. As opposed to this piecemeal procedure, in the next activity the recording keeps moving, forcing you to repeat everything as you hear it, including native pronunciation. It is assumed that you simply have no time to alter the intonation and rhythm of the utterances as you voice them over.

- Choose a recorded monologue of medium difficulty and speed. Listen to it once so as to get the hang of it. Stop it, listen again, and check for meaning, wherever necessary.

- When you listen for the second time, do not stop the recording. Voice-over the monologue after the speaker, with a delay of not more than two or three words. Should you become tongue-tied on occasion, don't stop and correct yourself. Catch up with the speaker as soon as you can.

- After you have had sufficient practice with monologues, you can try your tongue on texts with more than one speaker. Another variation is to substitute live programmes for recorded ones – carry on until you run out of breath.

☉³ Look at the techniques I recommended for listening and speaking (pp. 101-105). Which devices could now be replaced or supplemented with more recent technology?

☉⁴ Needless to say, since then, the IT revolution has caught up with ELT as well. How does this affect your work?

---

[1] In the 1950s, the broadcasts from Western radio stations were constantly jammed in Eastern Europe to 'protect people from the harms of bourgeois propaganda'.

Be more English than the English![2]

In my experience, adults are reluctant to parrot native-like pronunciation. We non-NESTs are no exception. Many of us fear that the harder we try to imitate native models, the more odd we sound. Why don't we try to break the barrier by means of self-irony and exaggeration?

- Choose a recorded text, preferably an easy one with several voices, such as an extract from a play. After you have listened to it once, identify the characters: their profession, age and sex, their relationship to each other and so on.

- Play the recording again, sentence by sentence this time. Repeat each utterance as it is produced, but try to overdo the acting. For example, be more pretentious than A, more threatening than B, more hysterical than C, and so on. But above all, exaggerate their pronunciation – sound more English than the characters do!

Focused listening ⊙[5]

When we listen to a radio programme, or watch TV, we are engaged in one-way communication. On such occasions, we can afford to devote all our attention to form.

- Before you start listening, choose one type of language element to focus on. This can be verb tenses, phrasal verbs, conditionals or any other language point. Alternatively, you may decide to listen for encouraging noises in dialogues (*Really? Uh huh. Does he?*) or fillers (*Er, erm... Anyway... You know...*)[3]

- Suppose it is adjective-noun collocations this time. Start listening and jot down every collocation as you hear it. At the end of the listening passage, your list contains, say, twelve collocations, such as *remarkable progress, full rewards* or *worthy goals*.

- Now give an oral summary of the passage, using all twelve collocations on your list. Tick them off one by one after you have uttered them.

Subtitled films[4]

When watching an English-language film with subtitles, we usually cannot help resting our eyes on the L1 text. However, as learners of English, we may feel guilty about missing a good chance of practising listening comprehension.

- Choose an English-language video or DVD with L1 subtitles. Start watching the film and stop the tape at approximately two- or three-minute intervals. View each sequence three times.

- At first viewing, turn off the subtitles, so that you can only hear the dialogue in English, some of which you may not be able to catch.

- At second viewing, turn on the subtitles, so that you can simultaneously hear the conversation in English and see its equivalent in L1. The L1 subtitles will promote the comprehension of grey areas.

- At third viewing, turn off the subtitles again. At this stage, the English text should become fully intelligible.

- Warning: Do not stop the recording within any one stage, or you might get bogged down in the details and never reach the end of the film!

⊙[5] It is now possible to find past programmes on the BBC and other catch-up sites, such as iPlayer.

Are these available in your country too?

If so, have you ever used them in your work?

---

[2] Incidentally, I found a similar activity called 'Sounds English' in Nolasco & Arthur (1987).

[3] An excellent book specifically designed to practise hesitation gaps and other such communication devices is Dörnyei and Thurrell's *Conversation and Dialogues in Action* (1992).

[4] This technique was originally devised by György Horlai (personal oral communication).

Strain your memory

In any communicative situation with a native speaker of English, our partner uses a number of words, collocations and structures that make us prick up our ears. As we cannot note them down on the spot, they fall into oblivion unless we do something about it.

- Withdraw for a few minutes soon after talking to a native speaker. Sit down and relax. With your eyes shut, try to recall the sound sequences containing eight to ten worthwhile items. Some of them will emerge with little effort, others may be retrieved only if you dig hard enough. The ones that you manage to pull out from the deepest pit stand the best chance of being retained in your long-term memory.

- You may do the same meditation exercise with respect to your oral performance. Consider the built-in monitor in your head, which often beeps when you make a mistake during a conversation. When by yourself, make conscious efforts to recall those beeps and the context in which the error was committed. Supply the correct version. If it was a mistake of a major item, such as the use of conditionals, allow time to practise the item.

10.3 Developing speaking skills ☉⁶

English-speaking countries and friends

'Stay in English-speaking countries as long as you can and meet English-speaking friends as often as possible!' – these two recurrent pieces of advice have been no big discoveries.

- Longer periods of time spent in English-speaking countries are not only a cost-effective way to practise your speaking abilities: such opportunities also provide the most genuine context for English-language communication. Unfortunately, relatively few of us can afford this luxury. 'I have been doing nothing all my life but save up money to go to Britain,' says one dedicated non-NEST.

- One more feasible way of practising oral communication is to meet friends who use English as a native language or as a *lingua franca*. Some respondents claim that they are continually on the lookout for foreign tourists. The trouble is that superficial contacts of this kind seldom lead to more than an exchange of well-practised cliches. To reach beyond this, one colleague likes to escape to the relaxed atmosphere of pubs with English-speaking friends, and another one often puts up native English speakers in her home.

- A less common place to practise the speaking skill is the British or American library. One respondent teaches part-time in a Hungarian-language programme run for American students. Acting as a surrogate mother, as it were, she has to speak English all the time. Another teacher regularly works in summer camps looking after a mixed group of Hungarian- and English-speaking children.

- One of the respondents continually takes notes while chatting with English speakers – I wonder how the conversation can roll on. Others insist on being corrected all the time. The trouble is that native English speakers outside our profession may not even understand how they are expected to react to our nagging. ☉⁷

☉⁶ In a plenary,'The privilege of the non-native speaker' TESOL Long Beach, CA, Kramsch (2002) quotes a Vietnamese student: 'As for English, I do speak the language, but I don't think I'll ever talk it'.

What does the student mean? Do you agree? Why (not)?

☉⁷ Today, most interactions in English take place between non-native speakers. Given this, is it still important for non-NESTs to visit English-speaking countries to improve their language abilities?

The monologue

Speaking is the only skill which cannot normally be developed without partners. I have come across a few unusual procedures, though.

- A standard practice among EFL teachers with little opportunity to use English outside the classroom is the silent monologue. This implies performing certain verbal tasks in your head. For example, you may give a retrospective account of your daily events on your way home from school or after going to bed or, conversely, make a mental plan of next day's schedule.

- Another form of monologue is when you actually start speaking aloud in English. If you record your monologue, you have the additional advantage of spotting the linguistic errors in your performance when you listen to it. One respondent admits that he always carries a dictaphone in his bag to record his soliloquy when there is nothing else to do.

What would I say if...?

In another oft-mentioned activity, we have to put ourselves in an imaginary situation and try to behave the way the characters in that situation would.

- As you are watching a real interview on TV, you may make up questions in English that you would ask if you were the reporter. Or conversely, you may decide how you would answer the reporter's questions if you were the interviewee. Or picture yourself walking past a shoe shop – if you had enough money, what kind of shoes would you ask for and how? What is the English word for the Hungarian 'méret' (*size*), 'tiszta bőr' (*genuine leather*), 'cipőkrém' (*shoe polish*), 'szűk' (*tight*), and so on?

The unsolicited interpreter

A genuine way of improving speaking skills is to work as a part-time interpreter. A few respondents, however, report that they often interpret 'uninvited'.

- We all have to attend meetings which we find useless and/or where the speaker drags on endlessly. Instead of dozing off or staring out of the window, a linguistically more rewarding activity is doing 'simultaneous interpreting'.

- Brace yourself for the task and then begin to translate the speaker's words in your head. If the speech is in English, translate it into L1, and vice versa. Do not waste time looking for the most appropriate term or structure, or you will fall behind. If you have missed a sentence or two, don't worry, catch up as soon as you can. Don't be upset if you get tired after a few minutes – even professional interpreters flake out after about half an hour.

- A less awkward form of simultaneous interpreting is when you do it at home, sitting in front of the television. Long speeches delivered by politicians lend themselves particularly well to this task.

- One respondent admits that he is in the habit of spontaneously translating his colleague's words in face-to-face communication to prevent himself from switching off.

'Just a minute!' ⊙⁸

Many of us complain about fluency problems which lead, among other things, to long pauses and lots of hesitation in our speech. 'Just a minute!' is a well-known radio game. The point is that you have to speak non-stop on a given topic for exactly one minute. Meanwhile, you must not stammer, hesitate, repeat the same words and phrases, or deviate from the point. The following is an adapted version of the game.

- Find an inspiring topic. Give yourself thirty seconds to plan your speech. Put your watch in front of you, take a deep breath and begin. As soon as the one minute is up, stop.
- It is particularly useful to record yourself. If you are dissatisfied with your production, have another go.

Sound off

The sound-off technique has been in use ever since the video moved into the classroom. It may be applied for self-study as well.

- Turn on the television and tune in to a channel where there is a movie or an interview on. Watch it for a few minutes.
- Once you have understood the gist of the topic and the setting, turn the sound off. Relying on the visual image only, narrate the events for as long as you can.
- Record a 10–15 minute extract from a programme with a lot of dialogues. Now decide to take over the role of one of the characters.
- Watch the same extract for the second time with the sound on. Concentrate on what your chosen character has to say.
- Play the recording again, but this time with the sound off. Speak when your hero is seen talking and try to use the words you heard him/her saying when the sound was on. Stop the recording if necessary.

Phoney debates

Generally speaking, communication is a two-way activity. But in our solitude at home, we cannot possibly conduct a real interaction in English: we have to make do with a faked one.

- Look for an interview or a debate in an English-language TV programme. While watching, record it and make a list of phrases being used by the participants, such as expressions of agreement and disagreement, turn-taking devices, hesitation gaps, and so on.
- Picture yourself in the studio as an extra participant. Set the recording at the beginning, then stop it whenever you agree/disagree or have something to add or comment on. Use the given phrases when necessary.
- If you only have L1 channels available, record an L1 programme, pretending to be an English-speaking guest joining the debate. ⊙⁹

⊙⁸ This radio programme is still running (after 30 years!). Listen to it to get a feeling for the game.

It is available here: www.bbc.co.uk/justaminute

⊙⁹ On YouTube, watch two versions of the sketch 'Do you speak English?' (2008 and 2016).

Roleplay the same situation, substituting your own L1 for German and Chinese.

☉¹⁰ If you read them, what are the advantages and disadvantages of e-books compared to printed books?

10.4 Developing reading skills

What to read and why? ☉¹⁰

The results of my survey show that reading comprehension is the most accessible skill to non-NESTs. When asked to identify the skill they practise most frequently in non-professional activities, nearly everyone selected the alternative 'reading books/newspapers in English'. Reading professional literature has also proved to be a popular occupation. Several respondents claim that they read English authors exclusively in the original and a few add that they hardly ever read in L1, because they wish to spend the little free time they have on developing their reading skills in English.

The respondents differ greatly in terms of their motives. Some read chiefly for pleasure and/or information, while others primarily with the intention of developing their reading skills. Incidentally, one respondent admits that, for him, the richest source of information about the world has been supplied by various teaching materials.

Line by line

When we read something in L1, we can predict the next sentence with a high degree of probability. Our predictive capacity is worth developing in English, too.

- Choose a relatively easy text. Take a sheet of paper and use it to cover the text. Uncover one line at a time but first try to guess the line hidden behind the mask.[5]
- A similar technique may be applied to improve our speed reading ability. This time, however, the purpose is to understand the gist of a text by moving the eyes in a series of stops and quick jumps, instead of a piecemeal progress to achieve full understanding.[6]

Read aloud!

Reading-aloud techniques have not been in vogue lately. Yet it cannot be doubted that we have never given up practising reading aloud – if not literally aloud, then in our minds. Respondents seem to agree that saying a language item out loud can help us to decipher its meaning and use, to store it in our memory, and to improve pronunciation and intonation. After all, as we read and speak at the same time, information is processed in two sensory channels: seeing *and* hearing.

---

[5] A variation of this technique has been mentioned in Ellis & Sinclair (1989).

[6] For your information, here is a table of estimated speeds of the general reading public (including native speakers only):

Words per minute	Scale of speeds
170-200	very slow
200-230	slow
230-250	average
250-300	above average
300-350	medium-fast
350-450	fast
450-550	very fast
550-650	exceptionally fast

Needless to say, reading rate only makes sense if it is compared against a pre-established comprehension criterion level.

- Read aloud a short article in English. What were you paying attention to as you were reading? To the form or, rather, to the content?
- Read the same text aloud a second time. Were you focusing on the same things?
- Read it aloud a third time, but now give special emphasis to certain linguistic features, such as new vocabulary items, certain phonemes or sentence structures.
- Put the article aside. Can you summarise the gist of the article? Do you remember the unfamiliar words and expressions? Can you recall the features you have highlighted?[7]

The ubiquitous dictionary ⊙[11]

The development of reading skills and vocabulary building are inseparable processes. We cannot improve our reading competence unless we make systematic efforts to enhance and update our lexis. Therefore, we should always have a dictionary at hand.

- No day should pass without consulting a dictionary of some kind, a few respondents warn. Others are in the habit of opening a dictionary at a random page and brooding over a few entries. One admits that she always keeps a dictionary on her bedside table, just in case. Don't be ashamed of perusing advanced vocabulary builders either, others argue. (But if no reference book should help you out, call your uncle in London, suggests somebody in jest.)
- Another teacher reports on a strange dictionary game he used to play. His friend would page through a large English-Hungarian dictionary and ask him the Hungarian meaning of 30 randomly selected English words within a time limit. If he wasn't able to supply the meaning of at least 25 items, he would lose his bet. If he was, it was his friend's turn to pay.
- On the other hand, several respondents warn against the unbridled use of the dictionary. 'We should always try to deduce the meaning of unfamiliar words from the context,' they contend. 'We'll never forget the words whose meaning we've managed to infer.' Only if the 'wicked word' repeatedly refused to unveil itself should we turn to a dictionary.

The card file system

Now let me present a step-by-step description of the most common technique for vocabulary learning and retention, called *the card file system*.

- Choose a text and underline or highlight as many useful words and expressions as you wish to learn (but not too many). Give priority to those items which appear to be the most relevant and/or crop up more than once. Set about the subsequent activities only after you have finished reading the text. Do not break the flow of reading!
- Look up the meaning, usage and pronunciation of each unfamiliar item. Use any dictionary or reference book available, but one of them should be an English-only dictionary to make the usage clear. Pay special attention to collocations.

⊙[11] My favourite dictionaries are dictionaries of collocations.

It is now possible to look up words on a corpus or concordance website and find how they have been used in context as examples of authentic English.

For example, the British National Corpus is freely available at:

www.natcorp.ox.ac.uk/corpus

Find collocations that have surprised you and/or you have used wrongly.

---

[7] This is an adapted version of 'A technique from Frieda' in Stevick (1989).

- Jot down each new item on a separate card.[8] Do not supply the mother-tongue equivalents. Each item should first be registered in isolation, then in the sentence in which it originally occurred. Copy one further model sentence from the dictionary to exemplify the usage.

- Clip or rubber band the cards which belong to the same text. Always have these sets within easy reach. Browse through them whenever an opportunity arises.

- Make conscious efforts to memorise the items. Use them in speech as soon as you can so that they build into your active vocabulary.

- Recycle the sets from time to time. Go back to a reference book for re-checking or clarification. Should an item recur in a different text, add the new sentence on the appropriate card.

- When plenty of sets have been collected, rearrange them according to new criteria, such as:
  - parts of speech (nouns, verbs, adjectives, and so on)
  - topic areas (transport, shopping, illness, and so on)
  - recall difficulties ('I simply cannot remember this word!')
  - degree of acquisition ('I've already used this one – it's almost in my active vocab.')
  - frequency.

- Continually eliminate those items you can already use in speech – if your collection grows too big, it becomes unmanageable.

Of course, there are several other ways of manipulating the card file system. One teacher always has a set of items blu-tacked on her bedroom mirror, changing the sets once a week. Another one keeps a few sets in the glove compartment of his car – in traffic jams, he likes to flick through them (he hasn't reported any accidents). A third respondent habitually spreads out a few cards on his classroom desk, determined to use every one of them before the bell rings.

10.5 Developing writing skills ☉¹²

Writing and translating

Since writing is undoubtedly the most time-consuming skill to practise, we cannot often resort to it in our hard-pressed lifestyle.

Nevertheless, the respondents report on various forms of writing in English. Most frequently, they correspond with friends and acquaintances. Only a small number of teachers pursue other forms of creative writing such as writing essays and professional articles or keeping a diary. One person admits to writing merely for her own satisfaction, without any desire to publish anything. An up-to-date motive for producing English texts is when you practise word-processing on the computer. A utilitarian reason is to prepare grant applications. Needless to say, translating in and out of the target language is a very effective way of developing writing skills. A few respondents remind us always to have our written productions checked by educated native speakers.

☉¹² Writing habits have changed radically in the era of emails, texting, blogs and other forms of written communication. Does this affect the way in which you teach writing?

---

[8] Alternatively you may keep a small notebook or store the new items in a digital computer diary.

The standard exercise[9] ⊙[13]

The following procedure is called 'the standard exercise', because it can be applied to any text. It is a combined reading and writing activity. Its guiding principle is to teach readers how they can avoid being bogged down in minute problems of vocabulary and grammar by harnessing their background knowledge and deductive capabilities.

- Choose a one-page article dealing with any topic.
- By reading the headline only, predict at least five key words you expect to find in the article. Write them down.
- Skim the article in one minute. Check how many of the key words you have predicted occur in the article.
- Summarise the main topic of the article in not more than fifteen words.
- Read the article closely enough to be able to perform the following tasks:
  - What is the author's main intention: to inform, persuade, report or instruct? Jot down any unknown words that appear to be important. Infer their meaning from the context.
  - Report on the main idea of each paragraph in one sentence each.
  - Analyse the *structure* of the article. Is there an introduction and a conclusion?
  - Analyse the *content* of the article: Whose interests does it reflect? Which country, social class, institution? Is the content relevant in your home situation, too?
  - Produce a one-sentence summary of what you have learned from the article.
  - On a scale from 1 to 5 (1=very boring; 5=very interesting), indicate to what extent you have found the article interesting.
  - In your estimate, what percentage of the article did you comprehend?

Predict and summarise ⊙[14]

We all read English-language papers and magazines, but we hardly ever try to analyse the articles from a linguistic point of view.

- Read the headline of a newspaper or magazine article.
- On the basis of the headline, predict the content of the article and summarise it in one paragraph.
- Now read the full article and check it against your prediction.
- Next, underline or highlight the first sentence of each paragraph.
- Link the first sentences in a way that they make a coherent summary.
- If there is a native colleague around, show her your summary and ask her to suggest improvements.
- Prepare the final draft of the summary.

⊙[13] Read one of these articles: Kubota 2001, Liu 2001 or Sasaki 2001. Identify the similarities and differences in how the authors learned to read and write in English.

⊙[14] Two edited volumes containing personal accounts of how non-native speakers became reputed academics in their field are worth reading.

Choose one paper and describe the way its author studied English.

Further reading:
Belcher & Connor (2001), Braine (2005)

---

[9] The name and some of the steps of the 'standard exercise' have been borrowed from Scott *et al.* (1984).

Stream of consciousness

People in psychotherapy are sometimes asked to sit down and write whatever comes into their mind, without bothering to think about or edit their product.

- Put an alarm clock or kitchen timer in front of you and then choose a topic of any sort.
- Set the alarm to ring in five minutes and then begin to write.
- Write non-stop without paying attention to either form or content and stop as soon as the clock starts ringing.
- Check your writing and edit it into a coherent text, but try to maintain its spontaneous flow.

Further reading

- **Belcher, D. & U. Connor** (Eds.)(2001). *Reflections on Multiliterate Lives*. Multilingual Matters.

  This collection reports on the language development of highly successful users of English. About half the contributors come from the world of language studies, the other half represents a variety of other disciplines. Despite the diversity of the tales, the common denominator is the narrators' high levels of language awareness.

- **Braine, G.** (Ed.) (2005) *Teaching English to the World: History, Curriculum, and Practice* Lawrence Erlbaum.

  This volume contains reports by ELT specialists from 15 countries. Each chapter follows the same structure. After chronicling the brief history of ELT in the respective country, it describes the current ELT curriculum. Each account ends with the contributor's (auto)biography, thus combining country-specific information with life stories.

CHAPTER 11

Natives and non-natives on video (with Valéria Árva[1])

Chapters 11 and 12 report on my research carried out after the first and second editions of *The Non-native Teacher* had been published. As such, they do not carry margin notes for discussion.

They can be used as extension reading to the main text.

11.1 Background to the study

In this chapter, we revisit the issue of the native versus the non-native speaker by reporting on the results of a fourth study we carried out. This study examines the validity of the assumptions that (a) native and non-native teachers use different teaching strategies, and (b) most of these differences lie in their divergent language backgrounds. Our primary aim, then, is to review the claims advanced in previous chapters. In order to ensure better validity, the scope of investigation has been expanded by employing a multiple research design. Whereas the data presented earlier (Chapter 4.2) were obtained solely from questionnaires and interviews, this ethno-cognitive study analyses the participants' behaviour at the chalkface through a series of video-recorded lessons and follow-up interviews. While the range of research tools has thus been widened, the sample is rather limited. Therefore, our findings are tentative at best, and call for replication on a larger population.

Our second aim is to find matches and mismatches between *stated* and *actual* teaching behaviours, because we subscribe to the belief that there is a distinct gap between them. Stated behaviour may be influenced, among other things, by one's belief system, which 'deals not only with beliefs about the way things are, but also with the way things should be' (Woods, 1996: 70). Clark and Peterson argue that 'the correspondence between teachers' espoused beliefs and classroom behaviour is not always high and is moderated by circumstances that are beyond the teacher's control' (1986: 291–292). This corresponds to the distinction Marton (1981), in a more general framework, made between first-order and second-order research, the former being concerned with what people do and the latter with what they *perceive* they do.

Finally, we wish to respond to the criticism raised by a reviewer of the first edition of *The Non-native Teacher*, who said that 'the author tends to overemphasize the linguistic deficit of non-native professionals while neglecting other equally significant factors related to professionalism' (Samimy 1997: 816), probably referring to EFL qualifications and length of experience. Our analysis, therefore, pays special attention to the relationship between language competence, professional expertise and the efficacy of instruction.

---

[1] This is an adapted version of a paper entitled 'Native and non-native teachers in the classroom' *System 28*: 355–372. I wish to thank my co-author for kindly agreeing to have our paper included in this volume. I am also indebted to all the teachers and students for their willingness to participate in the project. My special thanks are due to our technician, *Tamás Selmeczi*, as well as to *Katalin Deli* and *Christopher Ryan* for providing assistance in various stages of the project.

11.2 Research design

Research questions

This small-scale study analyses ten video-recorded language lessons and ten follow-up interviews with the recorded teachers. By combining first-order and second-order research, we seek to answer the following questions:

- What are the differences in teaching behaviour between NESTs and non-NESTs?
- To what extent are these differences ascribable to the participants' language background?
- What else may cause the differences?
- How do the participants' stated behaviour and actual behaviour differ?

Data collection

There were a number of decisions we had to take concerning the selection of the sample. First, we decided to restrict to ten the number of lessons to be observed and recorded. Apart from budgetary and time constraints, we assumed that the data to be obtained from ten participants would suffice to offer tentative answers to the research questions. The second decision concerned an equal distribution of NESTs and non-NESTs, with the rationale that this would secure a better ground for comparison. A further consideration was to limit the number of participating schools to five, with one NEST and one non-NEST in each; this would give us the opportunity to kill two birds with one stone (ie, two recordings at a time), as well as to reveal traces of collaboration between colleagues teaching in the same school. Finally, we planned to select a set of homogeneous student groups in terms of age and language level. The target was Year 10, because by that time, we supposed, (a) the linguistic differences between students would already have levelled out,[2] (b) the teacher and the students would know each other well, and (c) the students would not yet have started preparing for language examinations.[3]

With these objectives in mind, we set out to identify ten teachers. It was made clear to every candidate that the purpose of the survey was to compare the teaching styles of NESTs and non-NESTs, and that strict anonymity and confidentiality would be guaranteed. Nevertheless, quite a few teachers, especially experienced non-NESTs, refused to participate. Our situation was exacerbated by the limited choice of NESTs available in secondary schools. As a consequence, our original aim to include groups with students of roughly the same age and level of English-language proficiency was only partially fulfilled.

The visits took place in the course of November and early December of 1997. Prior to the recordings, we had asked the participants to 'teach as usual'. After the lessons, every teacher sat for a 30 to 45-minute-long guided interview. Each interview was recorded on an audio-cassette and subsequently transcribed for the sake of convenience. There were two almost identical sets of questions compiled in advance: one for each cohort. The questions focused on the following points: professional background (including foreign language competence), the native/non-native issue, group profile, and the assessment of the lesson they had taught (see **Appendix I**).

The participants

The study comprised five native/non-native pairs, who were teaching in five different schools.

With respect to the NESTs, the three males and two females all came to Hungary on a two-year contract, under the auspices of 'Services for Open Learning', a voluntary organisation in England. Two arrived in September 1996 and three in September 1997. Although all of them had a BA/BEd degree or a teaching certificate, they were poorly qualified as EFL teachers: prior to their arrival in Hungary they had only completed crash courses. While two participants had several years of experience in teaching other subjects, the cohort's TEFL experience was limited, ranging

---

[2] When students start secondary school, the differences between them in terms of their foreign-language competence may be quite significant, depending on their previous contact with the language. Even in so-called beginner groups, one will find students whose knowledge is well above elementary.

[3] Towards the end of secondary school, groups tend to break up: students who have passed the state language exam are exempted from having to attend English lessons, while the rest are busy preparing for either the state exam or the school-leaving examinations.

between one and two-and-a-half years. To compensate for the gaps in their professional training, however, they were eager to attend conferences and in-service training courses. None of them claimed to speak foreign languages beyond elementary level; they spoke survival Hungarian at best. Their teaching load averaged 20 lessons a week; with one exception, they also had a few hours to teach outside their school.

The four female and one male Hungarians were all qualified teachers of English; while two were university graduates, three had college certificates.[4] The length of experience ranged between one and ten years, the average being 5.6 years. As regards in-service training, two of the college graduates were studying for a full university degree, two teachers regularly attended conferences and in-service courses, and one had even run workshops. While two participants spoke no foreign languages other than English, three were intermediate-level users of Russian and/or German. All the non-NESTs were employed full-time, their weekly teaching load varying between 16 and 26 lessons. Two of them had no extra teaching duties, three were respectively teaching another 5, 16 and 20 lessons in private language schools, at companies and/or privately.[5]

The five schools involved in the study were all secondary grammar schools in Budapest.[6] Two of them were well-established schools in the city centre while the other three were up-and-coming schools in the outskirts, including an English-language bilingual school.[7]

The 139 participating students were aged between 15 and 17 and attended grades 9, 10 and 11, respectively. 58 per cent were girls, 42 per cent boys. Group sizes ranged between 10 and 18, with an average of 14 students per group. The number of lessons per week averaged 4.2 for

eight of the groups; the two bilingual groups had 20 English lessons per week. In their teachers' judgement, one group was at beginner, three at pre-intermediate, two at intermediate and four at upper-intermediate level. All the main books being used were standard contemporary coursebooks. (The chart in **Appendix J** summarises the main points described above.)

Data analysis

After the data gathering process, first we watched the video recordings to get a taste of the teachers' work. This was followed by a detailed analysis of the interviews in order for us to identify differences in perceived teaching behaviour between the NESTs and the non-NESTs, and the extent to which these differences correlated with the results shown in the **Table 8** (Chapter 6.3). As an offshoot of this stage of investigation, attempts at cooperation between the two cohorts were recorded. Finally, we examined the recorded lessons with the purpose of finding points of convergence and divergence between stated and actual teacher behaviour. It is in this order that we present and discuss the results below.

11.3 Results and discussion

The interviews

How the NESTs behaved

Not surprisingly, the primary advantage attributed to NESTs lies in their superior English-language competence (Chapter 5.1). Their superiority was found particularly patent in their capability to use the language spontaneously and in the most diverse communicative situations. It

---

[4] In Hungary, there are two forms of teacher education: universities award degrees, while colleges award certificates. Whereas university graduates may teach in any type of school, college graduates may only teach in primary education. Owing to the present shortage of English teachers, college graduates are also allowed to work in secondary schools.

[5] The compulsory teaching load for secondary school teachers is 20 contact hours a week. The load of the two university graduates included a few hours of teaching their other major subject, whereas the participant with 16 hours was a form-teacher, entitled to have a reduced load. Since it is impossible for school teachers to make ends meet on their salary, they are forced to moonlight. Only those financially assisted by their families can afford to do without second and third jobs.

[6] Before 1989, primary education covered students aged 6–14 and secondary education 15–18. Since then, the monolithic 8+4 structure has loosened up, and comprehensive schools with a 6+6 or 4+8 structure have become fairly common.

[7] In bilingual schools, there is a 'zero year' followed by four 'normal years'. In the 'zero year', the students have 20 English lessons a week so that they can cope with the subjects they are obliged to study in English by the time they begin their first 'normal year'.

was argued by a non-native that any NEST's stock of colloquial expressions, idioms and phrasal verbs was incomparably richer than any non-NEST's. 'Natives can answer any questions, even from the area of biology or chemistry,' she said. In addition, they serve as a vast source of cultural knowledge (Chapter 6.4).

A native participant mentioned that 'My presence in itself has a lot of value' – a presumptuous statement which was corroborated by a non-NEST: 'The mere presence of a native acts as a motivating factor.' NESTs were said to command respect, because 'Students *have to* speak in English when they're speaking to me [...], which is what it would be like if they travelled abroad anywhere.' 'Natives can say anything,' complained a non-NEST. 'They are even forgiven for their mistakes.' But the claim that really boggles the mind came from a NEST: 'In a sense you can throw away all your training and techniques and just be yourself. Being yourself is the central element.'

Nonetheless, a few handicaps were singled out, too. Among them, the gaps in the NESTs' grammatical knowledge ranked at the top (Chapter 6.3). As a native lamented, 'This is wrong and this is the correct way you should say it, I know, but I can't explain why it's wrong or right.' Another NEST remarked that 'Most native teachers I know never really came across grammar until they started teaching it. So you have to learn it as you go along.' However, most NESTs working in Hungarian secondary schools do not have to teach grammar. In our sample, too, except for the native in the bilingual school, dealing with grammar was the exclusive liability of the non-NESTs: 'I don't teach grammar, so I rarely get asked grammar questions.' This being the case, the snappiest native participant could afford to laugh away his ignorance like this: 'Of course I have no idea of grammar.'

In four out of the five participating schools, there was a distribution of work between the NESTs and the non-NESTs (Chapter 8). In this set-up, the natives were commissioned to teach conversation, usually in one or two lessons a week, whereas the non-natives, being the 'chief teachers', had to deal with everything else. This implied that the NESTs had as many as ten groups to teach without being in charge of any of them. 'This isn't right,' said a non-NEST, 'but

they shouldn't take responsibility for a group before they become aware of the needs of Hungarian students, or are clear about language examinations in Hungary' (Chapter 6.5). Another non-native added that 'native colleagues don't get groups because they are not qualified teachers; children sense this.'

Another glaring defect in the NESTs' repertoire was their lack of Hungarian (Chapter 6.6). Now that the rights of L1 use in the foreign-language classroom had been reinstated, the NESTs with no knowledge of Hungarian felt handicapped: 'I can't explain fully, especially with beginners, and it can be frustrating.' Precisely for this reason a non-NEST said: 'I wouldn't give a beginners' group to a native unless he speaks Hungarian.' With regard to error correction, another non-native said that 'If natives don't speak the students' mother tongue, they cannot really "interpret" the mistakes the students make.' This may explain why the natives, as a rule, were so reluctant to offer error correction (Chapter 6.4). A lack of Hungarian may also be conducive to a lack of empathy (Chapter 6.5), a remark paraphrased by a NEST like this: 'Being a native speaker, it is difficult for you to appreciate what the students are going through when they're learning English.' The NEST who speaks no Hungarian 'misses a lot, does not realise when students are being nasty or funny.' This leads on to the more general issue of cultural deficit that NESTs are bound to suffer from in a Hungarian school environment and beyond (Chapter 6.4).

The NESTs were also criticised for their casual attitude: 'The native is just making friends with the students,' said a non-native. 'The students don't view him as a teacher, but just as a young chap messing about in sneakers.' The NESTs were similarly lax in setting requirements. 'I don't force anybody to do anything,' said a NEST contentedly, only to be rebuked by a non-NEST: 'The students do not feel that they need to prepare from lesson to lesson.' Be that as it may, the fact that the NESTs were relegated to teaching conversation justifies their insouciant attitude to a certain degree.

Another characteristic feature of the NESTs was that, again, except for the teacher in the bilingual school, they did not use coursebooks (Chapter 6.3). This was due to two things, said a non-NEST: 'They don't like them and they feel coursebooks limit their work.' It is a pity, she went on, because 'students have difficulties storing photocopied handouts.' According to another non-native, the NESTs' permissive teaching style also featured in their reluctance to assign homework and give grades. The NESTs 'are used as "props" at the school or as "status symbols",' concluded a non-native.

How the non-NESTs behaved

Providing that the assumptions made in earlier chapters are valid, the reverse of what is said about NESTs should apply to non-NESTs. In fact, this proved to be particularly true in our example, where the intrinsic differences between the two groups were compounded by the discordances found in their training, foreign-language competence, experience and familiarity with the local context.

To begin with the cons, the non-NESTs' most conspicuous handicap, in their own judgement, was their faulty command of English (Chapter 5.1). 'Because this is a learned language, it doesn't come spontaneously,' said a non-native. In spite of the fact that all of them had been to English-speaking countries, with a duration ranging from two weeks to one-and-a-half years, they admitted to having problems with basically every aspect of competence, but especially with pronunciation, vocabulary and colloquial expressions. Since non-NESTs have far less contact with English as it is used in real communicative situations, their usage is often out-of-date and smacks of textbook language. As a native participant pointed out, 'You need to know not just the grammar, but where to use it, when it sounds right, when it sounds wrong, and a non-native speaker has to know a hell of a lot in order to be able to do that.' On the other hand, 'even natives argue and wonder a lot about both vocabulary and grammar,' noted a non-NEST, 'Children are aware of this and upset about it.' But the real trouble is that non-NESTs pass their mistakes and inappropriacies to their students. As a native observed, 'All students say *pullover*. It's not wrong but the more common word is *jumper*. But *pullover* is easier for students.' To make matters worse, said a non-NEST, 'non-natives mix the two languages indiscriminately while teaching'.

In the long list of assets, grammar occupied the pride of place (Chapter 6.3). Thanks to both their own learning experience and their training, most of our non-native participants claimed to have in-depth knowledge of the structure of English and

a meta-cognitive awareness of how it worked. This was acknowledged by the NESTs as well: 'The non-native teacher has learned grammar and is able to convey that to people very clearly with no wastage, whereas I would have to look things up more often to find out what it was I was being asked about.' And when push came to shove, non-NESTs might call on L1, too (Chapter 6.6). 'It must be wonderful to be Hungarian and if students have a problem to explain it in Hungarian,' said a native participant.

The interviews with the non-NESTs also revealed a high level of professional awareness. In recognition of their linguistic strengths and weaknesses, they knew how to make improvements (Chapter 10). The most readily available forms of language practice included reading books and magazines, watching films on video and TV, and talking to English-speaking friends. In addition, one participant considered his university studies, and another one the act of teaching itself, as a means to better their command of English (Chapter 9). The non-NEST in the bilingual school found that discussing professional issues in the staffroom was not only the best form of in-service training, but also an effective way of practising English.

Having moved along the same road as their students, non-NESTs 'may remember those difficulties from their own learning' (Chapter 6.2), which was supposed to make them more sensitive and understanding (Chapter 6.5). Furthermore, since they were more familiar with general educational goals, including curricular and exam requirements, as well as the students' individual goals, they were better prepared to produce more realistic and concrete teaching plans. Conscious of their linguistic deficiencies, the non-NESTs claimed to prepare more thorough lessons plans, and, as a non-NEST remarked, 'Maybe because I have three classes with the group, there's more continuity in my work.' The assumption that non-NESTs were stricter teachers may be explained by their enhanced feeling of responsibility as well as an awareness of being 'more limited by school regulations and administrative tasks like giving marks.' In this regard, a NEST formed a negative view: 'A disadvantage of being a non-native teacher is having been brought up in very forced educational circumstances and possibly sometimes passing that on.'

In summary, both the NESTs and the non-NESTs had mixed feelings about the teaching styles of colleagues from the opposite group. Their statements would have more face validity if it had not turned out that most of them had, in fact, little or no direct experience of observing each other's classes. It is only logical to suppose, therefore, that the views expressed in the interviews were based on a combination of previous experience, hearsay and hunches.

Cooperation between NESTs and non-NESTs

Once it turned out that the participants were not in the habit of attending each other's lessons, this question arose: Was there any cooperation at all between the two groups? (Chapter 8).

The picture received by the researchers was ambiguous. Cooperation was by far the closest in the bilingual school where NESTs and non-NESTs claimed to 'talk and coordinate a lot in general.' They would even swap higher-level groups in the middle of the term. A less close form of joint work was reported by a non-native participant: 'We report to each other and I tell him what I've covered and ask him to support that [...]. He supplements my work.' In similar vein, one of the natives said that 'I'm in constant contact every day, many times a day, with the non-native English teachers and the other teachers,' but then he added: 'They're doing their thing and I'm doing my thing'. Another NEST made it felt that their cooperation stopped at him being used as a language resource by non-native colleagues.

The remaining two reports from the NESTs were quite grim. A newly arrived native was left out on a limb by his non-native colleagues: 'I don't know what the students are doing until they tell me or I ask them [...]. The Hungarian teachers have organised meetings, but I just stand in the corridor, have coffee, talk to students, I never take part'. The other native felt no less deserted: 'I don't really know what I'm supposed to be doing [...]. I just ask the children where they are in the textbook because it's easier than trying to get any sense out of the non-native teachers'.

A few non-NESTs, on the other hand, would accuse their native colleagues of ignorance. One of them said that his partner knew nothing about the Hungarian state language examination, and another mentioned that her partner 'did not know that the class was compulsory also for those students who were frequently absent'. When asked whether there was any cooperation between him and his native colleague, a non-NEST tersely said: 'No. There's a lack of trust between us'.

There may be several reasons why, on the whole, there was only a low level of collaboration between the partners, the main reason being that the differences between the two cohorts were just too big and manifold. For one thing, the natives were neither qualified nor experienced, especially not in comparison with their non-native partners. Whereas the NESTs were typically monolingual, speaking 'idiot Hungarian', as one of them said, non-NESTs were proficient speakers of at least two languages (Hungarian and English). NESTs were typical backpackers urged to 'go East', except for the most senior teacher in the bilingual school, who came as a spouse. To make matters worse, they would only stay for a limited period of time.[8]

Another reason for limited cooperation may be that the non-NESTs were just too overburdened to engage in collaboration with anyone, let alone in a foreign language. Although the official teaching load of the two groups was the same, most non-natives were compelled to take on far more extra classes than their native colleagues, in addition to their extra-curricular school duties, postgraduate studies and family commitments. In short, the life of any non-NEST in our sample was more difficult and stressful than that of any NEST.[9]

---

[8] Owing to bad salaries, young Hungarian EFL teachers do not stick it out, either. Rumour has it that an elderly teacher went up to a young colleague and asked: 'Tell me, dear, do you plan to stay long enough for me to try and remember your name?'

[9] This may also explain, by the way, why several experienced non-NESTs refused to engage in our study.

A comparative analysis of the results

In this part of the discussion, the views of the participants in this study are compared with the views of the respondents featuring in **Table 8** (Chapter 6.3). The area of investigation is the perceived teaching behaviour of NESTs versus non-NESTs.

With respect to English-language proficiency, our study bore out the assumption put forward in the previous chapters of this book that the NESTs spoke better English than the non-NESTs. Their superiority embraced all four skills and all areas of competence. There was a great deal of correlation between the two sets of data specifying the NESTs' linguistic strengths and the non-NESTs' linguistic weaknesses.

In like fashion, both studies identified the differences in teaching style between NESTs and non-NESTs. With respect to the category labelled 'General attitude' in **Table 8**, most items in the two columns recurred in our study. Namely, as conversation teachers, the NESTs could afford to be innovative, flexible and casual, as opposed to the non-NESTs, who had to apply more middle-of-the-road, consistent and demanding teaching strategies in awareness of the prevalent educational constraints and their students' needs. At the same time, the fact that they were the sole bearers of responsibility strengthened their commitment, too. Having encountered the same obstacles during their own language learning career as their students, they were more likely to empathise with their difficulties; the NESTs were supposed to be in the dark about such hurdles.

Most of the specific attitudinal features in **Table 8** were reiterated in our study. Non-NESTs were said to have more insight into, and better meta-cognitive knowledge of, grammar, even though they could not manipulate linguistic structures with the same ease as NESTs; the distribution of work between the NESTs and the non-NESTs in our sample accentuated their divergent foci of attention. The non-natives in the present study, too, were found to stick to the textbook, whereas the natives were reported to use a variety of materials instead. It was also confirmed that the NESTs were more tolerant of student errors. For lack of

competence in Hungarian, they could not turn to it for help. While they were better informants of the cultures of the English-speaking world (and certainly of the cultural heritage of the British Isles) than their non-NEST colleagues, they felt culturally handicapped in the Hungarian environment.

There were two further issues that emerged in this study with particular force. One concerned the strong motivational effect the natives brought to bear on their students, by virtue of using English as a genuine vehicle of communication. The students simply had to use English if they needed to interact with their native teacher – this was obviously not the case with their non-native teacher. The other issue had to do with lesson planning: the non-NESTs were reported to be more conscientious in their preparation and their plans had more professional relevance. Their efforts may have been spurred in part by an awareness of gaps in their English-language competence.

On the other hand, certain features highlighted in **Table 8** were disregarded by our participants. For example, there was no mention of whether our NESTs, too, favoured oral skills, teaching items in context, free activities and group and pair work, as opposed to our non-NESTs, who would be expected to lend more emphasis to the printed word, teaching items in isolation, controlled activities and frontal work. More importantly, while it is clear that the two sources of results bear a good deal of resemblance, there is no way of establishing at this point the degree of correspondence between *perceived* behaviour and their *actual* teaching behaviour. The analysis of the video-recordings was designed to shed light on possible discrepancies.

However, it looks certain that the respective teaching behaviour of NESTs and non-NESTs is closely connected with linguistic matters, and at least some of the divergences perceived between the two cohorts are determined by their divergent language backgrounds. The school principals in our project are likely to have assigned to the NESTs the job of conversation classes on grounds of linguistic considerations alone. Such a selection criterion is of dubious value. Considering the NESTs' lack of EFL training and experience, however, there is no doubt that the principals' decision was ultimately right.

The video-recorded lessons

Observing the NESTs

The four conversation lessons given by the NESTs took us by pleasant surprise.[10] Instead of 'young chaps messing about in sneakers', four keen, active and relaxed teachers were observed in control of similarly disposed students. The success of their endeavours may be attributed to several factors.

First of all, the unqualified NESTs were timetabled to do what they knew best: to use English for communicative purposes (Chapter 6.1). All of them spoke some local variety of British English, and, judging by their reactions, the students were able to understand them without undue effort, even though the NESTs spoke at almost normal speech rate. They were able to express the desired message economically and clearly, but their linguistic advantage over the non-NESTs became especially palpable when instructions were being given.

In addition to serving as 'perfect language models', the NESTs were rich sources of cultural information, highbrow as well as lowbrow, about any topic around which the lessons were structured: the jury system in Britain, charity projects, the 'ideal world' of John Lennon, and the gimmicks of advertising. Meanwhile, in an effort to build cross-cultural bridges, they kept inquiring about Hungarian traditions, for example, folk art and the local version of Santa Claus. These 'debating societies' seemed to bring a welcome break in the students' daily routine.

Apart from the good choice of topics, the overall success of the lessons was ensured by thorough preparation – contrary to hints in the interviews. Since none of the NESTs were using coursebooks, they designed their own material in the form of newspaper cut-outs, posters and worksheets. Students were also required to prepare their own material for the projects to be presented. Thanks to meticulous planning, the NEST lessons had a clear structure with activities linked to each other in logical order.

The four NESTs proved to be good facilitators. Untrained they may have been as EFL teachers, but they were well-trained debaters, applying with dexterity the etiquette of agreeing, disagreeing, challenging, hesitating, and so on. They sometimes took up a contrary position just for the sake of stirring debate, but they did not hide their own personal opinions, either. For example, when a boy said that women should not be allowed on the jury, the teacher reminded him that the ancient symbol of justice was a woman, Justitia, with scales in one hand and a sword in the other. Our general impression was that the NESTs professed tolerant views, reflected in the selection of discussion topics as well as in comments such as 'John Lennon's world may not be realistic but still that's his dream'. Or, when a student said that Nazis should be barred from the jury, the teacher countered that, for all his personal aversion, nobody should be excluded on the basis of their political allegiances. But above all, the NESTs were good listeners who showed genuine interest in whatever the students had to say (Chapter 6.5).

The classes had a relaxed atmosphere, with the teachers behaving in an ostentatiously non-teacherly fashion. They discarded several elements of the educational culture customary in Hungarian schools. For example, they did not expect to be formally greeted upon entering and leaving the classroom, nor did they call on shy or reluctant students or correct errors unless they hindered understanding.[11]

The NESTs' casual attitude was manifest in other respects, too. For example, they were moving a lot between the blackboard and the students, their movement being facilitated by the horseshoe arrangement of desks. During pair and group activities, they often crouched before the student they wanted to listen or talk to, so that their eyes would be at the same level. Speaking of pair and group work, the researchers could not help noticing that, far more often than not, the students used Hungarian among themselves (Hancock 1997).

---

[10] As mentioned earlier, the fifth NEST was a 'normal' teacher in the bilingual school; her lesson is examined together with the non-NESTs.

[11] We wondered about the causes of the pidginised English that most of the students spoke – surely, NESTs had not spent a long enough time to be the culprits!

Humour was in great abundance in all four lessons. It typically featured in one-liners, like these: 'I'll give you one-and-a-half minutes because I'm generous'; 'Earnings, not earrings'; 'Unarmed doesn't mean that he has no arm' (while showing that the arms would not be cut off). On another occasion, the teacher deliberately put up a word with a spelling mistake, and when the mistake was spotted by a student, she said: 'Good, so you are listening!' A few minutes later, the same teacher praised those who had designed funny distractors for a multiple-choice exercise. Exchanges between teacher and student were often of a teasing kind, like this one:

> Teacher: We'll finish this the next time.
> Student: Sure?
> Teacher: Believe me.

The students were also allowed to make witty remarks – it is a pity that all of them were produced in Hungarian.

Finally, a caveat about the NEST lessons: they were found successful in comparison to our expectations, rather than in an absolute sense. As a matter of fact, the teachers' performances were rife with professional errors, big and small. Some activities were launched and never finished; the teacher spent an unduly long time with a certain group at the expense of the others; after the groups had dwelt on a task for ten minutes, some were not given the chance to present their project; discussions occasionally dragged on endlessly, stealing the time from other tasks; while one NEST ran out of time, another one ran out of ideas, and so on. But don't teachers with long experience commit the same mistakes?

Observing the Non-NESTs

Although the non-NESTs complained a lot about their language handicaps in the interviews, it turned out that all five of them were fluent speakers of English, two being what is often called near-native speakers (Chapter 2.3). Except for one teacher, the non-NESTs used English almost exclusively during their lesson. This is in stark contrast to the claim voiced in the interviews that a great advantage of non-NESTs over NESTs was their capability of drawing on the mother tongue for assistance (Chapter 6.6). It was only the fifth participant to whom the statement that 'non-natives mix the two languages indiscriminately while teaching' applied, as he was often caught code-switching even in mid-sentence. Incidentally, he was perhaps the most creative and energetic teacher in the non-NEST sample.

The teachers themselves insisted on using English all the time, but did not demand their students to follow suit. The use of Hungarian was most conspicuous during pair and group work – a case of unprincipled leniency shared by both cohorts. While acknowledging the laudable aims of this form of practice, one is bound to ask: What is the point of a group activity which, for instance, requires a twenty-minute-long preparatory discussion in Hungarian only to yield a one-sentence advertisement in English?

In consonance with the interview data, four of the five lessons were built around some aspects of grammar but, in contrast with the data in **Table 8**, practice was not dominated by controlled activities – a vast array of techniques and procedures, including communicative tasks, was applied to teach the structural patterns in context. In other respects, too, the non-NEST lessons were more varied than the NEST lessons, with the main stress falling on speaking skills throughout.

However, some other results of **Table 8** were corroborated. Thus, all five non-natives relied on one, or as many as four, different coursebooks, resorted to more error correction, checked the students' work more consistently and assigned more homework than their native colleagues. As expected, the non-native classes were poor in cultural content (Chapter 5.1): four lessons conveyed hardly any cultural information, whereas the information supplied in the fifth lesson about the British school system was some thirty years out of date.

With respect to class atmosphere, drawing any comparison between the two cohorts would be unfair, because conversation classes are freer by nature. Nevertheless, a congenial atmosphere was characteristic of three lessons. In addition to activities eliciting humour such as charades, tongue twisters and mimes, there were a lot of witty asides ('I'm like the Országh-dictionary. I just supply the words.'). One teacher exercised self-irony when he responded to a student correcting him, like this: 'You may draw my attention to my mistakes because I do make mistakes.' Some non-natives rounded off their classes with cheerful comments, such as 'You were great today. I liked working with you.' and 'Thank you for your cooperation. Have a nice day. See you on Monday.' In defiance of a prediction made by a NEST that the non-NESTs would keep their students sitting all the time, the students had ample opportunity to move among the desks arranged in a horseshoe shape.

In contrast, two NESTs imposed formal discipline, expecting the class to greet and take leave of them in chorus and the group monitor to report at the beginning of the lesson. Possibly also upset by the video-camera, they both looked rather impatient[12], especially after they had realised that they would run out of time. Blaming the students for their flop, one of them escaped into sarcasm: 'You're writing these down, aren't you? Of course you are', and 'Don't advertise your own personal problems because they're expensive'. Tension caused the students to stare at their books speechlessly, only to become unruly during group and pair work.

In our samples, two teachers stuck out like sore thumbs: the NEST from the bilingual school whose brief was to teach grammar and the non-NEST who was doing a conversation class. Both were misfits in their own ways. The trouble with the NEST was that she was unqualified to teach grammar, therefore she relentlessly plodded through the coursebook exercises. Strangely enough, she was the only NEST who adhered to classroom formalities, perhaps in an effort to compensate for being a foreigner. The non-NEST's conversation class was no less miserable; as her feeling of frustration grew, she gradually lost all sense of timing and touch with her students. Their failure may be due to the fact that they had taken on a role they were not fit for: the NEST might have been more successful had she held a conversation class, and the non-NEST might have done better had she focused on grammar.

---

[12] After several futile attempts to get across the meaning of the word *impatient*, the teacher asked with no feigned impatience: 'Now, shall I write impatient on the board or not?'

Summary

Even a glance at the particulars of the ten participants selected for the study reveals enormous differences: unqualified, inexperienced, monolingual, adventurous and relaxed natives on the one hand, and well-qualified, experienced, bi/plurilingual, settled and overburdened non-natives on the other. This may account for the looseness of cooperation between NESTs and non-NESTs, as well as for the adoption of considerably different teaching strategies. It would be more difficult to ascertain, however, the extent to which these differences are due to divergences in their language or professional backgrounds.

As for the differences in language proficiency, even though all five non-NESTs were fluent speakers of English, they were unable to emulate NESTs on any count of language competence. The NESTs' authenticity was ensured by representing a different cultural heritage: they were carriers of a set of values and ideas which were often at variance with the students' expectations. The students seemed to derive a great deal of motivation from the opportunity to operate at the interface of two cultures.

With respect to the differences in allocated roles, four NESTs had been pre-ordained to teach only conversation classes, leaving the lion's share for non-NESTs - this was a wise decision in our judgement. Although Seidlhofer is right in saying that 'There has often been the danger of an automatic extrapolation from *competent speaker* to *competent teacher* based on linguistic grounds alone, without taking into consideration the criteria of cultural, social and pedagogic appropriacy' (1996: 69), it appears to be a fair assumption that even untrained NESTs can be used effectively for certain teaching purposes – and not merely as 'status symbols'.

The differences in teaching style between NESTs and non-NESTs may be best characterised with two comments. At one point, a non-NEST said to her class: 'And now I'd like to teach you a tongue twister.' Compare this to what a NEST said in the interview: 'Well, there's nothing in particular I want to teach those kids.' Although both intended to teach their students to communicate, they clearly had two different kinds of commission. With tangible chunks to teach, the non-NESTs favoured a step-by-step approach. With no such handrails to hold on to, the NESTs kept pushing their students along a never-ending path. Hence the researchers' difficulty in making this comparative analysis any more transparent.

In an era of political correctness, one often reads references to classics of the profession. In a plenary lecture, van Essen (1994) reminded us, for example, that 'As long ago as 1899 Henry Sweet, quite unequivocally as was his wont, gave the following verdict: trained non-native teachers are better than untrained native ones.' It took us a hundred years to realise that the picture is more complex than that.

CHAPTER 12

Natives and non-natives – as seen by the learners (with Eszter Benke[1])

Here, as in many other sources, the abbreviations NSs and NNSs are used instead of NESTs and non-NESTs.

12.1 Introduction

The NS/NNS issue has come into the focus of professional attention: various aspects thereof have been discussed in recent years. This debate has produced several taxonomies and a special NS/NNS-related vocabulary has evolved. Even the legitimacy of the key term 'native speaker' has been called into doubt (Braine 1999, Kramsch 1997, Medgyes 1994, Paikeday 1985), and the number of professionals who assert that the separation of NSs and NNSs does not bear scrutiny is on the increase. Nevertheless, the NS/NNS dichotomy is still in current use.

In his seminal book, *Linguistic Imperialism*, Phillipson (1992a) tries to pull down the barriers between NS and NNS teachers, yet he strengthens the distinction by establishing the demarcation line between core and periphery countries. To the core belong countries, he claims, whose first language is English, whereas the periphery includes countries in which English is spoken as a second or foreign language. Phillipson argues that linguistic imperialism holds sway by maintaining six NS fallacies, one of which is the relative ineffectiveness of NNS teachers.

A similar division is offered by Holliday's (1994) categories of BANA/TESEP. While the BANA group typically comprises private sector adult institutions in Britain, Australasia and North America, the TESEP group includes state education at tertiary, secondary and primary levels in the rest of the world. By employing ethnographical research methods, Holliday asserts that an approach which works in BANA countries cannot necessarily be implemented in a culturally different environment. Although he is not directly concerned with the NS and NNS dilemma, his assumptions bear obvious relevance to the issue.

The acknowledgment of cultural differences and multiculturalism requires a critical examination of the profession's most fundamental beliefs about the role of the English language and about what constitutes native and native-like language ability. By questioning the idealised status of the NS, Kramsch highlights the benefits of being a NNS, maintaining that 'the linguistic diversity that learners bring to language learning can contribute to the multiple possibilities of self expression' (Kramsch 1997: 386). Learning a foreign or second language, therefore, does not constrain but, rather, enriches the mind.

This debate carries profound implications for the work of the classroom teacher as well. Most relevant from the perspective of the present study was the first full-length book (Medgyes 1994), which was wholly devoted to the NS/NNS dichotomy and its impact on teacher education. Investigating differences in teaching attitudes between the two groups of teachers, Medgyes relies on data obtained from comprehensive questionnaire surveys and interviews. The differences are discussed around the focal points of personal characteristics, language proficiency, attitude to teaching the language, as well as attitude to teaching culture. The results strongly suggest that these differences are in large measure due to linguistic factors.

[1] I would like to express my gratitude to my co-author for giving me the permission to re-publish our paper in this adapted version. The original paper, entitled 'Differences in teaching behaviour between native and non-native speaker teachers: As seen by the learners', was published in 2005 in E. Llurda (Ed.), *Non-native Language Teachers: Perceptions, Challenges and Contributions* (195-215). Springer. Many thanks also to the respondents of the study and to colleagues who kindly contributed to the administration of the questionnaires.

Another book primarily concerned with the NS/NNS teacher issue (Braine 1999) expounds hitherto unknown views held by NNS educators in ELT. This unique combination of autobiographical narratives, theoretical articles and research findings raises sociopolitical and sociocultural concerns and ponders their implications for teacher education.

While the NS/NNS issue has been extensively studied from the teacher's point of view, less has been written about learners' attitudes to teachers who come from divergent language backgrounds. Based on the findings of research elaborated in Medgyes (1994), the present study attempts to examine whether the differences as viewed by NS and NNS teachers respectively are in line with the learners' perceptions. A recent study (Árva & Medgyes, 2000, Chapter 11) suggests a possible mismatch between stated and actual behaviour, a fact which may well account for divergences in the results. Nevertheless, differences in language proficiency, allocated roles in the language class and teaching styles between NS and NNS teachers are confirmed by the empirical data obtained from classroom observations.

Thus far, this literature review has focused on theoretical findings concerning the NS/NNS issue, on the assumption that such findings can impinge on teaching practice. However, the reverse may also be true: practical problems may well designate areas for research. An area which has sparked off heated debate in the past decade concerns the sociopolitical constraints related to the employment and non-employment of NNSs. In defiance of NS superiority, numerous papers and research accounts in professional journals demand equal job opportunities. Regrettably, such voices often fall on deaf ears at the decision-making levels of educational institutions the world over.

The growing interest in the question of NS and NNS teachers is also acknowledged by the inclusion of the topic in the TESOL Research Agenda (June 2000) as an item in 'Priority Research Areas and Questions'. In this TESOL document, the following NS/NNS-related questions are offered for further research:

- What challenges do NNSs face in teacher education and professional development in and outside the United States?
- To what extent, if any, are issues related to NNS professionals addressed by the TESOL teacher preparation curriculum?
- What kinds of support system are in place to assist novice teachers (NSs and NNSs alike) to successfully make the transition from pre-service programs to the job situation?
- In what ways can TESOL programs capitalise on the skills and resources that NNSs bring to the TESOL classroom?
- How can collaboration between NNS and NS teachers be facilitated?
- Harking back to earlier research indicated above, the present study wishes to contribute to the NS/NNS debate by seeking answers to the following questions:
  - In the ESL/EFL learners' judgement, which are the most characteristic features of NS and NNS teachers?
  - In which aspects of teaching behaviour are the differences between the two groups the most apparent?
  - To what extent do learners' perceptions correspond to those held by the teachers themselves?

12.2 The study

The respondents

A total of 422 Hungarian learners of English, all NSs of Hungarian, participated in the study. The selection of respondents was determined by two factors:

- All of them had been exposed to more than a year of English language instruction offered by both NS and NNS teachers.
- They were at a proficiency level of low intermediate or above.

The characteristics of the respondents are reported in percentages in **Table 13**.

Table 13: Participant characteristics

		Frequency	Per cent
School type	Secondary school (vocational+grammar)	59	14.0
	Bilingual secondary school (vocational+grammar)	205	48.6
	College (teacher training, business)	26	6.2
	University	92	21.8
	Private language school	32	7.6
	Missing	8	1.9
	Total	422	100
Location of school	Budapest	305	72.3
	Outside Budapest	117	27.7
	Total	422	100
Age of participant	<20	276	65.4
	20 – 30	131	31.0
	30>	14	3.3
	Missing	1	0.3
	Total	422	100
Gender	Male	202	47.9
	Female	218	51.7
	Missing	2	0.5
	Total	422	100
Years of English studies	<5	82	19.4
	5-10	250	59.2
	10>	80	18.9
	Missing	10	2.5
	Total	422	100
Years of NS teacher's instruction	<2	219	51.8
	2-3	119	28.2
	4-5	51	12.1
	6>	10	2.5
	Missing	23	5.4
	Total	422	100
Level of language proficiency	Lower intermediate	27	6.4
	Intermediate	92	21.8
	Upper intermediate	179	42.4
	Advanced	100	23.7
	Missing	24	5.7
	Total	422	100

As shown in **Table 13**, the largest proportion of respondents came from ordinary or bilingual secondary schools, either grammar or vocational. Among the institutions of higher education, different kinds of colleges and universities were included. Language learners from private language schools are also represented in the study. (For a detailed list of participating schools, see **Appendix K**.)

To ensure easier access to data collection and a higher return rate, nearly three-quarters of the respondents were recruited from Budapest and the rest from the countryside. This imbalance may also be justified by the geographical distribution of native teachers: the capital city and other large cities offer better employment possibilities and more favourable conditions as compared to rural educational institutions. Since two thirds of the respondents were attending secondary school at the time of the survey, the majority of the population under study is below 20 years of age. In terms of gender, the proportion is well-balanced, with 47.9 per cent males and 51.7 per cent females. On average, the respondents were fairly experienced learners, and their English-language proficiency level ranged between intermediate and advanced. Considering the fact that all of them were studying English in Hungary, it is no surprise that they had been exposed to NS teacher instruction to a much lesser extent than to instruction provided by fellow Hungarians. The high percentage of the missing answers in relation to the years of NS teacher's instruction is the result of data omission. The categorisation of the apparent diversity of answers would have posed a serious threat to the reliability of the study. No subject, however, with less than a year's NS instruction was included in the sample.

The instrument

The research instrument applied was a multi-item questionnaire. (For a translated version of the questionnaire, which was done in Hungarian, see **Appendix K**.) As pointed out above, the main purpose of the study was to investigate learners' perceptions of the differences between NS and NNS teachers of English, and the process of questionnaire development was facilitated by the results of two earlier studies (Medgyes 1994, Árva & Medgyes 2000, Chapter 11). For fear of getting lost in detail, only those aspects of teaching which had been found relevant by the studies referred to above were included in the questionnaire.

After the draft questionnaire was piloted on a small sample, several modifications, prompted by expert validation as well as by verbal protocols, were carried out.

The final instrument was a four-page questionnaire broken down into five sections. The cover letter gave a brief rationale for the survey, instructions for the completion of the questionnaire, and a request that the questionnaire be completed and returned within a week. To increase the level of reliability, the researchers' own learners were not involved in the survey and personal identification was not required.

The first section of the questionnaire contained eight questions which asked for background information. The second and third sections each contained a set of 23 items, one designed for NNS and an identical set for NS teachers. The respondents had to apply a five-point Likert-type scale to assess the extent to which these statements, in their view, characterised NNS and NS teachers, respectively. The statements covered classroom management issues as well as personal, albeit teaching-related, characteristics. The fourth section comprised eleven provocative statements which referred to both NS and NNS teachers within the framework of a Likert-scale scoring design. The open-ended items in the last section elicited information about the potential advantages and disadvantages of NS and NNS teachers.

Procedures

The exceptionally high return rate (91 per cent) of the questionnaires was possibly due to the careful selection of respondents as well as to thorough preliminary arrangements. Colleagues willing to distribute the questionnaires were asked to perform in-class administration as this allowed continuous monitoring and immediate assistance with the completion if necessary. The informal and spontaneous feedback provided by colleagues both on the questions and their learners' reactions and verbal comments also proved helpful in interpreting the results. A number of respondents expressed their wish to read the final paper – an indication that the majority took their task seriously.

For the central part of the questionnaire eliciting differences between NS and NNS teachers, as well as for the concluding miscellaneous statements, means and standard deviations were calculated from students' perceptions marked on the Likert-scale. To test the significance of the observed differences, a paired-sample t-test was run on the data-set.

12.3 Results and discussion

In the sections below, the results of the data analysis of the questionnaire are presented and discussed.

Non-native speaker teachers

Table 14 presents learners' attitudes to, and opinions about, NNS teachers. The statements expressed in means and percentages are ranked according to the degree of agreement, in descending order.

Table 14: Responses for NNS teachers – as seen by the learners

Statement	Likert		answer %	strongly disagree----strongly agree %				
	Mean	SD	0	1	2	3	4	5
assigns a lot of homework	4.04	1.23	2.4	5.7	11.6	3.3	**29.6**	**47.4**
prepares conscientiously for the lessons	3.94	1.12	2.6	3.8	10.9	8.8	**37.4**	**36.5**
corrects errors consistently	3.72	1.22	2.1	3.3	20.9	7.8	**33.9**	**32.0**
prepares learners well for the exam	3.51	1.15	2.9	3.8	22.5	9.5	**43.1**	**18.2**
assesses my language knowledge realistically	3.50	1.20	3.1	5.2	19.9	15.6	**33.9**	**22.3**
relies heavily on the coursebook	3.22	1.36	2.6	12.3	27.5	2.1	**37.7**	**17.8**
is interested in learners' opinions	3.19	1.31	2.1	7.3	35.3	5.5	**30.8**	**19.0**
puts more emphasis on grammar rules	3.16	1.28	2.1	8.1	33.9	4.5	**36.7**	**14.7**
sticks more rigidly to lesson plan	3.13	1.13	2.4	4.5	36.5	5.2	**45.0**	**6.4**
is too harsh in marking	3.13	1.17	2.5	**13.0**	**47.6**	6.6	24.4	5.9
sets a great number of tests	3.09	1.33	2.6	11.1	33.2	4.5	**33.4**	**15.2**
prefers traditional forms of teaching	3.06	1.14	4.1	7.3	29.4	18.2	**32.5**	**8.5**
applies pair work regularly in class	3.05	1.35	2	12.1	34.8	2.8	**32.7**	**15.6**
uses ample supplementary material	3.03	1.28	2.6	**9.0**	**38.6**	3.1	33.9	12.8
applies group work regularly in class	2.81	1.30	2.4	**14.7**	**39.6**	2.8	30.8	9.7
directs me towards autonomous learning	2.73	1.19	2.3	**14.5**	**36.5**	13.5	27.5	5.7
runs interesting classes	2.7	1.21	2.1	**10.0**	**52.1**	1.2	26.5	8.1
is happy to improvise	2.64	1.22	2.4	**16.8**	**38.4**	12.6	22.5	7.3
speaks most of the time during the lesson	2.62	1.2	2.6	**13.5**	**49.1**	2.1	26.5	6.2
provides extensive information about the culture	2.6	1.28	2.1	**16.8**	**45.5**	6.2	18.5	10.9
focuses primarily on speaking skills	2.54	1.18	2.5	**15.9**	**47.2**	5.2	24.2	5.0
prefers teaching 'differently'	2.38	1.08	2.4	**19.4**	**43.8**	17.1	12.8	4.5
is impatient	1.99	1.15	2.6	**41.5**	**34.6**	6.2	11.1	4.0

The bold type in the table indicates the view of the majority of the respondents who agreed or disagreed with the statement. Thus, the top part of the table lists the most characteristic features of the NN teacher, whereas characteristics regarded as the least typical are presented in the lower part of the table. It is interesting to note that 77 per cent, 73.9 per cent and 65.9 per cent of the respondents claimed, on the one hand, that NNS teachers would always or often give a lot of homework, plan their lessons thoroughly, and consistently check for errors. On the other hand, the relatively low means for the last two items indicate that NNS teachers never or rarely lose their patience (76.1 per cent) and tend to apply middle-of-the-road methods (63.2 per cent).

Native speaker teachers

As opposed to **Table 14**, **Table 15** shows the learners' judgements about NS teachers.

Table 15: Responses for NS teachers – as seen by the learners

Statement	Likert		answer %	strongly disagree----strongly agree %				
	Mean	SD	0	1	2	3	4	5
focuses primarily on speaking skills	3.96	1.31	2.9	5.7	12.1	4.7	**32.2**	**42.4**
is happy to improvise	3.68	1.41	2.1	6.6	18.0	8.1	**32.5**	**32.7**
provides extensive information about the culture	3.62	1.38	2.4	8.1	22.0	4.0	**28.7**	**34.8**
is interested in learners' opinions	3.53	1.39	2.5	11.4	18.2	4.7	**33.6**	**29.6**
applies group work regularly in class	3.48	1.31	2.6	7.8	23.7	3.1	**39.3**	**23.5**
runs interesting classes	3.42	1.43	2.4	12.8	21.8	2.6	**32.9**	**27.5**
prepares conscientiously for the lessons	3.41	1.26	2.7	8.5	24.6	8.8	**28.9**	**26.5**
prefers teaching 'differently'	3.38	1.37	2.2	8.5	20.1	14.7	**34.8**	**19.7**
assesses my language knowledge realistically	3.36	1.17	3.3	5.9	20.9	19.2	**34.1**	**16.6**
applies pair work regularly in class	3.34	1.41	2.4	13.5	22.3	2.6	**36.0**	**23.2**
uses ample supplementary material	3.24	1.36	2.6	10.2	29.6	5.2	**31.8**	**20.6**
corrects errors consistently	3.21	1.26	3.0	7.1	30.8	10.0	**32.7**	**16.4**
speaks most of the time during the lesson	3.00	1.37	2.1	13.5	**35.8**	**2.4**	30.1	16.1
sticks more rigidly to lesson plan	2.76	1.46	2.4	21.8	**34.4**	**5.2**	17.5	18.7
prepares learners well for the exam	2.76	1.28	3.4	16.8	**34.1**	**9.7**	27.5	8.5
directs me towards autonomous learning	2.52	1.18	2.9	25.6	**29.4**	**13.0**	23.9	5.2
prefers traditional forms of teaching	2.36	1.19	2.6	26.5	**32.7**	**22.5**	8.1	7.6
assigns a lot of homework	2.33	1.27	2.5	28.0	**41.5**	**3.6**	16.6	7.8
is too harsh in marking	2.28	1.18	3.3	27.5	**39.3**	**10.0**	15.2	4.7
relies heavily on the coursebook	2.18	1.15	2.1	41.9	**29.6**	**3.6**	12.6	10.2
puts more emphasis on grammar rules	2.03	1.19	2.2	36.7	**41.2**	**4.5**	11.1	4.3
sets a great number of tests	1.97	1.46	2.6	42.9	**33.9**	**5.9**	10.4	4.3
is impatient	1.92	1.28	2.5	52.6	**24.6**	**4.7**	6.4	9.2

Not surprisingly, the NS teachers' preoccupation with practising the speaking skills figures at the top of the list ('strongly agree' and 'agree' together amounting to 74.6 per cent). This is followed by their preference for supplying cultural information and a flair for deviating from their lesson plan (63,5 per cent). The results at the bottom of the scale suggest that NS teachers are very patient, just as much as their NNS colleagues. In addition, it was generally agreed that the NS is a patient, permissive and experimenting type of teacher, reluctant to set tests and spend time on grammar development. Mention should also be made about the high proportion of indecisive answers that the statement 'prefers traditional forms of teaching' elicited. It seems that, in spite of the numerous modifications carried out during the validation process of the questionnaire, this statement remained a red herring for reasons unknown to the researchers.

Comparing results

Having performed the t-test, it turns out that with the exception of one item ('is impatient' $t = .809$, $p = .419$,), all the rest reveal statistically significant differences ($p < .05$) in teaching behaviour between NS and NNS teachers. Thus it may be said that NNS teachers, on the whole, are more demanding, thorough and traditional in the classroom than their NS colleagues, who are more outgoing, casual and talkative. An interesting point, noted above: both groups of teachers were found to be patient – equally patient, as a matter of fact!

Miscellaneous statements

As indicated earlier, the fourth section of the questionnaire consisted of provocative claims about NS and NNS teachers. **Table 16** shows the means and the percentages for each statement, arranged from the highest in descending order.

Table 16: Responses to miscellaneous statements

Statement	Likert		answer %	strongly disagree---strongly agree %				
	Mean	SD	0	1	2	3	4	5
It is important that we should be able to translate.	4.40	0.95	1.9	2.6	2.6	8.5	23.5	60.9
In an ideal situation both native and non-native teachers should teach you.	4.40	1.04	1.6	3.1	4.5	8.8	15.2	66.8
A non-native teacher can give more help for a beginner.	3.87	1.10	1.6	3.6	7.6	22.3	30.1	34.8
A native speaker teaches speaking skills and conversation more effectively.	3.78	1.11	1.9	3.6	9.5	23.9	29.1	32.0
Native speakers should teach at a more advanced level.	3.65	1.06	1.7	4.0	8.1	30.3	32.0	23.9
It does not matter what the teacher's native language is, the only thing that matters is how they teach.	3.53	1.13	1.7	3.3	14.9	32.2	22.5	25.4
There is no harm in the teacher using Hungarian every now and then.	3.43	1.22	1.9	5.2	20.9	23.2	23.9	24.9
It is essential that everything should be in English in an English lesson.	3.42	1.14	1.4	7.6	10.9	30.8	31.3	18.0
A non-native speaker teaches writing skills more effectively.	3.04	1.19	2	12.3	18.0	32.7	23.2	11.8
I would be ready to trade a non-native teacher for a native any time.	2.48	1.33	3.8	30.3	21.3	22.3	12.3	10.0
I wish I had only non-native teachers of English.	1.43	0.93	1.9	75.6	11.6	5.0	3.3	2.6

As **Table 16** shows, there are two statements with the same mean scores (4.40) at the top, which suggests that these items were agreed by the overwhelming majority of respondents. While the percentage of positive responses ('strongly agree' and 'agree' together) for 'It is important that we should be able to translate' was 84.4, 'In an ideal situation both native and non-native teachers should teach you' received 82 per cent. With respect to disagreements, 'I would be ready to trade a non-native teacher for a native any time' was the second least popular statement with a mean score of 2.48 (only 22.3 per cent of the respondents agreed or strongly agreed). The item bringing up the rear was 'I wish I had only non-native teachers of English' with a mean score of 1.43, and merely 5.9 per cent of the respondents agreeing or strongly agreeing. Apart from the statement referring to the importance of translation skills, the other three mentioned above carry the same message: both NS and NNS teachers play an important role in the classroom and neither group should be dispensed with. In this regard, one respondent commented on 'I would be ready to trade a non-native teacher for a native any time' with the expletive 'Rubbish!' in capital letters. This seems to express the general view.

Advantages and disadvantages

Non-native speaker teachers

Many features brought up by the earlier parts of the questionnaire were reiterated in the answers to the open questions in the last section. The advantage most frequently ascribed to the NNS teacher is related to teaching and explaining grammar. It was repeatedly claimed that NNS teachers have a more structured approach to teaching grammar and are better able to deal with grammatical difficulties, especially with those encountered by Hungarian learners. Thanks to their intimate familiarity with the local educational environment, NNS teachers can provide more thorough exam preparation and stand a better chance of detecting cheats. Being on the same wavelength as their learners, as one respondent put it, they can promote language learning more effectively. Furthermore, they are of invaluable help in supplying the exact Hungarian equivalent of certain English words and developing translation skills. On the other hand, the shared native language poses certain threats as well. Several respondents observed that NNS teachers are prone to use too much Hungarian during the lessons and to sidetrack in their mother tongue. A recurrent criticism was levelled against their bad pronunciation and outdated language use.

Native speaker teachers

With respect to NS teachers, learners spoke highly of their ability to teach conversation classes and to serve as perfect models for imitation. They were also found to be more capable of getting their learners to speak. Several respondents noted that NS teachers are more friendly, and their lessons are more lively and colourful than their NNS colleagues'. Lower level learners, however, often found NS teachers difficult to understand, nor was the explaining of grammar considered to be one of their strengths. In the absence of a shared native language, runs an argument, NS teachers tend to leave problems unexplained. On a more general plane, as NS teachers and their learners come from different cultural and language backgrounds, a communication gap between them is often created.

It must be admitted, though, that the picture is far more complex than the one described above, tainted with individual tastes and preferences. It often occurred that a feature highly appreciated by one learner was seen as a weakness by another. In addition, learners often expressed their views in crude and emotional terms, barely using modal auxiliaries as softeners. Here are a few quotations for illustration:

'I am absolutely positive that a native teacher is more confident and can teach the language much better.'
(a 22 year-old female university learner)

'I have been able to understand native English speech since I was taught by a native. It is an acoustic delight to listen to them. … Yet they are spoilt and are sometimes too casual.'
(a 22 year-old male university learner)

'Pronunciation, pronunciation, pronunciation!'
(a 17 year-old secondary school learner)

'A native speaker finds it more difficult to understand a sentence that was thought of in Hungarian but actually said in English.'
(a 32 year-old male from a language school)

'Non-natives take the English lesson too seriously – as if it was a question of life or death. If you make a mistake, you die.'
(a 28 year-old male college learner)

'They are sometimes not very accurate and they can't spell – especially Americans.'
(a 16 year-old secondary school learner)

Conclusion

The objective of the study was to conduct research on differences in teaching behaviour between NSs and NNSs, as perceived by their learners. Whereas earlier studies were grounded in teachers' perceptions, on the one hand, and classroom observation, on the other, this study investigated the differences from a third perspective, namely that of the learners of English.

Out of the three research questions asked in the Introduction, two were answered in the preceding sections. After the typical behavioural patterns were identified first for NNS teachers and subsequently for their NS colleagues, the results were compared against each other, with the aim of finding the distinguishing features between the two groups of teachers. In the light of these results, it may be said that NS and NNS teachers form two easily identifiable groups, who adopt distinctly different teaching attitudes and teaching methods.

There is only one question left unanswered: To what extent do learners' perceptions correspond to those held by the teachers? In order to be able to answer this question, the findings of Medgyes (1994: 58–59) need to be contrasted with the results obtained in the present study. It has to be admitted, however, that not all the features represented in the table by Medgyes (1994) were included in this study, just as there were certain items which were specifically designed for our questionnaire. Differences in wording for corresponding items also warrant caution in assessing the results.

For all these words of caution, it is legitimate to compare the two sets of data, and indeed the results yield very close correspondences: an item-by-item analysis of the respective features reveals that there is an almost perfect match between teachers' and learners' perceptions. The responses to the miscellaneous statements (**Table 16**), but especially the final part of the questionnaire inquiring about the respective advantages and disadvantages, provide persuasive evidence for the existence of distinctive features between the two cohorts of teachers.

Medgyes (1994) reiterated that the establishment of differences carries no value judgment: neither group is supposed to be better on account of their specific teaching styles. This assumption was confirmed by the learners' reactions to the provocative statements in the questionnaire: the results summarised in **Table 16** seem to prove that learners appreciate both groups of teachers for what they can do best in the classroom. An overwhelming majority of the respondents argued that in an ideal situation both NS and NNS teachers should be available to teach them, stressing that they would be ill-prepared to dispense with the services of either group.

This study aimed to complement the findings produced by an examination of teachers' perceptions and classroom observation with that of the learners, thus adding the third leg of a tripod. At the same time, it cannot be denied that the scope of this study was obviously limited as it canvassed a limited number of respondents, who cannot be considered to be a representative sample. It was also restricted in geographical terms: only the situation in Hungary was explored. Therefore, similar triangulative research projects should be launched before conclusive evidence concerning the NS/NNS distinction can be obtained. One aim of the project outlined above was precisely this: to induce further research in the area.

Conclusion

This book has been addressed to, and written about, non-NESTs, the problems we encounter and the challenges we have to meet. Some readers may close the book with the feeling that I have taken a fatalistic attitude: "You're born a non-NEST, you die a non-NEST!" They may argue that I have overemphasised inborn capacities at the expense of other, perhaps more important, aspects of the teaching profession.

I readily admit that, apart from passing remarks, I have paid less attention to many components of teacher education that contribute to the success of the language teaching operation. But, with the NEST/non-NEST distinction in focus, the issue of language proficiency has had to occupy pride of place. After all, most of the archetypal differences found between NESTs and non-NESTs in terms of their teaching behaviour are ultimately attributable, as I have attempted to prove, to their divergent language backgrounds. This is not the same as to suggest that a high degree of English-language proficiency alone is the guarantee for successful teaching. Indeed, despite the linguistic handicap, non-NESTs have an equal chance of success for reasons I have examined throughout the book.

While analysing the NEST/non-NEST discrepancy, I have consistently used the term *teacher education*, instead of *teacher training*. As I see it, 'teacher training' is restricted to institutionalised forms of teacher development, such as pre- and in-service training, in which the teacher is given external assistance by teacher trainers. A wider term, 'teacher education', goes beyond teacher training to include any voluntary, self-generated activity which a teacher, NEST or non-NEST, pursues with the intention of enhancing her professional expertise. Teacher education is about raising the teacher's self-awareness: it makes her conscious of what she is doing, and why she is doing whatever it is that she is doing. The essence of all forms of teacher education should be to help teachers develop a *teaching philosophy* which guides them in their daily activities. Lacking a set of principles, teachers are hopelessly exposed to the whims of fashion and are likely to lose their credibility as professional people.

I regard the ability to be *reflective* as a far more important condition for success than any other factor, including that of language proficiency. In writing this book, I set out to make my own contribution to raising the self-awareness of all teachers, particularly us non-NESTs. To the extent that I have achieved this goal, I am content.

APPENDIX A

⊙ If you are a non-NEST, you might like to do this questionnaire and compare your responses with other non-NEST colleagues.

Questionnaire Survey 1⊙

If you feel that any of these questions will identify you in a way you do not wish to be identified, feel free to avoid the question.

1   **Native language(s):** _____

2   **Age:**   20-30 ☐   30-40 ☐   40-50 ☐   50-60 ☐   60+ ☐

3   **Major area of study (specialisation):**

BA: _____

MA: _____

PhD: _____

4   **Are you currently preparing for a degree?**

YES ☐   NO ☐

If yes, specify field: _____

5   **Indicate the overall level of your foreign language proficiency. List all the languages you know.**

Languages:

low: _____

medium: _____

high: _____

near-native: _____

6   **Obviously not all learners are equally gifted in learning foreign languages. How do you rate yourself? Check the appropriate box. (1 is best.)**

1 ☐   2 ☐   3 ☐   4 ☐   5 ☐

7   **Concerning the foreign language you know best, have you spent any significant time in a country where this language is spoken as the native language?**

YES ☐   NO ☐

For how long?   _____ months

8   **Apart from possible longer stays in the target language country, what helped you most in becoming proficient in that language? Describe briefly.**

_____

_____

9 **Have you ever attended a School of Education?**

YES ☐   NO ☐

If yes, specify the duration of training and the degree/certificate you hold.

Duration: _____

Degree/certificate: _____

10 **For how long have you been teaching.....?**

English?   _____ years

other foreign languages?   _____ years

Specify languages: _____

11 **What has been your average teaching load in the past couple of years?**

_____ hours per week

12 **Do you regard teaching as your main professional interest?**

YES ☐   NO ☐

If not, why are you teaching?

to earn my living: _____

to study at USC: _____

because I enjoy teaching: _____

other: _____

specify: _____

_____

13 **Have you taught English abroad for any significant period of time?**

YES ☐   NO ☐

If yes, specify the three longest stays:

Country: _____

Duration: _____

Type of school: _____

Your job: _____

14 **What was the primary motive for your decision to teach overseas?**

_____

15 In the countries in which you taught, was there any organised cooperation between native-speaker teachers of English (NTs) and non-native-speaker teachers (NNTs), such as team-teaching, in-service training courses for NNTs?

YES ☐   NO ☐

If yes, briefly describe indicating who (or what agency) organized the cooperation and the exact nature and duration of the cooperative activity.

_____

16 Suppose you were the principal of a language school in a non-English speaking country. Would you prefer to hire:

more NTs than NNTs?   _____

an equal number of NTs and NNTs?   _____

more NNTs than NTs?   _____

Explain your preference: _____

_____

17 Undoubtedly there are differences between the teaching attitudes of NTs and NNTs. Based on your experiences and/or impressions, describe the major differences (max. 150 words).

_____
_____
_____
_____
_____
_____
_____
_____
_____
_____
_____
_____
_____
_____

If you have any further comments, please provide them on a separate sheet.

APPENDIX B

Questionnaire Survey 2

Your name (optional): _____

1   What is your native language (mother tongue)?

    _____

2   How many years/at what academic level did you study to qualify as a
     teacher of English as a foreign language?

    _____

3   How many years of experience do you have as an English teacher?

     one year: _____

     less than three years: _____

     three years: _____

     less than five years: _____

     five years: _____

     more than five years: _____

4   Type of school (e.g. academic, vocational, comprehensive, etc.):

    _____

5   Approximate number of students in your school:

    _____

6   What age-groups are you teaching?

     3-6 ☐   6-10 ☐   10-14 ☐   14-18 ☐   18-24 ☐   24+ ☐

7   What is your average teaching load per week?

     less than 10 hours a week: _____

     10-15 hours a week: _____

     15-20 hours a week: _____

     more than 20 hours a week: _____

8   On average, how many students are there in your classes?

     less than ☐   10-15 ☐   15-20 ☐   20-25 ☐   25-30 ☐
     30-35 ☐   40 ☐   more than 40 ☐

9　What do you consider the main aims/objectives of your teaching of English as a foreign language?

_____

10　Describe briefly the teaching methods you apply in your teaching of English as a foreign language.

_____

_____

_____

_____

_____

_____

11　The average level of learning ability of your students, in your opinion, is:

poor ☐　　mediocre ☐　　good ☐　　very good ☐　　excellent ☐

12　Among the teachers of English in your school, what is the proportion of those who are native speakers of English?

all of them:　　　　　　　　　　_____

about ... per cent of the staff:　　_____

none of them:　　　　　　　　　　_____

13　Do you see any differences between native and non-native speaker teachers of English in the way they teach the foreign language?

YES ☐　　NO ☐

If yes, what are the differences?

_____

14　Who do you think is more successful in teaching English as a foreign language:

the native speaker of English?　　　　_____

the non-native speaker of English?　　_____

Give your reasons to justify your answer.

_____

15 Is there any organised cooperation between native and non-native speaker teachers of English in your country?

YES ☐   NO ☐

If yes, briefly describe it.

_____

16 If no, in what form do you think the cooperation of native speaker and non-native speaker teachers of English could be established or made effective?

_____

17 If you were in charge of administering your school, what proportion of native speaker vs. non-native speaker teachers of English would you employ in the English department?

more native speakers of English: _____

an equal number of native speakers and non-native speakers: _____

more non-native speakers of English: _____

Give your reasons to justify your choice:

_____

18 Further comments:

_____

FOR NON-NATIVE SPEAKER TEACHERS

19 Indicate the amount of time you have spent in an English-speaking country:

none: _____

less than one month: _____

1-3 months: _____

about half a year: _____

about a whole year: _____

more than a year: _____

20 If you have studied in an English-speaking country, describe your studies briefly, in terms of time and level.

_____

_____

21 How often do you speak with native speakers of English?

every day: _____

once or twice a week: _____

once or twice a month: _____

a few times a year: _____

rarely: _____

never: _____

22 Compared to other non-native speaker teachers of English in your country, how would you rate your command of English? (5 is best!)

1 ☐   2 ☐   3 ☐   4 ☐   5 ☐

23 If you feel you have difficulties in the use of English,

a) What are they? Describe them briefly.

_____

_____

b) To what extent do they hinder you in your work as a teacher of English?

not at all: _____

a little: _____

quite a bit: _____

very much: _____

extremely: _____

Thank you for your kind cooperation!

APPENDIX C

Questionnaire Survey 3

1 **How many years ago did you start your teaching career?**

_____

2 **What age group do you teach primarily? (You may indicate more than one age group.)**

4-6 ☐   7-10 ☐   11-14 ☐   15-18 ☐   19-24 ☐   over 24 ☐

3 **In your judgement, has your overall command of English become better or worse since you graduated from university/college?**

better ☐   better in some respects, worse in others ☐   worse ☐

4 **Answer these questions only if your response to Question 3 is 'better' or 'better in some respects, worse in others'.**

4a For most of us, it is in the classroom that we use English most frequently. Our primary communicative partners are the students, whose English is far poorer than ours. On the whole, how does this affect your command of English?

It does _____ damage to my English.

no ☐   hardly any ☐   some considerable ☐   a lot of ☐

4b Outside the classroom, where else have you had the chance to use English ? (You may indicate more than one area.)

extended stays in English-speaking countries: _____

talking with native English-speaking friends: _____

reading books/newspapers in English: _____

reading professional literature in English: _____

corresponding with friends/acquaintances: _____

listening to English-language programmes on radio/TV: _____

frequent contacts with English-speaking friends: _____

other: _____

4c Specify those areas where your English has improved most considerably over the years. (You may indicate more than one area.)

pronunciation: _____

grammar: _____

vocabulary: _____

functions: _____

listening skills: _____

speaking skills: _____

reading skills: _____

writing skills: _____

Any other areas? _____

5 **Answer these questions only if your response to Question 3 is 'worse'.**

5a Do you think your loss of language is mainly due to your job as a teacher?

YES ☐   NO ☐

5b Specify those areas where you feel language loss has been particularly acute. (You may choose more than one area.)

pronunciation: _____

grammar: _____

vocabulary: _____

functions: _____

listening skills: _____

speaking skills: _____

reading skills: _____

writing skills: _____

Any other areas? _____

6 **Many colleagues complain that their command of English seems to have reached a plateau level, ie, they can make no further progress. Do you share this feeling?**

YES ☐   NO ☐

7 **If your answer is 'yes' to Question 6, which areas of your competence appear to be most fossilized? (You may indicate more than one area.)**

pronunciation: _____

grammar: _____

vocabulary: _____

functions: _____

listening skills: _____

speaking skills: _____

reading skills: _____

writing skills: _____

Any other areas? _____

8 **Do you do anything to prevent or slow down the process of fossilization? Suggest ways of overcoming it. (I would particularly appreciate techniques that have worked for you.)**

Thank you!

APPENDIX D

This is an extract from *Dracula*, a horror story written by the Irish novelist Bram Stoker. It was first published in 1897 and subsequently filmed several times.

The story is told by Jonathan Harker, a young English solicitor, who visits Count Dracula in his castle in the Carpathian mountains to give him legal advice. At first, Harker is dazzled by Dracula's gracious manners, but soon realises that he has become the vampire's prisoner.

Whilst I was looking at the books, the door opened, and the Count entered. He saluted me in a hearty way, and hoped that I had had a good night's rest. Then he went on.

"I am glad you found your way in here, for I am sure there is much that will interest you. These companions," and he laid his hand on some of the books, "have been good friends to me, and for some years past, ever since I had the idea of going to London, have given me many, many hours of pleasure. Through them I have come to know your great England, and to know her is to love her. I long to go through the crowded streets of your mighty London, to be in the midst of the whirl and rush of humanity, to share its life, its change, its death, and all that makes it what it is. But alas! As yet I only know your tongue through books. To you, my friend, I look that I know it to speak."

"But, Count," I said, "You know and speak English thoroughly!" He bowed gravely.

"I thank you, my friend, for your all too-flattering estimate, but yet I fear that I am but a little way on the road I would travel. True, I know the grammar and the words, but yet I know not how to speak them."

"Indeed," I said, "You speak excellently."

"Not so," he answered. "Well, I know that, did I move and speak in your London, none there are who would not know me for a stranger. That is not enough for me. Here I am noble. I am a Boyar. The common people know me, and I am master. But a stranger in a strange land, he is no one. Men know him not, and to know not is to care not for. I am content if I am like the rest, so that no man stops if he sees me, or pauses in his speaking if he hears my words, 'Ha, ha! A stranger!' I have been so long master that I would be master still, or at least that none other should be master of me […] You shall, I trust, rest here with me a while, so that by our talking I may learn the English intonation. And I would that you tell me when I make an error, even of the smallest, in my speaking."

From: Stoker, B. (1897) *Dracula (pp.*19-20) Archibald & Constable.

APPENDIX E

In a replication study, Davies (1996) measured differences between native and non-native speakers of English in terms of grammatical judgements. His sample consisted of applied linguists with experience as English teachers. All the non-native participants (18 persons) were highly proficient speakers of English; the native speakers (16 persons) were mostly speakers of British English. Davies included 12 sentences in his survey, and the participants were required to rate the sentences on a 4-point scale as follows:

1   The sentence sounds perfect. You would use it without hesitation.
2   The sentence is less than perfect – something in it just doesn't feel comfortable. Maybe lots of people could say it, but you never feel quite comfortable with it.
3   Worse than (2), but not completely impossible. Maybe somebody might use the sentence, but certainly not you. The sentence is almost beyond hope.
4   The sentence is absolutely out. Impossible to understand, nobody would say it. Un-English.

Here are the 12 sentences to be rated on the scale:

1   Under no circumstances would I accept that offer.
2   Nobody who I get along with is here who I want to talk to.
3   We don't believe the claim that Jimson ever had any money.
4   The fact he wasn't in the store shouldn't be forgotten.
5   What will the grandfather clock stand between the bed and?
6   I urge that anything he touch be burned.
7   All the further we got was to Sudbury.
8   That is a frequently talked about proposal.
9   Nobody is here who I get along with who I want to talk to.
10 The doctor is sure that there will be no problems.
11 The idea he wasn't in the store is preposterous.
12 Such formulas should be writable down.

The participants were asked to give 1 point for a perfect sentence and 4 points for one that was totally unacceptable. They were also asked not to look at the scores below.

Here are the results of Davies's study:

Sentence	Mean		Sentence	Mean	
	Natives (N=16)	Non-natives (N=18)		Natives (N=16)	Non-natives (N=18)
1	1.1	1.1	7	3.3	3.0
2	2.7	3.0	8	1.2	2.2
3	1.6	1.8	9	2.3	2.5
4	1.7	1.6	10	1.0	1.0
5	2.7	3.5	11	1.7	1.5
6	1.7	2.5	12	3.0	3.3

⊙ Compute your own score and compare it with the mean of natives and non-natives in Davies's sample.

Are you more or less tolerant than either group?

Note that the aggregate mean for all 12 sentences for natives and non-natives is 1.99 and 2.23, respectively. This suggests that natives are more tolerant of uncertainty with regard to grammaticality. ⊙

APPENDIX F

(adapted from Mohebbi & Alavi 2014)

I use L1 in the English classroom to:	always	usually	sometimes	seldom	never
- teach new vocabulary					
- explain grammar					
- provide clarification					
- provide feedback and explain errors					
- give written corrective feedback on compositions					
- explain instructions for assignments					
- give metalinguistic knowledge					
- negotiate the syllabus and the lesson					
- administer issues like exam announcements					
- deal with discipline problems in class					
- establish or assert authority					
- answer possible questions at the end of the class					
- encourage and comfort					
- build rapport					
- give personal comments					
- make humorous comments					
- present information about the target culture					
- supervise/guide with collaborative tasks					
- conduct pre-listening/ reading activities					
- give individual help					
- avoid lengthy task explanations					
- make contrasts between L1 and L2					

APPENDIX G

A TESOL Statement on Non-native Speakers of English and Hiring Practices

Whereas TESOL is an international association concerned with the teaching of English to speakers of other languages and composed of professionals who are both native and non-native speakers of English, and

Whereas employment decisions in this profession which are based solely upon the criterion that an individual is or is not a native speaker of English discriminate against well-qualified individuals, especially when they are made in the absence of any defensible criteria, and

Whereas such decisions, not based on sound criteria, must therefore be in contradiction to sound linguistic research and pedagogical practice.

Therefore be it resolved that the Executive Board and the Officers of TESOL shall make every effort to expunge from all publications of TESOL and its affiliated bodies all language supporting such discrimination, and

Therefore be it further resolved that the Executive Board and the Officers of TESOL shall make every effort to prevent such discrimination in the employment support structures operated by TESOL and its own practices, and

Therefore be it further resolved that the Executive Board of TESOL shall instruct the Committee on Professional Standards (and such other TESOL bodies as the Board sees fit to involve) to work towards the creation and publication of minimal language proficiency standards that may be applied equally to all ESOL teachers without reference to the nativeness of their English.

This resolution is moved by the Sociopolitical Concerns Committee, having been drafted by the Employment Issues Subcommittee and endorsed by the committee of the whole.

October 1991

APPENDIX H

TESOL's Position Statement Against Discrimination of Non-native Speakers of English in the Field of TESOL (2006)

For decades there has been a long-standing fallacy in the field of English language teaching that native English speakers are the preferred teachers because they are perceived to speak 'unaccented' English, understand and use idiomatic expressions fluently, and completely navigate the culture of at least one English-dominant society, and thus they will make better English as a second language (ESL) or English as a foreign language (EFL) teachers than nonnative English speakers. As a result, non-native English-speaking educators have found themselves often implicitly, and sometimes explicitly, discriminated against in hiring practices or in receiving working assignments in the field of teaching ESL or EFL.

However, as English language learners, non-native English-speaking educators bring a uniquely valuable perspective to the ESL/EFL classroom, and so can closely identify with the cross-cultural and language learning experience that their students are experiencing. Research has shown that students do not have a clear preference for either native English- speaking educators or non-native English-speaking educators, demonstrating that, in general, students do not buy into the 'native speaker fallacy'.

In many cases the non-native English-speaking educator may also be an immigrant to an English-language-dominant country, and thus had to master both a second language and a second culture. These personal experiences may be similar to those of their students, and thus the non-native English-speaking educator can serve as a powerful role model for students.

The distinction between native and non-native speakers of English presents an oversimplified, either/or classification system that does not actually describe the range of possibilities in a world where English has become a global language. More important, however, the use of the labels 'native speaker' and 'non-native speaker' in hiring criteria is misleading, as this labeling minimizes the formal education, linguistic expertise, teaching experience, and professional preparation of teachers. All educators should be evaluated within the same criteria. Non-native English-speaking educators should not be singled out because of their native language.

TESOL strongly opposes discrimination against non-native English speakers in the field of English language teaching. Rather, English language proficiency, teaching experience, and professionalism should be assessed along a continuum of professional preparation. All English language educators should be proficient in English regardless of their native languages, but English language proficiency should be viewed as only one criterion in evaluating a teacher's professionalism. Teaching skills, teaching experience, and professional preparation should be given as much weight as language proficiency.

APPENDIX I

The interview items

NOTE: These questions were in Hungarian.

1 Name _____

2 Native language _____

3 Length of teaching experience _____

4 Qualifications _____

5 Do you regularly participate in any form of in-service training?

6 Non-natives: How do you strive to improve your command of English?
  Natives: Do you speak any Hungarian?

7 Non-natives: What do you consider to be your strongest and your weakest points in your English language competence?

8 Knowledge of other foreign languages:

9 Non-natives: Length of stay in English-speaking countries /What did you do there?

10 Average teaching load per week:

11 What age group do you like teaching, and why?

12 Is there a specific teaching method that you prefer?

13 Other subjects you are teaching:

14 What helped you most to become a professional teacher?

15 Where else do you teach? Other occupations?

16 What do you regard as the advantages of being a native/non-native teacher?

17 What do you regard as the disadvanatages of being a native/non-native teacher?

18 In what sense do you think you teach differently from a native/non-native teacher?

19 Is there any organised method of cooperation between native and non-native teachers in the staff?

20 Is there any specific distribution of work between them?

21 If you were the principal of your school, would you prefer to hire natives to non-natives? What is the ideal ratio of natives and non-natives?

22 For how long have you been teaching this class?

23 Standard coursebook being used:

24 Level of class:

25 Short description of class/problems:

26 How satisfied were you with your lesson?

27 What would you do differently?

28 Did anything go wrong, in your judgement?

APPENDIX J

Data about the participants

Native

Gender	Male	Male	Female	Male	Female
Qualifications	BA	BA	PGCE	Certificate of further education	BEd
EFL teaching experience	1.5 years	2.5 years	1 year	1.5 years	1 year
Teaching load at school	20	20	20	20	21
Extra teaching	2	7	-	4.5	5
Number of students in class	18	15	11	14	12
Girl/boy ratio	8:10	13:2	4:7	7:7	5:5
Year students are in	10	11	11	10	9
Language level	upper-inter-mediate	upper-inter-mediate	upper-inter-mediate	upper-inter-mediate	inter-mediate
Number of lessons/week	4	4	5	4	20

Non-native

Gender	Female	Male	Female	Female	Male
Qualifications	College certificate	College certificate	College certificate	University degree	University degree
EFL teaching experience	5 years	2.5 years	2.5 years	10 years	8 years
Teaching load at school	16	20	20	26	20
Extra teaching	16	20	-	-	5
Number of students in class	15	15	18	10	12
Girl/boy ratio	5:10	10:5	14:4	6:8	9:3
Year students are in	9	10	10	10	9
Language level	pre-inter-mediate	beginner	pre-inter-mediate	inter-mediate	pre-inter-mediate
Number of lessons/week	4	3	6	4	20

APPENDIX K

List of schools participating in the study (in alphabetical order)

- Budapest Business School, Faculty of Commerce, Catering and Tourism
- Budapest University of Technology and Economics
- Calvinist Secondary Grammar School, Sárospatak
- ELTE Centre for English Teacher Training, School of English and American Studies, Budapest
- International House Language School, Budapest
- Karinthy Frigyes Bilingual Secondary School, Budapest
- Pázmány Péter Catholic University, English Department, Piliscsaba
- Technical Vocational and Secondary Grammar School, Budapest
- University of Veszprém, English Department, Veszprém

Questionnaire

Dear Participant,

With this survey we would like to obtain information on the attitudes of Hungarian learners of English to native and non-native teachers of English. We are interested to find out about the differences between native and non-native teachers as perceived by the learners. Please fill in the questionnaire by circling the appropriate answers and complete the questions in the final part. It will not take more than 20 minutes to answer the questions. The questionnaire is anonymous. All data will be handled confidentially, but we are happy to share our findings with you if you like.

Thank you for your help, Eszter Benke and Péter Medgyes.

I.   Age of respondent: _____

II.   Gender: male / female: _____

III. Years of English study: _____

IV. Level of language proficiency (based on course-book currently used):
     lower intermediate ☐   intermediate ☐
     upper intermediate ☐   advanced ☐

V.   How many non-native teachers of English have you had?

     _____

VI. How many native-speaker teachers of English have you had?

     _____

VII. How long have you been taught / were you taught by native-speakers?

     _____

VIII. Institution where you are currently studying English:

     secondary school ☐   bilingual secondary school ☐

     college ☐   university ☐   language school ☐

ON NON-NATIVE-SPEAKER TEACHERS

Please decide whether the following statements are typical/true of your non-native-speaker teachers of English and indicate the extent to which you agree with them.

strongly disagree - 1
disagree - 2
neither agree, nor disagree - 3
agree - 4
strongly agree - 5

THE NON-NATIVE SPEAKER TEACHER …

1.	NNS	sticks more rigidly to lesson plan.	1 2 3 4 5
2.	NNS	is too harsh in marking.	1 2 3 4 5
3.	NNS	prepares learners well for the exam.	1 2 3 4 5
4.	NNS	applies pair work regularly in class.	1 2 3 4 5
5.	NNS	applies group work regularly in class.	1 2 3 4 5
6.	NNS	prefers traditional forms of teaching.	1 2 3 4 5
7.	NNS	speaks most of the time during the lesson.	1 2 3 4 5
8.	NNS	sets a great number of tests.	1 2 3 4 5
9.	NNS	directs me towards autonomous learning.	1 2 3 4 5
10.	NNS	is impatient.	1 2 3 4 5
11.	NNS	is happy to improvise.	1 2 3 4 5
12.	NNS	focuses primarily on speaking skills.	1 2 3 4 5
13.	NNS	puts more emphasis on grammar rules.	1 2 3 4 5
14.	NNS	prefers teaching 'differently'.	1 2 3 4 5
15.	NNS	relies heavily on the coursebook.	1 2 3 4 5
16.	NNS	prepares conscientiously for the lessons.	1 2 3 4 5
17.	NNS	corrects errors consistently.	1 2 3 4 5
18.	NNS	runs interesting classes.	1 2 3 4 5
19.	NNS	assigns a lot of homework.	1 2 3 4 5
20.	NNS	uses ample supplementary material.	1 2 3 4 5
21.	NNS	assesses my language knowledge realistically.	1 2 3 4 5
22.	NNS	provides extensive information about the culture of English-speaking countries.	1 2 3 4 5
23.	NNS	is interested in learners' opinions.	1 2 3 4 5

ON NATIVE-SPEAKER TEACHERS

Please decide whether the following statements are typical/true of your native teachers of English and indicate the extent to which you agree with them.

strongly disagree - 1
disagree - 2
neither agree, nor disagree - 3
agree - 4
strongly agree - 5

THE NATIVE-SPEAKER TEACHER …

1. NS	sticks more rigidly to the lesson plan.	1	2	3	4	5
2. NS	is too harsh in marking.	1	2	3	4	5
3. NS	prepares learners well for the exam.	1	2	3	4	5
4. NS	applies pair work regularly in class.	1	2	3	4	5
5. NS	applies group work regularly in class.	1	2	3	4	5
6. NS	prefers traditional forms of teaching.	1	2	3	4	5
7. NS	speaks most of the time during the lesson.	1	2	3	4	5
8. NS	sets a great number of tests.	1	2	3	4	5
9. NS	directs me towards autonomous learning.	1	2	3	4	5
10. NS	is impatient.	1	2	3	4	5
11. NS	is happy to improvise.	1	2	3	4	5
12. NS	focuses primarily on speaking skills.	1	2	3	4	5
13. NS	puts more emphasis on grammar rules.	1	2	3	4	5
14. NS	prefers teaching 'differently'.	1	2	3	4	5
15. NS	relies heavily on the coursebook.	1	2	3	4	5
16. NS	prepares conscientiously for the lessons.	1	2	3	4	5
17. NS	corrects errors consistently.	1	2	3	4	5
18. NS	runs interesting classes.	1	2	3	4	5
19. NS	assigns a lot of homework.	1	2	3	4	5
20. NS	uses ample supplementary material.	1	2	3	4	5
21. NS	assesses my language knowledge realistically.	1	2	3	4	5
22. NS	provides extensive information about the culture of English-speaking countries.	1	2	3	4	5
23. NS	is interested in learners' opinions.	1	2	3	4	5

Please indicate the extent to which you agree with the following statements.

strongly disagree - 1
disagree - 2
neither agree, nor disagree - 3
agree - 4
strongly agree - 5

Please list some advantages and disadvantages emerging from being taught by a native and a non-native teacher.

24. A non-native speaker teacher can give more help for a beginner.   1   2   3   4   5

25. A native speaker teaches speaking skills/conversation more effectively.   1   2   3   4   5

26. It does not matter what the teacher's native language is, the only thing that matters is how they teach.   1   2   3   4   5

27. In an ideal situation both native and non-native teacher teach you.   1   2   3   4   5

28. It is essential that everything should be in English in an English lesson.   1   2   3   4   5

29. A non-native speaker teaches writing skills more effectively.   1   2   3   4   5

30. I wish I had only non-native teachers of English.   1   2   3   4   5

31. There is no harm in the teacher using Hungarian every now and then.   1   2   3   4   5

32. It is important that we should be able to translate.   1   2   3   4   5

33. Native speakers should teach at a more advanced level.   1   2   3   4   5

34. I would be ready to trade a non-native teacher for a native any time.   1   2   3   4   5

Advantages:

NS _____

NNS _____

Disadvantages:

NS _____

NNS _____

Bibliography

Aitchison, J. (1981) *Language Change: Progress or Decay?* Fontana Paperbacks.

Alexander, L. G. & J. Tadman (1972) *Target 1: Teacher's Book.* Longman.

Allwright, D. (1988) *Observation in the Language Classroom.* Longman.

Allwright, D. & K. M. Bailey (1991) *Focus on the Language Classroom.* Cambridge University Press.

Amin, N. (1997) Race and identity of the nonnative ESL teacher. *TESOL Quarterly 31* (pp. 580–583).

Ammer, C. (1992) *The Methuen Dictionary of Clichés.* Methuen.

Anderson, J. (2016) Initial teacher training courses and non-native speaker teachers. *ELT Journal 70* (pp. 261–274).

Antier, M (1976) Language teaching as a form of witchcraft. *ELT Journal 31* (pp. 1–10).

Atkinson, D. (1987) The mother tongue in the classroom: a neglected resource? *ELT Journal 41* (pp. 241–247).

Bárdos, J. (1984) Foreign-language teaching in the 80s. *Educational Review 34* (pp. 105–118).

Barduhn, S. (2014) Identity, imperialism and the role of the EFL teacher. In T. Pattison (Ed.) *IATEFL 2013: Liverpool conference selections* (pp. 40–51). IATEFL.

Beaven, B. (Ed.) (2008) *IATEFL 2007: Aberdeen Conference Selections.* IATEFL.

Beebe, L. M. (1983) Risk-taking and the language learner. In H. W. Seliger & M. H. Long (Eds.) *Classroom Oriented Research in Second Language Acquisition* (pp. 30–65). Newbury House.

Belcher, D. & U. Connor (Eds.) (2001) *Reflections on Multiliterate Lives.* Multilingual Matters.

Benson, M., E. Benson & R. Ilson (1986) *The BBI Combinatory Dictionary of English.* John Benjamins.

Bernat, E. (2008) Towards a pedagogy of empowerment: the case of 'impostor syndrome' among pre-service non-native speaker teachers. *ELTED 11* (pp. 1–8).

Berne, E. (1964) *Games People Play.* Penguin.

Bodóczky, C. and A. Malderez (1993) New style teaching experience and the training of supervisors in Hungary. *The Teacher Trainer 8 (9)* (pp. 11–17).

Bolitho, R. & P. Medgyes (2000) Talking shop: from aid to partnership. *ELT Journal 54* (pp. 379–386).

Borden, R. C. & A. C. Busse (1925) *Speech correction.* F. S. Crofts & Co.

Bowers, R. (1986) English in the world: aims and achievements in English language teaching. *TESOL Quarterly 20* (pp. 393–410).

Braine, G. (Ed.) (1999) *Non-native Educators in English Language Teaching.* Lawrence Erlbaum.

Braine, G. (Ed.) (2005) *Teaching English to the World: History, Curriculum and Practice.* Lawrence Erlbaum.

Braine, G. (2010) *Nonnative Speaker English Teachers: Research, Pedagogy, and Professional Growth.* Routledge.

Breen, M. P. (1985) The social context for language learning – a neglected situation. *Studies in Second Language Acquisition 7* (pp. 135–158).

British Council (1985) *Teaching and Learning in Focus.* The British Council.

Britten, D. (1985) Teacher training in ELT. *Language Teaching 18* (pp. 112–128; 220–238).

Broca, Á. (2016) CLIL and non-CLIL: differences from the outset. *ELT Journal 70* (pp. 320–331).

Brown, G. & G. Yule. (1983) *Teaching the Spoken Language.* Cambridge University Press.

Brown, H. D., C. A. Yorio & R.H. Crymes (Eds.) (1978) *On TESOL '77, Teaching and Learning English as a Second Language: Trends in Research and Practice* (pp. 278–294). TESOL.

Brumby, S. & M. Wada (1990) *Team-Teaching*. Longman.

Butler, Y. G. (2007) How are nonnative-English-speaking teachers perceived by young learners? *TESOL Quarterly 41* (pp. 731–755).

Byrne, D. (1976) *Teaching Oral English*. Longman.

Celce-Murcia, M. (Ed.) (2001) *Teaching English as a Second or Foreign Language*. Heinle & Heinle.

Chaudron, C. (1988) *Second Language Classrooms: Research on Teaching and Learning*. Cambridge University Press.

Clark, C. M. & P. L. Peterson (1986) Teachers' thought processes. In M. C. Wittrock (Ed.) *Handbook of Research on Teaching* (pp. 355–396). Macmillan.

Clark, E. & A. Paran (2007) The employability of non-native speaker teachers of EFL: a UK survey. *System 35* (pp. 407–430).

Claxton, G. (1989) *Being a Teacher*. Cassell.

Cogo, A. (2012) English as a lingua franca: concepts, use, and implications. *ELT Journal 66* (pp. 97–105).

Coleman, H. (Ed.) (2011) *Dreams and Realities*. British Council.

Cook, G. & B. Seidlhofer (Eds.) (1995) *Principle and Practice in Applied Linguistics*. Oxford University Press.

Cook, V. (2005) Basing teaching on the L2 user. In E. Llurda (Ed.) *Non-native Language Teachers: Perceptions, Challenges and Contributions to the Profession* (pp 47–61). Springer.

Coppieters, R. (1987) Competence differences between native and near-native speakers. *Language 63* (pp. 544–573).

Corder, S. P. (1973) *Introducing Applied Linguistics*. Penguin.

Corder, P. (1983) Strategies of communication. In C. Faerch & C. Kasper (Eds.) *Strategies in Interlanguage Communication* (pp. 15–19). Longman.

Coulmas, F. (1981) Spies and native speakers. In F. Coulmas (Ed.) *A Festschrift for Native Speakers* (pp. 355–367). Mouton Publishers.

Coulmas, F. (Ed.) (1981) *A Festschrift for Native Speakers*. Mouton Publishers

Cowley, S. (2001) *Getting the Buggers to Behave*. Continuum.

Crystal, D. (1985) *A Dictionary of Linguistics and Phonetics*. Basil Blackwell.

Crystal, D. (1987) *The Cambridge Encyclopedia of Language*. Cambridge University Press.

Crystal, D. (1995) *The Cambridge Encyclopedia of the English Language*. Cambridge University Press.

Crystal, D. (2000). On trying to be crystal-clear: a response to Phillipson. *Applied Linguistics 21* (pp. 415–421).

Das, B. K. (Ed.) (1987) Communication and learning in the classroom. *Anthology Series 19*: SEAMEO Regional Language Centre.

Davies, A. (1989) Is international English an interlanguage? *TESOL Quarterly 23* (pp. 447–467).

Davies, A. (1991) *The Native Speaker in Applied Linguistics*. University of Edinburgh.

Davies, A. (1995) Proficiency of the native speaker: what are we trying to achieve in ELT? In G. Cook & B. Seidlhofer (Eds.) *Principle and Practice in Applied Linguistics* (pp. 145–157). Oxford University Press.

Davies, A. (1996) What second language learners can tell us about the native speaker: identifying and describing exceptions. Presented at the *1996 American Association of Applied Linguistics (AAAL) conference in Chicago*.

De Oliviera, L. C. & S. Richardson (2004) Collaboration between native and nonnative English-speaking educators. In L. D. Kamhi-Stein (Ed.) *Learning and Teaching from Experience: Perspectives on Nonnative English-speaking Professionals* (pp. 294–306). The University of Michigan Press.

Dewey, J. (1929) *The Sources of a Science of Education.* Liveright.

Dickinson, L. (1987) *Self-Instruction in Language Learning.* Oxford University Press.

Dogancay-Aktuna, S. & J. Hardman (Eds.) (2008) *Global English Teaching and Teacher Education: Praxis and Possibility.* TESOL.

Dörnyei, Z & S. Thurrell (1992) *Conversation and Dialogues in Action.* Prentice Hall.

Dörnyei, Z. & M. Kubanyiova (2014) *Motivating Learners, Motivating Teachers: Building Vision in the Language Classroom.* Cambridge University Press.

Dry, D. P. L. (1977) Whose motivation and to what end? *ELT Journal 31* (pp. 190–203)

Dulay, H. C., M. K. Burt & S. D. Krashen (1982) *Language Two.* Oxford University Press.

Dunham, J. (1992) *Stress in Teaching.* Routledge.

Edge, J. (1988) Natives, speakers, and models. *JALT Journal 9* (pp. 153–157).

Eggington, W. (1992) On the sociopolitical nature of English language teaching *TESOL Matters 2* (p. 4).

Ellis, E. M. (2006) Language learning experience as a contributor to ESOL teacher cognition. *TESL-EJ 10* (pp. 1–20).

Ellis, G. & B. Sinclair (1989) *Learning to Learn English.* Cambridge University Press.

Ellis, R. (1985) *Understanding Second Language Acquisition.* Oxford University Press.

Enyedi, Á. (2008) The rather well-fed caterpillar and the very hungry butterfly. In B. Beaven (Ed.) *IATEFL 2007: Aberdeen Conference Selections* (pp. 38–47). IATEFL.

Enyedi, Á. & P. Medgyes (1998) ELT in Central and Eastern Europe. *Language Teaching 31* (pp. 1–12).

Faerch, C. & G. Kasper (Eds.) (1983) *Strategies in Interlanguage Communication.* Longman.

Ferguson, C. A. (1982) Foreword. In B. B. Kachru (Ed.) *The Other Tongue: English Across Cultures.* (pp. vii–xi). Pergamon.

Firth, J. R. (1957) *Papers in Linguistics: 1934-1951.* Oxford University Press.

Fishman, J. A. (1982) The sociology of English as an additional language. In B .B. Kachru (Ed.) *The Other Tongue: English across Cultures* (pp. 15–22). Pergamon.

Fishman, J. A., R. L. Cooper & A. W. Conrad (Eds.) (1977) *The Spread of English: The Sociology of English as an Additional Language.* Newbury House.

Flowerdew, J. (2001) Attitudes of journal editors to nonnative speaker contributions. *TESOL Quarterly 35* (pp. 121–150).

Forhan, L. E. (1992) Nonnative Speakers of English and hiring practices. *TESOL Matters 2* (p. 7).

Freudenstein, R. (Ed.) (1989) *Error in Foreign Languages: Analysis and Treatment.* FIPLV/Eurocentres.

Gaies, S. J. (1987) Research in TESOL: romance, precision, and reality. *TESOL Newsletter, February 87* (pp. 21–23).

Gallwey, W. T. (1979) *The Inner Game of Tennis.* Bantam Books.

Gardner, R. C. (1985) *Social Psychology and Second Language Learning: The Role of Attitudes and Motivation.* Edward Arnold.

Gardner, R. C. & W. E. Lambert (1972) *Attitudes and Motivation in Second Language Learning.* Newbury House.

Gee, J. P. (1988) Dracula, the Vampire Lestat, and TESOL. *TESOL Quarterly 22* (pp. 201– 225).

Ghanem, C. (2015) Teaching in the foreign language classroom: how being a native or non-native speaker of German influences culture teaching. *Language Teaching Research 19* (pp. 169–186).

Grabe, W. (1988) English, information access, and technology transfer: a rationale for English as an international language. *World Englishes 7* (pp. 63–72).

Graddol, D. (1997) *The Future of English?* The British Council.

Graddol, D. (2006) *English Next*. The British Council.

Gregg, K. R. (1984) Krashen's monitor and Occam's razor. *Applied Linguistics 5* (pp. 79–100).

Guiora, A. Z., R. C. L. Brannon & C. Y. Dull (1972) Empathy and second language learning. *Language Learning 22* (pp. 111–130).

Hancock, M. (1997) Behind classroom code switching: layering and language choice in L2 learner interaction. *TESOL Quarterly 31* (pp. 217–235).

Harboard, J. (1992) The use of the mother tongue in the classroom. *ELT Journal 46* (pp. 350–355).

Harmer, J. (1991) *The Practice of English Language Teaching*. (1st edition). Longman.

Harmer, J. (1992) Correspondence. *ELT Journal 46* (pp. 236–238).

Harmer, J. (2007) *The Practice of English Language Teaching* (4th edition). Pearson Education Limited.

Hayes, D. (2009). Non-native English-speaking teachers, context and English language teaching. *System 37* (pp. 1–11).

Hebb, D. (1972) *Textbook of Psychology*. Saunders.

Heidegger, M. (1968) *What is Called Thinking?* Harper Torchbooks.

Hermans, F. (2014) Near-native pronunciation? Who cares? *IATEFL Pronunciation Special Interest Group Newsletter 51* (pp. 42–46).

Highet, G. (1950) *The Art of Teaching*. Vintage Books.

Holliday, A. (1994) *Appropriate Methodology and Social Context*. Cambridge University Press.

Holliday, A. (2006) Native speakerism. *ELT Journal 60* (pp. 385–387).

Holliday, A. (2013) The politics of ethics in diverse cultural settings: colonising the centre stage. *Compare: A Journal of Comparative and International Education 43* (pp. 537–554).

Holt, J. (1971) *What Do I Do Monday?* Pitman.

Horwitz, E. K., M. B. Horwitz & J. Cope (1986) Foreign language classroom anxiety. *Modern Language Journal 70* (pp. 125–132).

Howatt, A. P. R. (1984) *A History of English Language Teaching*. Oxford University Press

Hoyle, E. (1969) *The Role of the Teacher*. Routledge.

Hughes, A. & C. Lascaratou (1982) Competing criteria for error gravity. *ELT Journal 36* (pp. 175–182).

Hughes, G. (1981) *A Handbook of Classroom English*. Oxford University Press.

Hughes, G. & J. Moate (2007) *Practical English Classroom*. Oxford University Press

Illés, É. (1991) Correspondence. *ELT Journal 45* (p. 87).

Janicki, K. (1985) *The Foreigner's Language: A Sociolinguistic Perspective*. Pergamon.

Jenkins, J. (1996) Native speaker, non-native speaker and English as a foreign language: time for a change. *IATEFL Newsletter 131* (pp. 10–11).

Jenkins, J. (1998) Which pronunciation norms and models for English as an international language? *ELT Journal 52* (pp. 119–126).

Jenkins, J. (2000) *The Phonology of English as an International Language.* Oxford University Press.

Jersild, A. T. (1955) *When Teachers Face Themselves.* Teacher's College: Columbia University.

Johnston, B. (1999) The expatriate teacher as postmodern paladin. *Research in the Teaching of English 34* (pp. 255–289).

Kachru, B. B. (1977) The new Englishes and old models. *English Teaching Forum 15 (3)* (pp. 29–35).

Kachru, B. B. (Ed.) (1982) *The Other Tongue: English across Cultures.* Pergamon.

Kachru, B. B. (1985) Standards, codification and sociolinguistic realism: the English language in the Outer Circle. In R. Quirk & H. G. Widdowson (Eds.) *English in the World – Teaching and Learning the Language and Literature* (pp. 11–30). Cambridge University Press/The British Council.

Kachru, B. B. (1992) World Englishes: approaches, issues and resources. *Language Teaching 25* (pp. 1–14).

Kamhi-Stein, L. D. (Ed.) (2004) *Learning and Teaching from Experience: Perspectives on Nonnative English-speaking Professionals.* The University of Michigan Press.

Kamhi-Stein, L. D. (2016) The non-native English speaker teachers in TESOL movement. *ELT Journal 70* (pp. 180–189).

Kaplan, R. B. (1983) Language and Science Policies in New Nations. *Science 221* (p. 913).

Kaplan, R. B. (1987) English in the language policy of the Pacific Rim. *World Englishes 2* (pp. 137–148) *English in the World – Teaching and Learning the Language and Literature* (pp. 7–8) Cambridge University Press/The British Council.

Kennedy, C. (Ed.) (1999) *Innovation and Best Practice.* Longman.

Kennedy, G. (1985) Commentator. In R. Quirk & H. G. Widdowson (Eds.).

Kershaw, G. (1990) When intuition isn't enough. *EFL Gazette, December 9* (pp 8–10).

Kershaw, G. (1996) The non-native teacher by Péter Medgyes. *ELT Journal 50* (pp. 364–367).

Klein, W. (1986) *Second Language Acquisition.* Cambridge University Press.

Kobayashi, T. (1992) Native and nonnative reactions to ESL compositions. *TESOL Quarterly 26* (pp. 81–112).

Kramsch, C. (1993) *Context and Culture in Language Teaching.* Oxford University Press.

Kramsch, C. (1995) The privilege of the non-native speaker. *Plenary address, TESOL Conference.*

Kramsch, C. (1997) The privilege of the nonnative speaker. *Publications of the Modern Language Association of America 112* (pp. 359–369).

Kramsch, C. (2002) Language thieves. In H. Barkowski & R. Faistauer (Eds.) *Sachen Deutsch als Fremdsprache* (pp. 91–103). Schneider Verlag.

Kramsch, C. (2014) Teaching foreign languages in an era of globalization: introduction. *The Modern Language Journal 98* (pp. 296–311).

Krashen, S. D. (1981) *Second Language Acquisition and Second Language Learning.* Pergamon.

Krashen, S. D. & T. Terrell (1983) *The Natural Approach.* Pergamon.

Krasnick, H. (1986) Images of ELT. *ELT Journal 40* (pp. 191–195).

Kubota, R. (2001) My experience of learning to read and write in Japanese as L1 and English as L2. In D. Belcher & U. Connor (Eds.) *Reflections on Multiliterate Lives* (pp. 96–109). Multilingual Matters.

Kuhn, T. (1962) *The Structure of Scientific Revolutions.* Princeton University Press.

Kumaravadivelu, B. (2001) Toward a postmethod pedagogy. *TESOL Quarterly 35* (pp. 537–560).

Lado, R. (1957) *Linguistics across Cultures: Applied Linguistics for Language Teachers.* Ann Arbor.

Lazaraton, A. (2003) Incidental displays of cultural knowledge in the nonnative-English-speaking teacher's classroom. *TESOL Quarterly 37* (pp. 213–245).

Lee, W. R. (1995) 'Natives' and 'non-Natives': much ado about something. *IATEFL Newsletter 126* (pp. 8–9).

Leech, G. & J. Svartvik (1975) *A Communicative Grammar of English.* Longman.

Lewis, L. W. (1971) The American and British accents of English. *ELT Journal 25* (pp. 239–248).

Li, X. M. (1999) Writing from the vantage point of an outsider/insider. In G. Braine (Ed.) *Non-native Educators in English Language Teaching* (pp. 43–55). Lawrence Erlbaum Associates.

Littlejohn, A. P. (1992) *Why Are English Language Teaching Materials the Way They Are?* PhD Thesis: Lancaster University.

Littlewood, W. (1981) *Communicative Language Teaching.* Cambridge University Press.

Littlewood, W. & B. Yu. (2011) First language and target language in the foreign language classroom. *Language Teaching 44* (pp. 64–77).

Liu, D. (1999) Training non-native TESOL students: challenges for TESOL teacher education in the West. In G. Braine (Ed.) *Non-native Educators in English Language Teaching* (pp. 197–210). Lawrence Erlbaum Associates.

Liu, J. (2001) Writing from Chinese to English: my cultural transformation. In D. Belcher & U. Connor (Eds.) *Reflections on Multiliterate Lives* (pp. 121–131). Multilingual Matters.

Llurda, E. (Ed.) (2005) *Non-native Language Teachers: Perceptions, Challenges and Contributions to the Profession.* Springer.

Llurda, E. (2008) The effects of stays abroad on self-perceptions of non-native EFL teachers. In S. Dogancay-Aktuna & J. Hardman (Eds.) *Global English Teaching and Teacher Education: Praxis and Possibility* (pp. 99–111). TESOL.

Lortie, D. (1975) *Schoolteacher: A Sociological Study.* University of Chicago Press

Lowe, T. (1987) An experiment in role reversal: teachers as language learners *ELT Journal 41* (pp. 89–96).

Lowe, R. J. & M. Kiczkowiak (2016). Native-speakerism and the complexity of personal experience: a duoethnographic study. *Cogent Education 3(1).*

Luo, W-H. (2010) Collaborative teaching of EFL by native and non-native English-speaking teachers in Taiwan. In A. Mahboob (Ed.) *The NNEST Lens: Non-native English Speakers in TESOL* (pp. 263–284). Cambridge Scholars Publishing.

Ma, L. P. F. (2012) Advantages and disadvantages of native- and nonnative-English-speaking teachers: student perceptions in Hong Kong. *TESOL Quarterly 46* (pp. 280–305).

Macaro, E. (2005) Codeswitching in the L2 classroom: a communication and learning strategy. In E. Llurda (Ed.) *Non-native Language Teachers: Perceptions, Challenges and Contributions to the Profession* (pp. 63–84). Springer.

Mackey, W. F. (1965) *Language Teaching Analysis.* Longman.s

Maggioli, G. D. (Ed.) (2012) *Teacher training and education. The newsletter of the Teacher Trainers and Educators Special Interest Group (Special Issue).* IATEFL.

Mahboob, A. (2004) Native or nonnative: what do students enrolled in an intensive English program think? In L. D. Kahmi-Stein (Ed.) *Learning and Teaching from Experience: Perspectives on Nonnative English-speaking Professionals* (pp. 121–147). The University of Michigan Press.

Mahboob, A. (Ed.) (2010) *The NNEST Lens: Non Native English Speakers in TESOL.* Cambridge Scholars Publishing.

Mahboob, A., K. Uhrig, K. L. Newman & B. S. Hartford (2004) Children of a lesser English: status of nonnative English speakers as college-level English as a second language teachers in the United States. In L. D. Kamhi-Stein (Ed.) *Learning and Teaching from Experience: Perspectives on Nonnative English-speaking Professionals* (pp. 100–120). The University of Michigan Press.

Maley, A. (1984) I got a religion – evangelism in language teaching. In M. S. Berns & S. J. Savignon (Eds.) *Initiatives in Communicative Language Teaching* (pp. 79–86). Addison-Wesley.

Maley, A. (1992) An open letter to the 'profession' *ELT Journal 46* (pp. 96–99).

Mantell, M. (1996) *Don't Sweat the Small Stuff: PS It's All Small Stuff.* CreateSpace Independent Publishing Platform.

Marton, F. (1981) Phenomenography: describing conceptions of the world around us. *Instructional Science 10* (pp. 177–200)

Marton, W. (1988) *Methods in English Language Teaching: Frameworks and Options.* Pergamon.

Maslow, A. H. (1968) *Toward a Psychology of Being.* D. Van Nostrand Company Inc.

Matsuda, A. & P. K. Matsuda (2004) Autonomy and collaboration in teacher education: journal sharing among native and nonnative English-speaking teachers. In L. D. Kamhi-Stein (Ed.) *Learning and Teaching from Experience: Perspectives on Nonnative English-speaking Professionals* (pp. 176–189). The University of Michigan Press.

McArthur, T. (Ed.) (1992) *The Oxford Companion to the English Language.* Oxford University Press.

McLaughlin, B. (1978) The monitor model: some methodological considerations *Language Learning 28* (pp. 309–332).

McKay, S. L. (2002) *Teaching English as an International Language.* Oxford University Press.

McNeill, A. (2005) Non-native speaker teachers and awareness of lexical difficulty in pedagogical texts. In E. Llurda (Ed.) *Non-native Language Teachers: Perceptions, Challenges and Contributions to the Profession* (pp. 107–128). Springer.

Medgyes, P. (1983) The schizophrenic teacher. *ELT Journal 37* (pp. 2–6).

Medgyes, P. (1986) Queries from a communicative teacher. *ELT Journal 40* (pp. 107–112).

Medgyes, P. (1989) Error and the communicative approach. In R. Freudenstein (Ed.) *Error in Foreign Languages: Analysis and Treatment* (pp. 70–79). FIPLV Eurocentres.

Medgyes, P. (1992) Native or non-native: who's worth more? *ELT Journal 46* (pp. 340–349).

Medgyes, P. (1993) The national L2 curriculum in Hungary. *Annual Review of Applied Linguistics 13* (pp. 24–36).

Medgyes, P. (1994) *The Non-Native Teacher* (1st edition). Macmillan.

Medgyes, P. (1995) The solitary learner – the solitary teacher. *The Polish Teacher Trainer 3 (1)* (pp. 22–25).

Medgyes, P. (1997) *A nyelvtanár [The Language Teacher].* Corvina Publishing House.

Medgyes, P. & A. Malderez (Ed.) (1996) *Changing Perspectives in Teacher Education.* Heinemann.

Medgyes, P. & E. Nyilasi (1997) Pair-teaching in pre-service teacher education. *Foreign Language Annals 30* (pp. 352-368).

Medgyes, P. (1999a) Language training: a neglected area in teacher education. In: G. Braine (Ed.) *Non-Native Educators in English Language Teaching* (pp. 177–195). Lawrence Erlbaum.

Medgyes, P. (1999b) The fifth paradox: What's the English lesson all about? In C. Kennedy (Ed.) *Innovation and Best Practice* (pp. 133–145). Longman.

Medgyes, P. (2001) When the teacher is a non-native speaker. In M. Celce-Murcia (Ed.) *Teaching English as a Second or Foreign Language* (pp. 429–442). Heinle & Heinle.

Medgyes, P. (2004) Out of the box: the ventriloquist. *The Essential Teacher 1(5),* (pp. 42–44).

Medgyes, P. (2012) Why won't the little beasts behave? In: G. D. Maggioli (Ed.) *Teacher Training and Education, Proceedings of the 2012 Pre-Conference Event, Special issue* (pp. 5-25). IATEFL.

Mitchell, R. & C. Brumfit (1991) Research in applied linguistics relevant to language teaching: 1990. *Language Teaching 24* (pp. 137-142).

Mohebbi, H. & S. M. Alavi (2014) An investigation into teachers' first language use in a second language learning classroom context: a questionnaire-based study. *Bellaterra Journal of Teaching & Learning Language & Literature 7 (4)* (pp. 57-73).

Moskowitz, G. (1978) *Caring and Sharing in the Foreign Language Class.* Newbury House.

Mousavi, E. S. (2007) Exploring 'teacher stress' in non-native and native teachers of EFL. *ELTED 10* (pp. 33-41).

Moussu, L. (2010) Influence of teacher-contact time and other variables on ESL students' attitudes towards native- and nonnative-English-speaking teachers. *TESOL Quarterly 44* (pp. 746-768).

Moussu, L. & E. Llurda (2008) Non-native English-speaking English language teachers: history and research. *Language Teaching 41* (pp. 315-348).

Murdoch, G. (1994) Language development provision in teacher training curricula. *ELT Journal 48* (pp. 253-265).

Naiman, N., M. Fröhlich, H. H. Stern & A. Todesco (1978) *The Good Language Learner.* Ontario Institute for Studies in Education.

Nemtchinova, E. (2005) Host teachers' evaluations of nonnative-English-speaking teacher trainees – a perspective from the classroom. *TESOL Quarterly 39* (pp. 235-261).

Nickel, G. (1987) How 'native' can (or should) a non-native speaker be? *JALT: The Language Teacher 11 (11)* (pp. 14-23).

Nolasco, R. & L. Arthur (1987) *Conversation.* Oxford University Press.

Norton, B. (1997) Language, identity, and the ownership of English. *TESOL Quarterly 31* (pp. 409-429).

Norton, B. & C. Tang (1997) The identity of the nonnative ESL teacher on the power and status of nonnative ESL teachers. *TESOL Quarterly 31* (pp. 577-580).

Nunan, D. (1987) Communicative language teaching: the learner's view. In: B. K. Das (Ed.) *Communication and Learning in the Classroom, Anthology Series 19* (pp. 176-190). SEAMEO Regional Language Centre.

Nunan, D. (Ed.) (1992) *Collaborative Language Learning and Teaching.* Cambridge University Press.

Omaggio, A. C. (1978) Successful language learners: what do we know about them? *ERIC/ CLL News Bulletin, May/2-3* (pp. 101-104).

O'Malley, J. M., A. U. Chamot, G. Stewner-Manzanares, L. Küpper & R. Russo (1985) Learning strategies used by beginning and intermediate ESL students. *Language Learning 35* (pp. 21-46).

O'Neill, R. (1991) The plausible myth of learner-centredness: or the importance of doing ordinary things well. *ELT Journal 45* (pp. 293-304).

Oxford, R. L. (1990) *Language Learning Strategies.* Newbury House.

Oxford, R. (2011) Strategies for learning a second or foreign language. *Language Teaching 44* (pp. 167-180).

Pacek, D. (2005) Personality not nationality: foreign students' perceptions of a non-native speaker lecturer of English at a British university. In E. Llurda (Ed.) *Non-Native Language Teachers: Perceptions, Challenges and Contributions to the Profession* (pp. 243-262). Springer.

Paikeday, T. M. (1985) *The Native Speaker is Dead!* Paikeday Publishing Inc.

Pajares, M. F. (1992) Teachers' beliefs and educational research: cleaning up a messy construct. *Review of Educational Research 62* (pp. 307–332).

Palfreyman, D. (1993) 'How I got it in my head': conceptual models of language and learning in native and non-native trainee EFL teachers. *Language Awareness 2* (pp. 209–223).

Palmer, H. E. (1921 & 1964) *The Principles of Language Study.* Harrap/Oxford University Press.

Park, G. (2012) 'I am never afraid of being recognized as an NNES': one teacher's journey in claiming and embracing her nonnative-speaker identity. *TESOL Quarterly 46* (pp. 127–151).

Pattison, T. (Ed.) (2013) *IATEFL 2012 Glasgow conference selections.* IATEFL.

Pattison, T. (Ed.) (2014) *IATEFL 2013: Liverpool conference selections.* IATEFL.

Phillipson, R. (1992a) *Linguistic Imperialism.* Oxford University Press.

Phillipson, R. (1992b) ELT: the native speaker's burden? *ELT Journal 46* (pp. 12–18).

Phillipson, R. (1999a) Voice in a global English: unheard chords in crystal loud and clear. *Applied Linguistics 20* (pp. 265–276).

Phillipson, R. (1999b) Closing word. *The European English Messenger VIII(1)*, 65.

Pirsig, R.M. (1974) *Zen and the Art of Motorcycle Maintenance – An Inquiry into Values.* Bantam Books.

Politzer, R. L. & L. Weiss (1969) *The Successful Foreign-Language Teacher.* The Center for Curriculum Development.

Popper, K. (1968) *Conjectures and Refutations.* Harper and Row.

Postman, N. & C. Weingartner (1969) *Teaching as a Subversive Activity.* Penguin.

Povey, J. (1977) The role of English in Africa. *English Teaching Forum 15 (3)* (pp. 25–29)

Prabhu, N. S. (1990) There is no best method – why? *TESOL Quarterly 24* (pp. 161–176).

Preston, D. R. (1984) How to milk a native speaker: an essay in TES/FL husbandry. *English Teaching Forum 22 (1)* (pp. 11–23).

Quirk, R. (1985) The English language in a global context. In: R. Quirk & H. G. Widdowson (Eds.) *English in the World - Teaching and Learning the Language and Literature* (pp. 1-6). Cambridge University Press/The British Council.

Rajagopalan, K. (2005) Non-native speaker teachers of English and their anxieties: ingredients of EFL teachers. In E. Llurda (Ed.) *Non-native Language Teachers: Perceptions, Challenges and Contributions to the Profession* (pp. 283–303). Springer.

Rampton, M. B. H. (1990) Displacing the 'native speaker': expertise, affiliation and inheritance. *ELT Journal 45* (pp. 97–101).

Ren, W. (2014) Can the Expanding Circle own English? Comments on Yoo's 'Nonnative teachers in the Expanding Circle and the ownership of English'. *Applied Linguistics 35* (pp. 208–212).

Reves, T. and P. Medgyes (1994) The non-native English speaking EFL/ESL teacher's self-image: an international survey. *System 22* (pp. 353–367).

Richards, J. C. & T. S. Rodgers (1986) *Approaches and Methods in Language Teaching: A Description and Analysis.* Cambridge University Press.

Richards, J. C., J. Platt & H. Weber (1985) *Longman Dictionary of Applied Linguistics.* Longman.

Rivers, W. M. (1981) *Teaching Foreign-Language Skills.* The University of Chicago Press.

Rives, F. C. (1979) The teacher as a performing artist. *Contemporary Education 51* (pp. 7–9).

Roberts, J. T. (1982) Recent developments in ELT. *Language Teaching, 15* (pp. 174–193).

Rogers, C. R. (1983) *Freedom to Learn for the 80s.* Charles Merrill Publishing Company.

Rogers, J. (1982) The world for sick proper. *ELT Journal 36* (pp. 144–151).

Rubin, J. (1975) What the 'good language learner' can teach us. *TESOL Quarterly 9* (pp. 45–51).

Rubin, J. & I. Thompson (1982) *How to Be a More Successful Learner*. Heinle & Heinle.

Ruecker, T. & L. Ives (2015) White native English speakers needed: the rhetorical construction of privilege in online teacher recruitment spaces. *TESOL Quarterly 49* (pp. 733–756).

Safadi, M. (1992) Correspondence. *TESOL Matters December 92/January 93* (p. 10).

Salzberger-Wittenberg, I., G. Henry & E. Osborne (1990) *The Emotional Experience of Learning and Teaching*. Routledge.

Samimy, K. (1997) A Review on 'the non-native teacher'. *TESOL Quarterly 31* (pp. 815–817).

Samimy, K. K. & J. Brutt-Griffler (1999) To be a native or non-native speaker: perceptions of 'non-native' students in a graduate TESOL program. In G. Braine (Ed.) *Non-native Educators in English Language Teaching* (pp. 127–144). Lawrence Erlbaum.

Sasaki, M. (2001) An introspective account of L2 writing acquisition. In D. Belcher & U. Connor (Eds.) *Reflections on Multiliterate Lives* (pp. 110–120). Multilingual Matters.

Savignon, S. (1976) On the other side of the desk: teacher attitudes and motivation in second language learning. *Canadian Modern Language Review 32* (pp. 295–304).

Savignon, S. J. & M. S. Berns (Eds.) (1984) *Initiatives in Communicative Language Teaching*. Addison-Wesley.

Schaefer Fu, G. & M. Chase (1991) Team-teaching as a form of staff development: or when are two teachers better than one? *Guidelines RELC 13* (pp. 81–87).

Schön, D. A. (Ed.) (1991) *The Reflective Turn: Case Studies in and on Educational Practice*. Teachers College: Columbia University.

Schumann, J. H. (1978) *The Pidginization Process: A Model for Second Language Acquisition*. Newbury House.

Schumann, F. M. & J. H. Schumann (1977) Diary of a language learner: an introspective study of second language learning. In: H. D. Brown, R. H. Crymes & C. A. Yorio (Eds.) *On TESOL '77. Teaching and Learning English as a Second Language: Trends in Research and Practice* (pp. 241–249) TESOL.

Schwarzer, R. (Ed.) (1986) *Self-Related Cognition in Anxiety and Motivation*. Erlbaum Associates.

Scott, M., L. Carioni, M. Zanatta, E. Bayer, & T. Quintanilha (1984) Using a 'standard exercise' in teaching reading comprehension. *ELT Journal 38* (pp. 114–120).

Scovel, T. (1978) The effect of affect on foreign language learning. *Language Learning 28* (pp. 129–142).

Scrivener, J. (2011) *Learning Teaching (3rd edition)*. Macmillan Education.

Seidlhofer, B. (1996) 'It is an undulating feeling...' the importance of being a non-native teacher of English. *Views 5* (pp. 63–80).

Seidlhofer, B. (1999) Double standards: teacher education in the Expanding Circle. *World Englishes 18* (pp. 233–245).

Seidlhofer, B., J. Akoha, Z. Ardo, J. Simpson & H. G. Widdowson (1991) 'Nationalism is an infantile disease' (Einstein). What about native-speakerism? *BAAL Newsletter 39* (pp. 21–26).

Seliger, H. W. (1979) On the nature and function of language rules in language teaching. *TESOL Quarterly 13* (pp. 359–369).

Seliger, H. W. & M. H. Long (Eds.) (1983) *Classroom Oriented Research in Second Language Acquisition*. Newbury House.

Selinker, L. (1972) *Interlanguage. International Review of Applied Linguistics 10* (pp. 219–231).

Selinker, L. & J. Lamendella (1978) Two perspectives on fossilization in international learning. *Interlanguage Studies Bulletin 3* (pp. 143–191).

Selvi, A. F. (2010) All teachers are equal, but some teachers are more equal than others: trend analysis of job advertisements in English language teaching. *WATESOL NNEST Caucus Annual Review 1* (pp. 156–181).

Selye, H. (1974) *Stress without Distress.* Lippincott.

Sharle, A. & A. Szabó (2000) *Learner Autonomy: A Guide to Developing Learner Responsibility.* Cambridge University Press.

Sheorey. R. (1986) Error perceptions of native-speaking and non-native-speaking teachers of ESL. *ELT Journal 40* (pp. 306–312).

Siriwardena, A. (1992) *Collaborative Teaching and Teachers as Collaborative Learners: A Contribution to Teacher Development.* MA Thesis: Lancaster University.

Skehan, P. (1989) *Individual Differences in Second-Language Learning.* Edward Arnold.

Smit, U. (1997) Looking beyond the native/non-native contrast in ELF teaching. *Views 6 (1)* (pp. 67–69).

Smith, L. E. (1983) English as an international language: no room for linguistic chauvinism. In: L. E. Smith (Ed.) *Readings in English as an International Language* (pp.165–171). Pergamon.

Snow, M. A., M. Omar & A. M. Katz (2004) Collaboration among native and nonnative English-speaking professionals. In L. D. Kamhi-Stein (Ed.) *Learning and Teaching from Experience: Perspectives on Nonnative English-Speaking Professionals* (pp. 307–323). The University of Michigan Press.

Soudek, M. and L. Soudek (1985) Non-verbal channels on language learning. *ELT Journal 39* (pp. 109–114).)

Sowden, C. (2012) The overnight growth in English as a lingua franca. *ELT Journal 66* (pp. 89–96).

Sowden, C. (2012) A reply to Alessia Cogo. *ELT Journal 66* (pp. 106–107).

Spock, B. M. (1946) *Baby and Child Care.* Pocket Books: Simon and Schuster.

Spolsky, B. (1989) *Conditions for Second Language Learning.* Oxford University Press.

Stern, H. H. (1975) What can we learn from the good language learner? *Canadian Modern Language Review 34* (pp. 304–318).

Stern, H. H. (1983) *Fundamental Concepts of Language Teaching.* Oxford University Press.

Stevick, E. W. (1976) *Memory, Meaning and Method.* Newbury House.

Stevick, E. W. (1980) *Teaching Languages: A Way and Ways.* Newbury House.

Stevick, E. W. (1984) *Teaching and Learning Languages.* Cambridge University Press.

Stevick, E. W. (1989) *Success with Foreign Languages.* Prentice Hall.

Stevick, E. W. (1990) *Humanism in Language Teaching.* Oxford University Press.

Stoker, B. (1897) *Dracula* (pp.19–20) Archibald & Constable.

Swales, J. (1985) English as the international language of research. *RELC Journal 16* (pp. 1–7).

Swire, H. (1899) The Practical Study of Languages: A Guide for Teachers and Learners. JM Dent and Company.

Szesztay, M. (1992) *From a Self-Aware Learner to an Empathetic Teacher.* MEd Thesis: Exeter University.

Tatar, S. & S. Yildiz (2010). Empowering nonnative-English speaking teachers in the classroom. In A. Mahboob (Ed.) *The NNEST Lens: Non-native English Speakers in TESOL* (pp. 114–128). Cambridge Scholars Publishing.

Thein, M. M. (1994) A non-native English-speaking teacher's response to a learner-centred program. *System 22* (pp. 463–471).

Thomas, J. (1999) Voices from the periphery: non-native teachers and issues of credibility. In G. Braine (Ed.) *Non-native Educators in English Language Teaching* (pp. 5–13). Lawrence Erlbaum.

Tobias, S. (1986) Anxiety and cognitive processing of instruction. In R. Schwarzer (Ed.) *Self-Related Cognition in Anxiety and Motivation* (pp. 35--54). Erlbaum Associates.

Tom, A. R. (1984) *Teaching as a Moral Craft.* Longman.

Tough, A. (1971) *The Adult's Learning Projects.* The Ontario Institute for Studies in Education.

Underhill, A. (2013) Mess and progress. In T. Pattison (Ed.) *IATEFL 2012 Glasgow Conference Selection* (pp. 242–250). IATEFL.

Ur, P. (2012) *A Course in English Language Teaching.* Cambridge University Press.

Van Els, T., T. Bongaerts, G. Extra, A. M. Janssen-van Dieten & C. Van Os (1984) *Applied Linguistics and the Learning and Teaching of Foreign Languages.* Edward Arnold.

Van Essen, A. (1994) Language Imperialism. *Plenary address, NELLE Conference.*

Wallace, M. J. (1991) *Training Foreign Language Teachers: A Reflective Approach.* Cambridge University Press.

Waters, A., J. Allwright, T. Bray & J. Sunderland (1990) Getting the best out of 'the language learning experience'. *English Language Teaching Journal 44* (pp. 305–315).

Wenden, A. L. & J. Rubin (1987) *Learner Strategies in Language Learning.* Prentice-Hall.

Wesche, M. B. (1979) Learning behaviours of successful adult students on intensive language training. *Canadian Modern Language Review 35* (pp. 415–427).

Widdowson, H. G. (1978) *Teaching Language as Communication.* Oxford University Press.

Widdowson, H. G. (1990) *Aspects of Language Teaching.* Oxford University Press.

Widdowson, H. G. (1994) The ownership of English. *TESOL Quarterly 29* (pp. 377–389).

Willis, J. (1981) *Teaching English through English.* Longman.

Woods, D. (1996) *Teacher Cognition in Language Teaching.* Cambridge University Press.

Wyld, H. (1934, 1991) The best English: a claim for the superiority of Received Standard English. In Tony Crowley (Ed.) *Proper English? Readings in Language, History and Cultural Identity.* Routledge (pp. 207–218).

Yoo, I. W. (2014) Nonnative teachers in the Expanding Circle and the ownership of English. *Applied Linguistics 35* (pp. 82–86).

ONLINE SOURCES

You Tube videos:

Davies, A. Discussing the concept of the native speaker: Retrieved 1 March, 2017, from https://www.youtube.com/watch?v=EzRvVg1o8i0

The Two Ronnies Four Candles (sketch): : Retrieved 1 March, 2017, from https://www.youtube.com/watch?v=OCbvCRkl_4U

Various Do You Speak English?: Retrieved 1 March, 2017, from https://www.youtube.com/watch?v=EzRvVg1o8i0

German coast guard (Chapter 5): Retrieved 1 March, 2017, from https://www.youtube.com/watch?v=yR0lWICH3rY

Grammar police (Chapter 6): Retrieved 1 March, 2017, fromhttps://www.youtube.com/watch?v=_Lb3n37q7Zs

TED Talks:

Burchfield, J. (2003) Playing invisible turntables

De Posada, J. (2015) Don't eat the marshmallows

Efromovich, S. (2013) 5 techniques to speak any language

McGonigal, K. (2013) How to make stress your friend

Mitra, S. (2013) Build a school in the cloud

Moore, T. (2011) How to tie your shoes

Patel, H. & Y. Rau (2013) Who am I? Think again

Robinson, K. (2010) Bring on the learning revolution!

Walker, J. (2009) The world's English mania

Other online sources:

British National Corpus (2007) www.natcorp.ox.ac.uk/corpus.

Just A Minute (VARIOUS) BBC Radio programme: http://www.bbc.co.uk/programmes/b006s5dp

Richardson, S (2016) The Native Factor, the haves and the have-nots. Plenary address, IATEFL Annual Conference.

https://iatefl.britishcouncil.org/2016/session/plenary-silvana-richardson

VOICE (2013). The Vienna-Oxford international corpus of English (version POS online 2.0). Available at http://voice.univie.ac.at/pos/. Retrieved 22 August, 2016

Lowe, R. J. & M. Kiczkowiak (2016).: (http://teflequityadvocates.us13.list-manage.com

Subject index

Name index

LOOKING AHEAD

Extracts from a conversation between a non-NEST (Péter) and a NEST (Susan)

Then and now

Susan: Péter, what for you was the motivation behind doing a third edition?

Péter: The internal motivation was that since the book first came out in 1994 there have been a lot of new findings relating to the native/non-native issue, even though the basic concept hasn't changed all that much.

Language and culture

Susan: The idea that there are these two different groups, NESTs and non-NESTs, do you think that has changed?

Péter: Well, it's a controversial issue. There're a lot of people who argue that there's no way you can define who's a native speaker and who's a non-native speaker and there's quite a bit of truth in that. It's really difficult, linguistically speaking, to tell the difference. There's no clearcut division-line between natives and non-natives.

Susan: One of the differences is as much of attitude as actual linguistic ability, don't you think?

Péter: That's right. And a matter of self-description too. If I take my own example I consider myself a non-native speaker of English and at the same time a native speaker of Hungarian.

Susan: One of the things that worries me about the labels 'NEST' and 'non-NEST' is that it seems to be isolating language proficiency from the ability to communicate with people from another culture. Communication is more than just words, it seems to me.

Péter: Absolutely. We're linguistically 'handicapped' as non-native speakers of English, but we can benefit a great deal by being immersed in two cultures or more. While my roots are in Hungarian culture, over the years I've learned a lot not only about British and American culture but also about the cultures of all the people with whom I've been able to communicate – in English. So I'm definitely enriched by being a bilingual speaker of English and Hungarian. Anyway, it's great fun to slide from one language to another, from one culture to another.

Susan: One of the things that struck me when we were talking about the new edition of the book is that a lot of people now have more opportunities to come into contact with English than was the case 25 years ago – through travel, the Internet, websites, Facebook and so on. English has become an international language, which for a non-native speaker can cause quite a few problems, because there isn't a 'right or wrong' any more.

Péter: I beg to differ slightly! Nowadays there're people who would say: 'We don't actually need a norm. Everybody can speak English the way they wish.' Not quite. Because if I go into the classroom to teach a group of complete beginners, then I have to pronounce the word 'table' in some way, and probably the way I will teach them this word will be approximating a British, American, Australian or Indian standard. I have to stick to some kind of norm. And I certainly don't want my kids to pronounce it in a Hungarian way. So there is a norm although it's rather elusive, very difficult to pin down. The other reason is that I want them to be successful.

Different contexts, different norms

Susan: Of course. The problem is that what they're producing – writing a message, posting on Facebook or writing an email – would be totally acceptable in the real world, but if you've got a class who are going to have to do an exam at the end of the year then there is a norm, something which is accepted as right or wrong. And when we talk about NESTs and non-NESTs we should also be talking about the context which they're teaching in, the objectives of their pupils, the school principal, the parents and so on. In other words, you can't isolate language from the context in which it's taught and learned… Another thing. 'Equal but different', you stress throughout the book. And that non-NESTs need to get a confidence boost.

Equality and discrimination

Péter: Yes, but these days I begin to wonder: don't NESTs also need a boost? I mean the ones who decide to go and find a job in a foreign country and they're suddenly thrown in at the deep end. Different culture, different education system, different mentality – everything is different. Some of them even make the bloody effort to learn the local language…

Susan: Yes, and that brings us on to another tricky topic, the question of payment, doesn't it? Because there's a lot of criticism of the fact that in some places NESTs are earning more than the locals, and emotionally one's reaction is: 'This is wrong, it shouldn't be like that!' But as an alien you do need more money to survive, don't you? So you have to give NESTs financial security…

Péter: (laughs) Says the NEST… But I agree. Look, I agree that discrimination is not fair. However, let's not forget that this only applies to a very small minority. 99 per cent of non-NESTs stay put in their home countries partly because that's where they feel at home and maybe because they're not mobile enough to search for a better-paid job abroad. Anyway, my sympathy mainly lies with those millions of fellow non-NESTs who teach locally in their home countries.

Younger and younger

Susan: Now looking ahead, when the first edition of the book came out, in 1994, teaching English wasn't so different from teaching any other foreign language.

Péter: Look, I no longer consider English a foreign language. It's a basic skill today. Like mathematics.

Susan: Yes, English obviously has become part and parcel of mainstream education. Children begin to learn English as a lingua franca at an early age, often as early as the nursery school. I think this has implications for teachers and teacher training.

Péter: Exactly. One of them is that you have to train teachers for primary education, kindergarten education, because you mustn't teach a 6-year-old like you teach a 14-year-old. There's a huge difference! But since there are very few trained teachers for the kindergarten or for the lower primary school, qualified secondary school teachers are teaching the young. Teaching them the present perfect, for instance. A disaster! …

In a digital world

Susan: There are two things that come to mind about this. One is that today more and more parents speak English and so they've got expectations of what goes on in the classroom. This can be a negative as well as a positive development. The other thing is ICT. Nowadays more and more 3-year-olds have a tablet or a smartphone and by using that they're being exposed to English. In a very haphazard way but still. So anybody, whether a NEST or a non-NEST, who's teaching that emerging age group is going to have to take notice of this. It's not enough just to do songs and games.

Péter: Indeed, computers are not just tools, they open up an entirely different world. A multicultural world…

Future directions?

Susan: … in which they'll probably use English as the means of communication… Finally, Péter, what about the future?

Péter: Well, there're several scenarios and it's impossible to tell which will gain the upper hand. However, one thing is certain: If a government won't invest in education, then that country's doomed. In the long run, for sure, but maybe even in the short run.

Susan: So looking ahead your perspective is more positive than negative, right?

Péter: Oh yes, the trend is positive, no doubt. For both NESTs and non-NESTs. And their students, of course.

Susan: And what if your 16-year-old son suddenly announced that he wanted to be an English teacher? Would you encourage or discourage him?

Péter: (laughs) My two daughters are English teachers. My wife is an English teacher. Most of my friends are English teachers! I'm surrounded by English teachers. So if my son decided to become an English teacher, I'd say 'Welcome to the club. And here are my English books, they're all yours.' It's his decision, his life.

Budapest, October 2016

Looking further ahead ...

The concerns raised by Péter Medgyes nearly a quarter of a century ago are still relevant and alive. This recent policy statement by a teachers' association in Spain (NESTs and non-NESTs) is an example of ways in which awareness can be raised and the discussion widened. The critical importance of professional training, not nationality or language background, needs to be explained and emphasised.

TESOL-SPAIN

POSITION STATEMENT AGAINST DISCRIMINATION

In compliance with Article 21 of the Charter of Fundamental Rights of the EU, TESOL-SPAIN stands in opposition to discrimination against teachers on the basis of their national, ethnic or lin-guistic background, religion, gender, gender identity and sexual orientation, in terms of hiring, pro-motion, recruitment for jobs, or employment conditions.

With respect to the common, long-standing notion, unsupported by research, that a certain ethnici-ty, accent, or national background gives a person an advantage as a teacher of English, TESOL-SPAIN firmly believes that all teachers should be evaluated and valued solely on the basis of their teaching competence, teaching experience, formal education and linguistic expertise. Therefore, TESOL-SPAIN does not condone job announcements that list "native English," "native command of English," "native-like fluency," "standard accented English," or similar, as required or desirable qualities.

Reproduced by permission of TESOL Spain, March 2017

Over to you ...